D0330900

Praise for *Graduating with Honor*

"What a wise and wonderful book! The team of Plante & Plante focus on one of the most important and challenging issues in higher education—how best to bake sound ethical precepts into the identity of college students so that they follow those precepts in later life. Every arena of college life is covered. With numerous telling illustrations of what to do and why, the coauthors give concrete advice to faculty, staff, and administrators. This is a book that belongs not on their bookshelves, but rather distilled into the daily education of their students."

Thomas Ehrlich, Consulting Professor, Stanford Graduate School of Education and President Emeritus, Indiana University

"I have been in higher education for over thirty years. The Internet, among other changes, has introduced ethical challenges that did not exist when most ethics textbooks were written—everything from instant pornography to hookup apps to made-to-order term papers. The ethical landscape for today's college student is a virtual minefield of life-shaping decision points. The Plantes' book provides a map through that minefield and addresses a need too long unattended to. This textbook is replete with real-life dilemmas and thoughtful considerations of how to approach them. The authors deliver on their promise to 'provide a model for imparting the skills of ethical decision making to college students during a time of great transition, temptation and unprecedented freedom.' This book offers life skills whose worth extends far beyond the college years and provide a framework for lives of responsibility, integrity, and compassion."

Stephen A. Privett, S.J., Chancellor and President Emeritus University of San Francisco

"True education, as noted by Martin Luther King Jr., brings forward intelligence and character. In *Graduating with Honor*, Professors Thomas Plante and Lori Plante seek to advance true education in this sense by defining best practices for nurturing ethics—ethical formation—among college students. The authors provide guidance to students as well as educators, parents, and leaders, illuminating the path for creating an optimal environment for ethical development on college campuses. Situated in the realities of dorms, athletics, and classrooms, this beautifully written text offers insights and practices that are of immediate value to those engaged in campus life. Rather than bringing ethical theory 'down' to the real world, however, Professors Plante and Plante elevate the discussion of college life to enrich our understanding of the hardest moral issues of the day: dishonesty, sexual exploitation, violence, injustice.

Martin Luther King Jr. also reminded us that a person has 'not started living until he can rise above the narrow confines of his individualistic concerns to the broader concerns of all humanity.' Professors Plante and Plante, through their words and example, invite their readers to live more fully by recognizing the role of ethical formation in college students who will shoulder many of the responsibilities of humanity in the future."

Laura Roberts, M.D., M.A., Katharine Dexter McCormick and
Stanley McCormick Memorial Professor and Chairman
Department of Psychiatry and Behavioral Sciences
Stanford University School of Medicine and
Editor-in-Chief (Books), American Psychiatric
Association Publishing

"Amid a chorus of pessimism and disillusionment about our colleges and universities, Lori and Tom Plante offer up a refreshing critique that takes an honest look at our contemporary challenges and suggest practical steps for faculty, administrators, and parents. Graduating with Honor calls us to imagine how we can deliver on higher education's promise for today's young people as they search for honorable lives of meaning and consequence."

David Quigley, Provost and Dean of Faculties
Boston College

"*Graduating with Honor* is a comprehensive resource offering practical options for the ethical formation of college students. The authors have captured the subtle complexities of the college student experience and offer a range of formation practices that are accessible to students, parents, and student affairs professionals alike."

Jeanne Rosenberger, Vice Provost for Student Life
Santa Clara University and President, Jesuit Association
of Student Personnel Administrators (JASPA)

Graduating with Honor

BEST PRACTICES TO PROMOTE ETHICS DEVELOPMENT IN COLLEGE STUDENTS

Thomas G. Plante, PhD, ABPP,
and Lori G. Plante, PhD

 PRAEGER™

An Imprint of ABC-CLIO, LLC
Santa Barbara, California • Denver, Colorado

Library of Congress Cataloging-in-Publication Data

Names: Plante, Thomas G., author. | Plante, Lori G., author.
Title: Graduating with honor : best practices to promote ethics development in
  college students / Thomas G. Plante, PhD, ABPP and Lori G. Plante, PhD.
Description: Santa Barbara, California : Praeger, an Imprint of ABC-CLIO,
  LLC, [2017] | Includes bibliographical references and index.
Identifiers: LCCN 2016030131 (print) | LCCN 2016045639 (ebook) |
  ISBN 9781440841996 (acid-free paper) | ISBN 9781440842009 (eISBN) |
  ISBN 9781440842009 (ebook)
Subjects: LCSH: Moral education (Higher)
Classification: LCC LC268 .P54 2017 (print) | LCC LC268 (ebook) |
  DDC 378/.01—dc23
LC record available at https://lccn.loc.gov/2016030131

ISBN: 978-1-4408-4199-6
EISBN: 978-1-4408-4200-9

21 20 19 18 17   1 2 3 4 5

This book is also available as an eBook.

Praeger
An Imprint of ABC-CLIO, LLC

ABC-CLIO, LLC
130 Cremona Drive, P.O. Box 1911
Santa Barbara, California 93116-1911
www.abc-clio.com

This book is printed on acid-free paper ∞
Manufactured in the United States of America

Contents

Preface   xi

Acknowledgments   xv

**I. Establishing the Foundation for Ethical Development
     in College**

1. Introduction to Ethical Issues in College   3

2. The Four I's: Developmental Goals and Challenges
   in College   13

3. Ethics 101: Moral Philosophy in a Nutshell   27

4. The RRICC Model: Five Ethical Principles for
   Decision Making   37

**II. What Colleges, Parents, and Students Can Do to
     Nurture Ethical Development**

5. Creating an Organizational Culture of Ethics   51

6. How Universities Can Teach and Embody Ethical Thought   59

7. What the Faith Communities Can Do to Promote
   Student Ethics   67

8. How Parents Can Help Young Adults Prepare Ethically
   for College   75

9. What Students Can Do to Nurture Their Own Character
   Development in College   85

10. In Their Own Words: Students Offer Their Views on Ethics
    Development at College   91

III. Best Practices in Ethical Development on Campus

11. Best Practices: Curricular   105

12. Best Practices: Extracurricular   113

13. Best Practices: Residential Life   123

14. Best Practices: Athletics   133

15. Best Practices: Campus Judicial Procedures   141

16. Best Practices: Alumni, Donor, and Community Relations   153

IV. Conclusions and Resources

17. Putting It All Together: Best Ways to Nurture Ethical
    Development in Colleges   161

Appendix A. Sample Syllabi for Applied Ethics Classes   171

Appendix B. Sample Syllabi for Freshman 100/101 Classes   182

Appendix C. Sample Honor Codes   191

*Appendix D. Sample Paradigm for University Judicial
   Procedures*   199

Appendix E. A Framework for Ethical Decision Making   202

*Appendix F. Fifteen Principles for the Design of College Ethical
   Development Programs*   208

Appendix G. Additional Resources   218

References   223

Index   227

To and for Zach . . .
and all other college students seeking to lead a life of honor.

Honor

That which rightfully attracts esteem, respect, or consideration; self-respect; dignity; courage; fidelity; especially, excellence of character; high moral worth; virtue; nobleness

—Webster's 1913 Dictionary

Ethics

The science of human duty; a particular system of principles and rules concerning duty, whether true or false; rules of practice in respect to a single class of human actions; as, political or social ethics; medical ethics

—Webster's 1913 Dictionary

The function of the university is to help men and women save their souls, and in so doing, to save their society: from what? From the hell of meaninglessness, of obsession, of complex artifice, of systematic lying, of criminal evasions and neglects, of self-destructive futilities.

—Thomas Merton

Preface

The college years are rife with opportunities and challenges that rarely come without ethical implications. Most compelling are high-risk choices that involve decisions made in the throes of temptation. Specifically, decisions regarding drug and alcohol consumption, sexual activity, and academic honesty can be argued to hold the greatest potential to disrupt or even derail one's college experience. Extensive data is available on the incidence of these problematic behaviors on college campuses, as well as their potentially dangerous repercussions. Universities across the country have been undergoing extensive self-evaluations and developing action plans to confront the blight of excessive drinking, sexual assault, and cheating. Most recently, governmental policies related to Title IX for the protection of students against sexual victimization and discrimination highlight the stakes and new demands confronting students embarking on their first years away from home.

United States government data provides a glaring account of these problematic behaviors on college campuses. First, in regard to drinking, data released by the Task Force of the National Advisory Council on Alcohol Abuse and Alcoholism (National Institutes of Health, 2002) provides startling statistics. More than 1,400 college student deaths are linked to alcohol each year. In addition, 500,000 students are accidentally injured while intoxicated, and more than 600,000 students experience physical assault by another inebriated student, while more than 70,000 students are victims of alcohol-related sexual assault. The list of alcohol-linked difficulties extends to unsafe sex, academic difficulty, suicide attempts, and drunk driving, as well as the staggering report that 31 percent of college students meet the criteria for a diagnosis of alcohol abuse. Clearly, neither students nor university officials can ignore the massive scope of this problem.

Alcohol has been in the forefront of numerous college tragedies and scandals. At Penn State in 2014, students photographed and posted pictures of a female student incapacitated by alcohol and being sexually assaulted by male students. Also in 2015, a UC Berkeley student left a fraternity party at USC, drunk and disoriented. He became lost, wandered into traffic, and was struck and killed by a car. These two cases are sadly only a small sampling of the untold problems linked with excessive alcohol consumption on college campuses. Would these outcomes have been different had the students involved been steeped and trained in the ethical implications of their own and others' drinking, and educated consistently in ethical decision making throughout their college experience? We would argue that the outcomes could only have been improved.

Similarly, sexual assault on college campuses is finally receiving greater attention. A recently released report by the White House Task Force to Protect Students From Sexual Assault (April 2014) indicates that one in five female students are victims of sexual assault, usually inflicted during the freshman or sophomore year. In 75–80 percent of cases, the woman knows her attacker, and college men are certainly not immune to this threat. Furthermore, campus rape and assault are vastly underreported, with only an estimated 2 percent of incapacitated sexual assault survivors and 13 percent of forcible rape survivors reporting the crime to authorities.

All college campuses face the specter of sexual assault. Stanford University expelled a student for allegedly raping a drunk and unconscious classmate in 2015. Penn State, in 2012, entered the national spotlight when failing to protect children from the serial sexual predation of one of their football coaches. While these problems are complex and defy simple safeguards and solutions, students and university officials need to heed these statistics and develop ways to better equip students and officials to protect against such crimes. Perhaps even more importantly, students themselves need to be armed with the knowledge, skills, supports, and ethical contexts for best protecting themselves.

In terms of academic integrity, cheating is epidemic on college campuses. Perhaps exacerbated by increasing levels of competition and pressure for high grades, 36 percent of undergraduates admit to "paraphrasing/ copying a few sentences" without referencing the source, while 24 percent of graduate students self report this as well. Also, 14 percent of students admit to "fabricating/falsifying a bibliography," 7 percent report copying from sources word for word, 3 percent obtain papers from term paper suppliers, and a whopping 43 percent admit to outright cheating on tests and written assignments. These statistics are all reported in a February 2015 document ("Facts & Stats").

Numerous large-scale cheating scandals have been reported by national news outlets, including recent scandals spanning military academies, the Ivy League, and a host of highly publicized cases throughout the United States. For example, in October 2014, the University of North Carolina was exposed for providing fake classes for athletes and other students, a scandal that spanned two decades and approximately 3,100 students. In March 2015, Stanford University also suffered a widely publicized cheating scandal in which as many as 20 percent of students in an introductory course were caught cheating (Korn, 2015). Ethical violations come into sharp relief in light of these figures, demanding that colleges actively address the underlying ethical goals and decision-making processes of students. Furthermore, whether colleges choose to educate and rehabilitate violators rather than simply punish or expel serves as an example of their own ethical commitment to humanely and constructively teaching their young charges.

In addition to these hot-button issues, and perhaps most importantly, we are all called upon to make ethical decisions every day. Some of these may seem small and easily resolved, others wrenching and extremely complicated. Ethical implications of dating, for example, can be fraught with a multitude of ethically charged choices. How honest should I be about my desire for a quick hookup versus an ongoing relationship? If I know my friend's girlfriend is cheating on him, should I tell him? I don't want to use a condom and she's not insisting, so should I ignore the issue? On every relational level and throughout an unlimited range of everyday choices and actions, ethical issues come into play. Having a model for personal ethical decision making enables these choices to be thoughtful, intentional, and more likely to maintain one's self-defined moral integrity and best interests.

During the college years, young adults are called upon to develop their own controls in the context of sudden and vast freedoms and temptations. The desire to socialize and experiment with drugs and alcohol, the opportunity and drive toward sexual gratification, and the pressure to succeed academically inevitably challenge the most well-meaning student. In a model of adolescent development presented in 2007 (L. Plante), four fundamental challenges confront youth. Young adults are confronting core developmental challenges in the areas of identity, intimacy, independence, and impulse control, also referred to as "the Four I's." All emerging adults, to various extents, are contending with identity formation, intimacy needs, skills needed for increased independence, and greater control over impulses. Helping both students and school officials understand the healthy developmental underpinnings of poor ethical choices can illuminate a process of teaching conscious decision making that humanizes college students at this formative time in their lives.

Colleges are well equipped to confront these issues in an educative, humanizing, and safeguarding manner. Universities need to create communities where students emerge from college as more ethical citizens than when they entered, and are in an ideal position to teach, support, and guide students toward this goal. A wide variety of approaches to moral ethics have been articulated, such as those emphasizing justice, utilitarianism, common good, absolute moral rules, and many others. In this book we refer to the RRICC model of ethical decision making, developed in 2004 by Thomas Plante, emphasizing the core values of respect, responsibility, integrity, competence, and concern as the foundations of sound ethical behavior. It is imperative that colleges expand their view of higher education to address the whole individual, and personal ethical decision making is critical to students' success and positive contributions to society.

In brief, we believe that the rampant rates of problematic college behavior demand intervention at the individual and institutional levels. Underlying the choice to participate in excessive drinking, sexual assault, and academic cheating involve core issues of personal morality and personal ethics, which all students must define for themselves. Learning how to make ethical decisions in an intelligent, intentional, ethically literate manner consistent with one's personal goals can only be accomplished with direct teaching, conversation, guidance, and modeling within the college environment. Our book provides a model for imparting the skills of ethical decision making to college students during a time of great transition, temptation, and unprecedented freedom. The developmental imperatives toward intimacy, identity, independence, and impulse control are integral to an understanding of the conflicts inherent to making ethical choices as young adults, and they need to be integrated into the understanding, teaching, and mentoring of students.

Acknowledgments

Many people other than the author or authors assist in the completion of a book project. Some contribute in a direct way while others help in a more supportive manner. We would like to acknowledge the assistance of the many wonderful people who helped us to make this book idea a reality.

First, we would like to thank our wonderful colleagues at the Ethics Institute at Dartmouth College for hosting us while on sabbatical during the Spring 2016 academic term while working on this project. Professor and Institute Director Aine Donovan and administrative assistant Diane Belback provided enormous assistance and support as well as terrific advice about all things Dartmouth and the Upper Valley, New Hampshire, and Vermont. We also wish to express appreciation for colleagues at Santa Clara University who provided sabbatical and grant support, allowing the time and resources for this book project to be completed. Special thanks to the Markkula Center for Applied Ethics director and professor, Kirk Hanson. Thanks also to SCU faculty colleagues who teach ethics, including Shannon Vallor, Margaret McLean, and David DeCosse. Additionally, SCU staff members Matthew Duncan, Lester Deanes, and Dana McCusker all offered invaluable advice on ethical formation within student life and athletics in particular. Many thanks to our dear friend and colleague, Miriam McKendall, a Boston-based higher education attorney for Title IX and other legal related advice.

Many thanks to Santa Clara University students who have taken Ethics in Psychology over the years, and especially the following students who offered helpful and extensive quotes about ethics formation on campus that we used in chapter 10: Zach Hines, Megan Schiel, Evangeline Yang, Ian Maltzer, Teresa Wickstron, Allison Byrne, Christian Deamer, Jessica Olhausen, Michael Turgeon, and Sonya Chalaka. Thanks also to the following Dartmouth College students who were interviewed about campus ethics as part of this book project: Noah Goldstein, Chris Dalldorf, James Fair, Phil Gomez, and Mary Sieredzinski.

It is also important to recognize the terrific people at ABC-CLIO who published this book. Most especially, many thanks go to our editor, Debbie Carvalko, for her efforts not only with this book project but with many other book projects that we have published with her assistance during the past several decades.

Finally, we would like to acknowledge our son, Zach, who is a constant reminder that life is good and sacred and that we are blessed beyond words to have him in our lives. As a college student at Dartmouth himself, he well epitomizes an interest in and model of good ethical citizenship and strivings. As we have often said to each other, in so many ways, we want to be just like him when we grow up!

Part I

Establishing the Foundation
for Ethical Development
in College

Chapter 1

Introduction to Ethical Issues in College

We are convinced that most emerging adults have been poorly educated about how to think about moral issues.
—Christian Smith, *Lost in Transition*, p. 21

What exactly is so unique about the college years? Developmentally, it is a watershed period rich with growth and equally rich with challenges. First, college is notoriously an adolescent's first launching point from their parents and homes, and as such embodies a sudden encounter with a host of adult-like choices. Upon leaving home, college students begin emerging adulthood on still-shaky legs. Some are fully aware of their inexperience, while others are naively overconfident and sail headlong into trouble, harming themselves and others. Second, college is a critical period of making wholly independent choices about their adult future, with decisions regarding their lifestyle and future career direction thrust directly in their paths. Defining one's intellectual and career trajectory is central to self-definition itself, as students must decide between many of those proverbial diverging roads. Third, issues of core identity are consolidated during college, as students gain insight into their central goals, passions, values, affiliations, and declarations of whom they want to be in the world. Finally, relationships take on a new intensity while students are surrounded 24-7 by same-age peers, often far away from family, and beliefs and choices regarding intimacy, sexuality, and commitment become imperative. All told, the college years are often a defining moment in the life-span, uniquely formative to adult identity.

College students (usually) are no longer living under their parents' roofs. They are no longer reliant on parents for everyday needs: transportation, eating, sleeping, purchasing supplies, studying, going to class on time, and determining who to spend time with, when, and doing what. Choices regarding drugs, alcohol, sexual behavior, and academic performance are purely within the college student's control to choose and regulate. Some young adults are better prepared to function independently, possessing experiences and character traits that provide greater stability and sound judgment. Many others are ill prepared and must error, flounder, and learn difficult lessons through regrettable choices and actions. As stated by Christian Smith (2011), youth are provided with "few useful intellectual tools for working on moral questions" (p. 21). It is incumbent upon colleges to correct this greatly overlooked intellectual and character-defining realm by teaching these very skills to their students. The typical four-year span of college affords all students a significant runway toward finding their direction, values, and internal controls.

This same four-year span of college also presents unique opportunities to develop ethical attunement and skills, complete with lessons learned through trials and successes. Where do ethics figure into this key life stage? The answer is: everywhere. Especially outside their parents' and high school teachers' purview, college students are forced to confront difficult ethical dilemmas on their own. Away from the fishbowl of high school, college students have greater freedom to do what they want, and have only their own consciences, well-beings, and moral codes to rely upon. Issues ranging from whether to report a fellow student for cheating and the justness of sneaking extra food out of the dining hall, to sexual choices in the throes of passion and/or intoxication are all commonplace. The stakes in college are higher now, as students must answer to law enforcement as full adults, and futures often hinge on critical choices. The imperatives of Title IX policies designed to protect against sexual assault and discrimination (discussed in chapter 15) now confront students from the moment they arrive on campus, requiring ethical integrity, awareness, and practical skills to navigate. Ethical issues pervade all of our lives, but for college students, their sudden independence places them at risk for making uninformed and impulsive choices. Thus, integrating education regarding ethical decision making into curriculums and campus communities provides guidance and a structural framework for developing one's own ethical code during this critical life passage of emerging adulthood.

EXAMPLE ONE: ONE DECISION, TWO SCENARIOS

A. Anna arrives as a newly minted freshman to immediately become swept up in the giddy socializing and partying on campus. She has been clearly informed in her orientation materials that hard alcohol is strictly banned on campus. While beer and wine are less strictly enforced, consequences for violating the hard liquor ban are quite severe.

Three weeks into her first term, Anna attends a fraternity party where word is spread of vodka shots being generously dispensed in the upstairs room of an upperclassman. While not particularly interested in pounding shots, she nonetheless follows a stream of students up the staircase and into the appointed room. Since she is not drinking, a bottle is thrust into her hands and she is asked to help pour drinks. It's a fun atmosphere and she's happy to be a part of the festivities, and after all, she isn't drinking any of the stuff herself. The night seems to have gone well until iPhone video of the event is posted on Facebook. Students seen in the room are summoned by administrators and summarily suspended until next fall term.

B. Now let's view this same scenario under different circumstances. Prior to arriving at college, Anna has been required to view an online video spelling out campus rules and resources regarding alcohol consumption and the many health, interpersonal, and legal risks at stake with excessive drinking. This is a strictly educational video that Anna, along with most students, watches reluctantly. Also in the materials is an outline of the school's Ethical Development Program. Many decisions students make are discussed through various ethical models, and Anna is alerted to the fact that student life involves a number of modes of integrating ethical thinking throughout the college years. Included are examples of some of the programs provided to teach ethical decision making and discuss ethical issues, places she can seek support and counsel regarding ethical quandaries, and information about a disciplinary board that responds to rule violations as teachable opportunities to help students evaluate their own ethical beliefs and serve restitution that corrects their violation through meaningful action. Individual follow-up consultation with a school official to check in regarding the student's ethical growth is not only available but mandatory.

It hadn't occurred to Anna that so many simple to complex decisions held ethical implications, and that making good decisions involves a great deal more than simply knowing right from wrong. She also learned that making such decisions intentionally and thoughtfully, and in fact being on the lookout for ethical dilemmas, could greatly enhance her ability to live consistently within her personal ethical standards. The ensuing seminars and dorm-based discussions about ethics helped her begin to develop this awareness along with practical skills that helped to implement her own personal ethical beliefs.

Three weeks into the term, Anna attends a fraternity party where word quickly spreads about available hard alcohol upstairs. Anna immediately realizes that even if the chances of getting caught are low, her subsequent decisions have significant ethical implications regarding not only her personal well-being but also her respect for the restrictions deemed necessary to function as a citizen of the college in good standing. Despite her friends' objections, and her appeal to them to leave with her, Anna chooses to leave the party and find something else to do.

These two examples illustrate the potential shift in awareness and decision making that can result from integrated efforts to educate students from the moment of admission. Declaring ethical behavior a campus-wide priority from the get-go, colleges help encourage students toward this highly valued aspect of campus culture and education. Awareness, strategies, structure, support, and ongoing programming can greatly enhance college students' ethical formation and successful decision making through college and beyond.

Ethical quandaries also emerge repeatedly throughout college in regard to interpersonal relationships. The complexities of sharing a living space with a new roommate, the often chaotic and intrusive environment of dormitory life, and the constant exposure to the intimate relationships of fellow students generate daily challenges to personal conduct and interpersonal relationships. Is it ethical to "borrow" a roommate's jacket, or read his journal, or make out with her boyfriend? Should one report the fellow student selling Ecstasy or look the other way? If a dorm mate "borrows" his roommate's car without permission, is that his business or something to be addressed? So many daily dilemmas emerge in such close proximity to so many young people that it's virtually impossible to survive a day without one.

EXAMPLE TWO

Tom and Varun are freshman roommates. Tom has been together with Maya for two months, often kicking Varun out at night so they can sleep together. Varun is conflict averse, and graciously sleeps on the couch in the common area more nights than not. Maya feels badly for Varun and tells Tom that they should spend more nights apart. Tom is torn between his desire to sleep with Maya and his responsibility to his roommate.

What ethical model can be drawn on to work out this dilemma? Which developmental striving is at stake in this scenario?

EXAMPLE THREE

Alejandro is at a sorority party and sees his friend's girlfriend, Yvonne, sitting alone, looking dazed and intoxicated. She's totally hot. He talks to her and quickly sees that she's had too much to drink. In fact, she's coming on to him and telling him that he's way cuter than her boyfriend. Alejandro is certainly tempted to hook up with Yvonne, but does not want to take advantage of her vulnerable and inebriated state. He helps her walk to her roommate, who takes her back to the dorm.

Alejandro knows he did the right thing, but should he tell his friend about Yvonne's attempted infidelity? Should his friend know that his girlfriend was hitting on him, or should he keep it to himself? Alejandro feels very conflicted.

Both of these examples portray extremely common situations confronted by college students. Neither dilemma offers a clear, black-or-white solution, and both require nuanced reasoning and communication. An understanding of ethical decision making and the developmental imperatives at play for students provide invaluable tools and agency at this otherwise confusing time of life.

Here again is an example that students and parents often face.

EXAMPLE FOUR

Sue loves college and has enjoyed a thriving social life. Often, her priority on friends and parties trumps her commitment to study, resulting in the need to drop classes rather than fail them. She hasn't wanted to tell her parents about the dropped number of classes because she's supposed to be graduating in the spring, and they'll freak out if they hear she won't be graduating. The embarrassment and the additional costs of another term of college feel overwhelming, and Sue puts off dealing with these realities until it is almost too late.

Sue needs to recognize the varied ethical issues at stake. First, by withholding information from her parents, she risks damaging their trust and may cause them to feel actively deceived. Her denial of not having enough credits to graduate further risks her self-respect and the way her peers view her. Also, the wasted tuition fees and prospective costs of another semester of college will be judged as irresponsible and result in anger and even some punishment from her parents.

EXAMPLE FIVE

Sue has also used her parents' credit card to purchase alcohol for dorm parties on multiple occasions. She made the purchases at Walmart and led her parents to believe that she was purchasing necessary school and self-care supplies. How can Sue respond when her parents finally confront her about these escalating purchases? Or is there a way to approach them prior to their discovering it on their own?

In both of these examples, which are all too common among young people adjusting to increased freedoms and lowered accountability, issues of integrity, respect, responsibility, concern, and competence are at stake. How can an ethical model of decision making, combined with teaching strategies of parents and colleges, be employed to minimize the negative consequences and allow Sue a path toward restitution and the salvation of her moral code? This book sets out to provide exactly such a guide.

This book provides a roadmap for students to partner with their colleges in acquiring tools to recognize and respond to ethical challenges. The RRICC model elaborates on five key principles to consider when confronting any ethical dilemma, assisting students in evaluating how respect, responsibility, integrity, competence, and concern can all be upheld and fulfilled through each complex decision. In order to help students recognize and humanize their struggle, an enhanced understanding of the four key developmental challenges underlying college-age drives are identified and explained in the "Four I's." Identity, independence, intimacy, and impulse control are the healthy underlying strivings of developing young adults, and it is critical that students appreciate these drives within each ethical conflict. Finally, the means by which colleges can integrate instruction and guidance on ethical decision making into the very fabric of college life is discussed. When finished, educators and students will be armed and ready to partner in maximizing ethical choices that best uphold personal values and lead toward the successful attainment of their goals.

MORAL DEVELOPMENT THROUGH ADOLESCENCE

Moral development refers to an individual's sense of right and wrong, justice and injustice, and corresponding behavior. Throughout childhood and adolescence, cognitive and social maturation enables youth to deepen and strengthen their moral understanding of complex situations. Understanding the developmental process relevant to college-age students in their moral thinking and evolution is important for college personnel in order to best educate and assist students in this ongoing process. A summary of major theorists' perspectives on how moral development occurs throughout childhood and adolescence is helpful. The precise age range of emerging adulthood, the lengthy and eventful phase between childhood and adulthood, is imprecise. For example, the stages of adolescence can be defined as early adolescence (ages 10–13), middle adolescence (14–17), and late adolescence (18–22). Furthermore, adolescence has been getting longer as a result of social changes that have extended the length of time youth depend on their families for the adult tasks of financial independence, life management skills, and career development, as well as the increasing age when young adults partner in marriage. Tracing the moral evolution through this time span will help to inform our subsequent discussion of moral and ethical reasoning and behavior among college-age youth.

Each major approach to moral development provides a rough and imperfect model of how children become increasingly sophisticated in assessing morality as they grow up. Jean Piaget (1932) provided one of the earliest comprehensive theories of children's cognitive development, with their moral development paralleling cognition in terms of complexity and acuity. Piaget posited ages four through seven as the earliest formal stage of moral thinking, which he termed "heteronomous morality." During this period, children view rules as rigid and invariant and believe that games can be played in one, and only one, way. Once children transition from between ages seven to 10, the "incipient cooperation" stage enables them to view games more socially, and rules are accepted as generally the correct way to play in order to enhance a shared experience. By the "autonomous cooperation stage," occurring after age 10, children become cognizant of rules being available to modification if the players all agree to the new rules. This reflects children's growing understanding that rules are created by people and thus changeable by individuals agreeing to a new set of parameters.

Lawrence Kohlberg's model of moral reasoning was largely influenced by Piaget's emphasis on cognitive development. Kohlberg focused on the reasoning underlying the progression of moral reasoning, developing his stage theory based on subjects' responses to moral dilemmas (1984). His stage theory traces one's sense of justice based on evolving forms of reasoning associated with advancing cognitive development. The three major levels of moral reasoning—preconventional, conventional, and postconventional—correspond to an evolution from young children's focus on punishment and reward as the indicators of what is right and wrong. Gradually, children observe right and wrong based on others' approval or disapproval, and a rigid adherence to laws. During adolescence, society's rules are viewed in more abstract ethical terms, which emphasize ultimate justice and fairness. Importantly, this latter adolescent phase involves developing a personal code of ethics, requiring flexible thinking and identity integration. This is the stage at which most adolescents enter college, and their efforts to wrestle with and define their own morality become tested and refined throughout their emerging adulthood.

It is also notable that youth who function at higher stages of moral reasoning are more likely to be altruistic and honest (Fabes, Carlo, Kupanoff, & Laible, 1999) and less likely to engage in antisocial behavior (Carpendale, 2000). Nonetheless, research has uncovered a gap between knowing what is right and doing what is right, as there is often a discrepancy between the two (Hart, Burock, London, & Atkins, 2003). Kohlberg's theory has been criticized for being based solely on observations of Western cultures, and for its lack of data obtained from females. This bias led to an alternative view of female moral development developed by Carol Gilligan.

In the 1980s, Carol Gilligan (1982) suggested that moral behavior among men and women differed as a result of societal attitudes in childrearing. She observed that broad concepts such as justice and fairness determined boys' morality, while girls viewed morality more in terms of self-sacrifice and responsibility to others. In her model, girls' moral behavior is based more on compassion than it is for boys. She suggested a three-stage process beginning with an "orientation toward individual survival" stage. This self-serving perspective is limited to what is best for oneself with little consideration of others. During stage two, girls begin to value "goodness as self-sacrifice" and therefore strive to overlook their own wishes in order to provide what others want. Gradually, however, this stage leads to an integration of what is best for the needs of both the self and others.

During stage three, the "morality of nonviolence" emerges, where more sophisticated forms of reasoning view hurting anyone, including oneself, as immoral. This leads to a greater relational perspective on morality, emphasizing cooperation and compromise based on an equal view of the rights of others and themselves. Gilligan views this understanding of equivalent rights as the highest level of moral reasoning.

Gilligan's model has been criticized as too sweeping in its conclusions about gender differences and too dismissive of Kohlberg's approach (Damon & Colby, 1987). Nonetheless, gender and other cultural variations in moral reasoning deserve serious attention.

For the purposes of our emphasis on how colleges can assist students in their ethical and moral development, we will emphasize the social learning perspective on morality. This approach focuses primarily on how the environment in which adolescents live influences and even produces behavior, moral or otherwise. Helping colleges generate environments wherein high ethical standards are advocated, taught, modeled, and rewarded is the most powerful means of influencing students' character and behavior. Adolescents are capable of generalizing from ethical principles that are taught and modeled within their college into their own beliefs and behavior. Integral and inseparable from children's development of character is the school environment within which they are immersed and influenced. As noted by William Damon in his seminal work, *The Moral Child: Nurturing Children's Natural Moral Growth* (1988):

The overall goal of any (educational) program must be to help children reason autonomously about moral problems. No amount of rote learning or indoctrination will prepare children for the many diverse situations that they will face in life. The child must learn to identify the moral issue in an ambiguous situation, to apply basic moral values to unfamiliar problems, and to create moral solutions when there is no one around to give the child direction. . . . Moral education programs must keep as their first goal the fostering of such an ability and above all must do nothing to hinder its development. (p. 149)

CONCLUSION

Few colleges provide coherent, integrated programs for addressing the ethical development of their students. At a time of life when young people are seeking to define themselves and make independent decisions outside the influence and oversight of their families, colleges are remiss in ignoring the needs of students in learning how to think about and resolve ethical dilemmas. After all, college life is replete with difficult decisions that involve moral and ethical challenges. This book seeks to provide a path for colleges to provide such ethical instruction as well as suffuse their campuses with models and resources for students as they endeavor to define their own ethical paths through college and in life.

Chapter 2

The Four I's: Developmental Goals and Challenges in College

American emerging adults are a people deprived, a generation that has been failed, when it comes to moral formation.
— Christian Smith, *Lost in Transition*, pp. 68–69

What makes the college years special in the grand scheme of lifelong development? What are the primary goals and challenges faced by the developing young adult during this formative life phase? In this chapter, we discuss the Four I's described by Lori Plante in 2007. These consist of four developmental imperatives with which virtually every young adult struggles. Identity, independence, intimacy, and impulse control are the siren calls of young adult development, and challenges from which we suffer and celebrate throughout the remainder of our lives. The wholesale transition during college from adolescence to emerging adulthood can be fraught with great tumult and conflict, and at the same time rewarded with enormous personal benefits. College is a particularly rich and immersive training ground for the ethical developmental growth of emerging adults, who are facing these challenges in a milieu populated by thousands of their peers and overseen by scores of adults charged with their education and formation.

Today, the path between adolescence and adulthood is more confusing and ambiguous than it was in past decades, extending the ages defined by adolescence well into the 20s, and perhaps even beyond. As a result, many labels are applied, including "adultolescence," "emerging adulthood," "young adulthood," and "extended adolescence." This phase of emerging adulthood situated between the teenage years and adulthood proper encompasses a broad range of developmental milestones and challenges set within societal context. For example, widespread economic changes have made it more difficult for youth to begin stable, lifelong careers, resulting in increased financial dependency on parents and loans. Many sociological changes have also occurred to further complicate this transition. For example, today's median age of first marriage for women has risen from 20.3 in 1960 to 25.9 years old in 2006, while men have delayed marriage during the same time period from 22.8 to 27.5 years old (Smith, 2011, p. 15). According to Smith, this shift is partly attributed to the greater number of youth seeking college and post-college educations as opposed to beginning their working careers at age 18. Inherent to these changes has been American parents' willingness, and often necessity, to extend financial support to their emerging adult children, including the growing phenomenon of these same children residing with parents well into their 20s. Thus, a variety of sociocultural and economic shifts have increased the sense of instability and anxiety that accompanies the emerging adult through this long, confusing transition.

A combination of terror and exhilaration often confronts the new college freshman. The dual temptations and challenges of sudden independence make students open to positive or negative influences in many forms. When colleges overtly proclaim and demonstrate the values and goals they seek to instill, young adults in search of direction and meaning can be offered positive models for attaining similar character goals. Inherent in all aspects of young adult development is the ongoing process of determining a personal code of ethics for operating in the adult world. Some students emerge inspired and practiced in the ethical skills and values that underlie so much of their subsequent professional and personal conduct, whereas others can be misguided and ultimately ethically stunted or damaged. It is therefore imperative for colleges and students to work together explicitly in defining and exploring the often unspoken framework for personal ethics, and in providing a context for humane guidance in the fine art of ethical decision making.

THE FOUR I'S: IDENTITY, INDEPENDENCE, INTIMACY, AND IMPULSE CONTROL

Identity

Identity is the consistent sense of one's core sense of self. Identity is the ultimate integration of an acceptable, realistic, and consistent sense of who one is, how one relates to others, and what roles, aptitudes, and values form the structure of one's life. The fundamental question "Who am I?" is answered by one's self-knowledge of the totality of values, qualities, strengths, weaknesses, beliefs, and passions that consistently define and direct us. Emerging adults are immersed in a hotbed of identity formation during college, where their professional, interpersonal, and ethical goals are constantly challenged and decisions must be made. Having a realistic sense of self, and of what one values and the manner in which one pursues these values, is central to a successful career and relational and self-care decisions. College students must increasingly ask the question "Who am I and who do I want to be in the world?" and ethical values are inevitably tested and defined in the answers.

In coming to terms with one's identity, replete with one's flaws and abilities, college students frequently test out a range of behaviors and affiliations. In seeking to determine and proclaim their identities, students often make poor choices and falter, hopefully learning more about themselves in the process. For example, a shy student might want to adopt a more outgoing identity, and by drinking heavily at social gatherings discovers a wildly less inhibited side of him- or herself. However, sometimes this drinking leads to embarrassing behavior, followed by throwing up, until the shy student learns to accept his or her core nature and take more sustainable steps toward a meaningful social identity. Thus, while the excessive drinking might be the wrong choice, the goal of gaining greater knowledge of one's core personality and social needs is in the healthy service of identity formation.

Similarly, students may commit terrible ethical violations in a poorly formed effort to ultimately pursue this quest for identity. A student might cheat on a test in an effort to fulfill their identity as a successful student, purchase alcohol for an underclassman in order to appear cool, or otherwise stumble into damaging behavior without considering both the ethical implications and the potential consequences. Thus, integrating an *awareness* and *strategy* for ethical decision making into the college curriculum and lifestyle can alert and arm students to *intentionally* think through ethical implications before diving headlong into misguided assertions of their identities.

By harnessing the innate motivation of young adults to establish a self-respecting and responsible identity, schools can champion their own culture of values. Emphasizing to students the centrality of a personal code of ethics in defining themselves, while also teaching the practical skills and strategies to consciously make informed ethical choices, colleges assist students in their quest for identity and integrity.

Independence

Nothing evokes heady independence and freedom like the college years. Seemingly unleashed into a world of independent choices and never-before-seen freedoms, college students nonetheless simultaneously confront the reality of owning responsibility for their decisions and actions. College students often walk a tightrope between easing yet not severing parental attachments and the proverbial net they provide. On this journey, young adults inevitably face decisions that test their ethical values apart from their parents' observing eyes. Thus, college students are learning to function independently, which means preserving and casting off certain beliefs and values their parents espouse. This journey of independence is often synonymous with learning through one's mistakes, and with the high stakes of many decisions during college, efforts to minimize destructive errors are invaluable.

By examining core ethical attitudes and developing a process for ethical decision making on their own, college students can benefit greatly from active instruction and reflection. Young adults often make poor ethical decisions without even knowing it in the eager pursuit of independence. Helping to attune students to the ethical aspects of acting independently can greatly facilitate their successful functioning into adulthood.

Example: Jamal has been eager to study abroad for many years. He particularly wants to explore environmental science programs in third world nations, and his university offers intriguing semesters in rural India and Somalia. Jamal's parents do not think these countries are safe and tell him that they won't support his education unless it occurs in first world nations. Without their support, Jamal has no funds to pay for such an endeavor.

Jamal values his parents' approval but strongly disagrees with their narrow views on international travel. He feels passionate about his interest in improving agricultural self-reliance in the third world and has no interest in a semester in Rome or Barcelona. He decides that he has several options in dealing with his parents in this situation.

Scenario 1: Jamal doesn't grasp that he's in a healthy, age-appropriate conflict with his parents over his autonomous decision making. He can only reason that his parents pose an obstacle to something he wants and that they don't have a right to control his life. Jamal takes a stand and poses an ultimatum: "Pay for me to study where I want or I'm leaving college." This threat so angers his parents that the conflict escalates to a point where Jamal and his parents stop speaking to one another, and Jamal feels he has no choice but to drop out of school. Jamal feels defiantly independent from his parents control yet abjectly distressed by the self-destructive outcome.

Scenario 2: Jamal understands that he and his parents are confronting a classic developmental conflict over his growing independence. Jamal tries to explain to his parents that he appreciates their concerns but also feels compelled to make some difficult choices that align with both his values and his career goals. He provides his parents with literature on the program and encourages them to call the program's lead professor with specific safety questions. Jamal says that if his parents are uncomfortable funding such a program, he understands, but he will look into other funding sources since this is such an important opportunity for him. His parents are sympathetic but stick to their guns. Jamal applies for a student loan to fund the trip. While worried sick, his parents respect his commitment and willingness to independently choose and finance his education. Jamal feels excited to be making his own decision and maintains integrity by behaving in a respectful and responsible manner. Though the financial implications worry him, he feels pleased to maintain an open dialogue with his parents along with a growing sense of sound independence.

These two scenarios illustrate that in recognizing, normalizing, and humanizing the conflict, Jamal and his parents ultimately were able to disagree yet maintain mutual fondness and respect. By rejecting the options of threatening his parents or lying outright, Jamal was able to accept both the benefits and the responsibilities and consequences of his independent choices. This proved to be a huge learning and growing moment for both Jamal and his parents, with ethical values preserved.

Intimacy

The third "I" involves the healthy developmental striving for intimacy. Intimacy encompasses the need to fit in and feel accepted, and the ability to enjoy a secure sense of friendship and bonding with peers. It can also mean romantic and sexual intimacy, and the two can become frequently confused. During college, it is common for students to experiment with a variety of friendships and sexual relationships, and from these gain self-knowledge into what one desires, values, and defines as meaningful intimacy.

Often in this pursuit, college students choose friends or sexual partners poorly. These can prove to be benign mistakes or catastrophic alliances. Students can descend into drug and alcohol abuse by seeking to fit into a particular group of friends or engage in sex impulsively and dangerously. Ultimately, college can serve as an essential practice field for students to discover themselves in relation to others and define what constitutes healthy, gratifying, and sustainable relationships in their lives ahead. Unbeknownst to most students is even a rudimentary awareness that how they choose to interact with others involves constant ethical choices that reflect their core identities, values, and integrity. Having a meaningful way to spot ethical choices within relationships and resolve inevitable conflicts through a rational and thoughtful analysis can have huge positive implications for students' ability to relate to others in a manner consistent with who they want to be in the world.

Intimacy and sexuality pose developmental challenges throughout our lives, but during college, away from the protective embrace of home, young adults experience a renewed imperative to seek acceptance and affiliation and to define one's sexual needs, forms of expression, and boundaries. During a time of newfound freedom, such tasks can lead to tumultuous trial-and-error decisions, often with hazardous outcomes. Furthermore, in the era of 21st-century sexual norms, the concept of hooking up can cloud genuine experiences of intimacy. Hookups—or casual, no-strings-attached sexual contacts—are often devoid of emotional investment. While allowing for immediate gratification of sexual impulses, hookups largely fail to satisfy needs for affection, love, security, and closeness. While some young adults revel in these superficial sexual experiences, others are left with feelings of vulnerability, emptiness, and regret. Hookups are particularly rife for exploitation, and in alcohol-fueled environments, often lead to the all-too-frequent sexual assaults reported on college campuses. Unwanted pregnancies and sexually transmitted diseases are further casualties of encounters devoid of commitment, emotional investment, and interpersonal accountability.

Example: Someone in Joe's freshman dorm has commandeered a keg and is inviting everyone to a field adjacent to the school for a spontaneous party. Joe arrives to find at least 100 kids, and not just one keg but cases of vodka being consumed from plastic cups. Joe particularly notes the presence of scores of really cute girls, all in various stages of inebriation. Joe begins catching up on the drinking and soon finds himself swept up in the drunken revelry around him. Couples are making out, girls are dancing provocatively, and Joe finds himself draped around a very friendly co-ed. Joe enjoys the spontaneous hookup yet realizes that both he and the girl are very drunk. She seems willing to be as sexual as he desires, and suddenly Joe is faced with a choice: take this rare opportunity to lose his virginity, or consider the implications for (1) his own sexual safety and deeper relational goals, (2) the girl's impairment and vulnerability, and (3) the opportunistic aspects of having sex with her.

Joe reluctantly decides to enjoy kissing this girl but to stop there and make sure she gets back to her dorm safely. While he feels partly like a chump for passing up this alluring opportunity, he also feels a deep sense of pride and justice in how responsibly he chose to behave.

Example: Natasha has been in a monogamous relationship with her girlfriend Sami for several months. She's been a bit disenchanted lately but hasn't wanted to rock the boat. She cares deeply for Sami but feels that the relationship is growing stagnant, and that she's outgrown the dependency that initially bonded her to Sami. Also, she has been getting close to a girl named Meg on her tennis team. During a team trip, Meg opens up to Natasha and reveals that she has never had a relationship with a woman but now longs for one with her. Natasha finds Meg super attractive and hasn't felt such a rush of lust since the early days of her relationship with Sami. Suddenly, she is contemplating cheating on Sami.

Scenario 1: Natasha realizes that Sami doesn't even know Meg and is extremely unlikely to find out if they slept together. They are, after all, sharing a hotel room during the team trip. Natasha feels so much attraction that she doesn't even want to think about Sami. She allows herself to "be in the moment" and has a sexual encounter with Meg. Natasha returns to school feeling guilty, conflicted, and frankly confused. She barely studies for her engineering exam because she is so distracted, and is very irritable around Sami.

Scenario 2: Natasha really wants to explore sexual intimacy with Meg but knows that it would really hurt Sami. She realizes that she could indulge her attraction to Meg and tell herself it was no big deal, keeping it from Meg. She knows, however, that this is one of those "ethical dilemmas" her college is always harping about. Would engaging in sex with Meg show respect, responsibility, integrity, concern, and competence toward her relationship with Sami? No, no, no, no, and no. She realizes that she can't justify sex with Meg without violating clear ethical standards that she's painfully aware are important to her.

Natasha reluctantly tells Meg that even though she's greatly tempted, she better hold off until she comes to some honest resolution about her relationship with Sami. She may have a set of very difficult conversations ahead, but in reality she'll have to confront her dissatisfaction at some point. Natasha opens up to Meg but holds the line from becoming physical, with great restraint, and makes it back to campus to start the arduous conversation with Sami.

These two scenarios depict the drive for intimacy at a moment of great temptation, first blindly without a structure for considering ethical implications, and in the second scenario, when armed and fully aware of such issues. While no student is always going to make the decision they know is ethical, a chance to appraise and intentionally soul search can certainly increase the chances of an outcome most consistent with one's ethical goals.

Impulse Control

Perhaps one of our most important life skills, impulse control can lead to fruitful self-discipline and goal achievement, and stave off self-destructive, poorly considered, and even catastrophic life decisions. Impulse control requires the ability to delay gratification and postpone immediate desires in the service of sustained well-being and long-term ambitions. Clearly, those of us who can avoid impulsive sexual behavior, excessive eating, drinking and drugging, and a host of other temporary means of fulfilling immediate needs have a better prospect of remaining healthy, protecting relational commitments, and working steadily toward long-term goals. The ability to resist small immediate rewards in favor of larger delayed rewards is the hallmark of impulse control.

As stated by Daniel Goleman: "There is perhaps no psychological skill more fundamental than resisting impulse. It is the root of all emotional self-control, since all emotions, by their very nature, lead to one or another impulse to act" (1997, p. 81). Impulse control requires tolerating frustration and inhibiting action. The infamous marshmallow test studies begun by Walter Mischel in the 1960s provide a foundation for the huge life benefits of impulse control. In the study, researchers told children that they could have two marshmallow if they waited for 15 minutes, or if they couldn't wait, they could have a single marshmallow right away. In follow-ups with these subjects at high school graduation, those individuals who were able to earn the two marshmallows by employing impulse control were superior students, with SAT scores 210 points higher on average than those students who opted for the immediate single marshmallow. As teenagers, this latter group of students was described as more stubborn, indecisive, easily frustrated, and more prone to fights (Goleman, 1997, pp. 80–82).

Impulse control has everything to do with ethical decision making. Impulsivity has two key characteristics: quick, unplanned reactions, and lack of concern for the consequences of those actions. College students dive headlong into temptation without even pausing to think through the consequences of their behavior. With even a modicum of impulse control, college students can learn to be aware and alerted to enter thoughtfully into decisions of ethical consequence. Weighing their choices, and at the very least making an informed ethical decision prior to acting, automatically raises the internal stakes of impulsive choices. Despite awareness of ethical failure, students may ultimately choose immediate gratification nonetheless. Knowing that one is cheating does not alone prevent indulging in it. Awareness of the risks of excessive drinking in violation of school rules does not necessarily result in temperance. However, a process of careful instruction and discernment regarding one's personal ethical goals, integrated throughout the course of college, can provide that extra awareness and impetus for students to make the right decision for themselves.

Example 1: Aaron has a huge exam tomorrow in his statistics class. He hates this course and does not feel like studying hard. However, he is a pre-med major, and his grade in the class is important. His fraternity brothers invite Aaron to join them in a movie night, and Aaron expresses hesitation because of his need to study. One of his friends tells him not to sweat it; he already hacked into the department secretary's computer file and knows the questions and the answers for the exam. He's happy to share them with Aaron, guaranteeing an A in the class plus a fun night away from studying.

Aaron is tempted mightily. He knows that this constitutes cheating, but he rationalizes that since his friend is already taking that advantage, and he hates the class anyway, it's not such a big deal . . . as long as he doesn't get caught. Then he considers what it would mean if he did get caught: possible suspension, expulsion or an F in the class, plus the shame and embarrassment. He reflects on the RRICC model and is painfully confronted with how lacking in integrity, competence, respect, concern, and responsibility such an act of cheating represents. He doesn't want to be that guy who cheats on exams, and even if he gets away with it he'll feel guilty. Aaron swallows hard, suspends his desire for a fun night and an easy A, and commences to study with a renewed sense of integrity despite the misery of statistics.

Example 2: Devrick attends a university that has banned hard liquor on campus. He and his friends think it's a dumb rule and insulting to their freedom and independence as young adults. Devrick knows that the penalties for drinking hard liquor are harsh, but he also knows that it's unlikely he and his friends will be discovered with vodka dispensed from water bottles. He justifies his decision by asserting his right to make his own choices and his disagreement with the merits of the alcohol ban. He and his friends get completely trashed, throw up all over the dorm, and piss off the other students on their floor. While no authorities discover their violation, they become known in the dorm as the guys who spurn university rules and act irresponsibly toward themselves and their peers.

Example 3: Shauna has been lusting after a water polo player named Isaac. He hasn't expressed much interest in Shauna until they discover each other high on Ecstasy and marijuana at an off-campus rave. Isaac is all over Shauna, and she is completely thrilled and turned on. She isn't, however, taking any birth control, and she's too embarrassed to ask if Isaac has a condom. She realizes that she faces a classic conflict of impulse control: she longs to surrender to temptation yet realizes that she doesn't believe in abortion and has no desire to have a child right now. What are the chances? she thinks. Then she remembers her ethics advisor talking about Responsibility, Respect, and some other stuff, and how clear she felt about maintaining those ethical standards. With great disappointment and restraint she realizes that risking a pregnancy is all wrong in her personal moral code and she draws the appropriate boundary with Isaac. The next day, after the effects of the drugs wear off, she is grateful not to be worried that she might be pregnant.

Impulse control is a matter of degrees, and all of us exhibit it to varying extents on a continuum. Its judicious deployment can greatly assist college students in their studies, career goals, interpersonal relationships, athletic and creative pursuits, and overall maintenance of mental and physical health. Often the temptations that steer us toward impulsive action have ethical ramifications, with implications for one's personal integrity, competence, responsibility, respect, and concern for others. For college students, without an awareness and a set of skills to problem solve through ethical dilemmas, the risk of stumbling into damaging situations is accentuated. By instilling ethical literacy into the college environment, positive decisions and behaviors that require impulse control can only be enhanced.

THE VULNERABLE, HIGH-RISK COLLEGE STUDENT

Not all young adults are equally well equipped to process ethical choices and make thoughtful, healthy decisions. Many students enter the college environment on shaky legs, not yet in possession of the emotional, cognitive, and social skills necessary to traverse from family support to authentic independence. Who are these more fragile adolescents? How can they be identified, supported, and helped to remain safe and ethical people?

Developmental crises can erupt during college when the normative tasks of identity formation, independence, intimacy, and impulse control hit roadblocks that the young adult lacks the resources to confront. The

Four I's evolve from foundations that may be strong, weak, or wildly divergent in maturation. Assessing each young adult through the lens of their developmentally appropriate levels of identity formation, independent functioning, interpersonal relating, and ability to control impulses can provide an invaluable window into which youth are most vulnerable, and in respect to which challenges in particular. Boosting resilience with the practical tools to problem solve around difficult choices can arm students to make responsible decisions in the face of adversity.

The increasing phenomenon of college students lacking resilience and the capacity to independently tackle life's demands is well documented. In her recent book *How to Raise an Adult* (2015), Julie Lythcott-Haims describes an epidemic of overprotected, overparented youth who lack the basic life skills and resilience to make effective decisions and contend with challenges. Colleges are dealing with more and more such students, and parents, who are appealing for support around challenges that are typically managed independently by students. Thus, given this generation of more dependent and less resilient youth (particularly from middle- and upper-middle-class homes), it behooves colleges to teach and educate students to problem solve and make decisions that are consistent with their goals and ethics.

College students struggling with identity confusion are particularly at risk for poor decision making. These young adults are easily led, or misled, and may grasp on to behaviors or experiment with personas that ultimately fail them. Students who lack sufficient identity consolidation are vulnerable to impairments in self-esteem and may generally feel lost and overwhelmed by the vast options and array of diverse demands and individuals in the college setting. In addition, many students entering college with a diffuse and changing sense of their own core identities are more at risk for anxiety and depression, academic setbacks, and venturing into behavior and affiliations that are largely experimental and poorly chosen. Young adults with fluctuating identities can lack direction, lasting attachments, and the ability to make consistent choices.

Students who enter college still highly dependent can find the transition especially difficult. Without parents or familiar others available to guide, advise, set limits, or otherwise support them, students can become overwhelmed with the many decisions they immediately encounter at college. Which courses should I take? Which groups or activities appeal to me? How do I divide and manage my time? How do I manage my budget? Do I want to do shots just because I can? When should I sleep, study, eat, and socialize? How do I cope with homesickness? The decisions are limitless, and when rules, boundaries, safeguards, and the vigilance of parents are suddenly removed, college students can feel extremely confused, vulnerable, and unmoored. These students are at risk for poor self-regulation and have great difficulty essentially caring for their basic needs and equilibrium. They may also feel like neophytes in the realms of drug and alcohol use, sexuality, and self-discipline. Students who enter college with little experience or confidence in independent living can quickly find themselves in serious trouble academically, medically, emotionally, sexually, and otherwise.

College students also vary in their ability to satisfy their needs for friendship and intimacy in healthy ways. Many students have poor boundaries, unsatisfactory relational histories, and encounter great difficulties negotiating the social world of college. Some may be simply shy, socially anxious, or have undergone damaging traumas. Others may have such a high need to affiliate that they engage in indiscriminate sexual liaisons, participate naively in risky rituals such as drinking games or fraternity initiations, join friends in shunning certain groups, or otherwise dive headfirst into all manner of social invitation. Similarly, impaired impulse control clearly places students at high risk for missteps in college, and thrill seekers may be at especially heightened risk for a variety of damaging outcomes. Identifying students who exhibit impaired or damaging relational histories can help to better equip vulnerable students to contend with these challenges.

Not surprisingly, there are also plenty of college students who blithely believe that they have all the answers. The narcissism of young adults can sometimes be astonishing, as they on one hand insist that they know exactly what's best for themselves while on the other hand demonstrate self-destructive outcomes in many of their choices. Even those students who appear arrogant or overtly confident tend to have a vulnerable underbelly of insecurity and self-doubt. Again, when colleges can normalize the struggles inherent to college life *and* offer concrete, practical tools for contending with difficult choices, students are empowered to better assess their strengths, weaknesses, and ultimate decisions.

Finally, impulse control is a very useful predictor of college success and the capacity to make thoughtful, ethical decisions. Impulsivity is clearly a risk factor in a range of detrimental behaviors, including suicide and self-harm, excessive alcohol and drug use, high-risk sexual behavior, poor academic performance, and aggressive or abusive behavior. Young adults who have an unresolved history of poor impulse control and associated problematic behaviors are clearly at heightened risk of continued vulnerability in college. These are the students who will benefit from additional education, support, supervision, and skills aimed at improving their ability to think before acting, delay gratification, and say no to unhealthy temptation.

The Four I's are accessible reference points for understanding students, and for students to self-reflect and gain awareness of their own developmental strengths and areas for growth. Importantly, even young adults who display immaturity or previous missteps can develop into ethical individuals capable of making thoughtful decisions that integrate their personal values, beliefs, and goals. It is imperative, however, that students receive the preparation, education, compassion, and assistance they need in order to facilitate such positive development.

UNDERSTANDING WHY COLLEGE STUDENTS MISBEHAVE

Oddly enough, young adults are notorious for making the wrong decisions, often for the right reasons. The implication here is that young people often make the wrong choices in their well-meaning striving to grapple with the goals of intimacy, identity, independence, and impulse control. Thus, a student may choose to restrict her eating in an effort to control impulses and fears of overeating, resulting in a classic eating disorder. Another student may engage in unsafe sexual relationships with the ultimate aim of feeling close and intimate. A student may fail to seek tutoring or help from a professor, trying to be independent. Quite commonly, a student may try to affiliate and socialize with a group that does not truly fit his or her personality and goals, all in an effort to achieve a false image of identity. Thus, it is critical that college staff, parents, and ultimately students understand what drives them and how these healthy drives can often lead to both positive and negative choices. Most importantly, equipping students with the skills to identify and resolve these dilemmas in an intentional and rational manner can greatly reduce the risk of misbehavior.

CONCLUSION

The Four I's—identity, independence, intimacy, and impulse control—were defined in this chapter as the central developmental challenges confronted by young adults. The Four I's are developmental imperatives that can underlie and precipitate poor choices on the path to more mature decision making. Ethical underpinnings of these decisions can lend valuable information and awareness to students in the throes of compelling drives, allowing for more conscious and thoughtful choices. Students at high risk can be assessed along the continuums of the Four I's, and by identifying and understanding their influence, lessen their chances of danger. When faced with these drives, ethical decision-making strategies enable students to first consider whether their actions will reflect the standards of respect, responsibility, integrity, competence, and concern that they seek to personally uphold.

Chapter 3

Ethics 101: Moral Philosophy in a Nutshell

A man without ethics is a wild beast loosed upon this world.
—Albert Camus

Ethical decisions are far more nuanced and complicated than simply distinguishing right from wrong. Most often, the small and large ethical dilemmas we face are neither black nor white, and require careful thought and difficult decision making. In addition, people typically assume that ethical decisions revolve only around large-scale issues involving infidelity, theft, cheating, lying, criminal behavior, and violations of firmly held religious principles. However, it is our facility with recognizing and thoughtfully resolving everyday ethical decisions that builds the skills necessary to resist capitulation to greater risks and temptations. College students who are taught to develop an ethical framework and practice these skills continually develop something akin to a "muscle memory" for choosing more wisely when confronted with highly consequential and challenging dilemmas. Thus, by paying back the five dollars a roommate lent, aware that it is an ethical issue, a student is more prepared to contend honestly with financial commitments on a larger scale, such as paying taxes or "cooking the books" within a business.

This book is not intended to prescribe specific dos and don'ts or moralistic judgments. The intention is not to preach or judge or generate guilt. It is not to tell people what to do and which code of ethics they should follow. Rather, the goal is to outline options and models for personal ethical decision making that are grounded in solid research and centuries of moral philosophy, along with a clinical understanding of how emerging adults in particular can make highly personal and satisfying decisions for themselves. At least being armed with the knowledge and skills to approach thorny issues provides young adults an alertness to conflicts and a structure and process for making more informed and intentional choices while wrestling with difficult, ethically charged decisions. This book is designed for colleges to help students obtain practical tools and experience in order to recognize, think through, and problem solve challenges that they face in life. They are then far better equipped to live by the ethical standards they set for themselves and to act thoughtfully and consistently in living with honor as they define it.

Ethical choices confront us everywhere. Should I give money to the homeless person asking desperately on the street? Should I stop and help someone having car problems on a freeway? Should I tell a store clerk that I was given too much change? Should I fudge a bit on my taxes since everyone else does? Should I choose plastic, paper, or no bag at the store? Should I serve stale food as directed by my boss or refuse to endanger customers? Should I be true to my own sexual needs or honor my commitment to my partner? Should I bother reducing my daily water use when so much is wasted by poor governmental policies? Should I agree to work as a research assistant in a lab that experiments on animals? And which types of animals? Each of these decisions can be resolved from a variety of ethical perspectives originating in the field of moral philosophy. Few of us are likely to invoke Aristotle, Plato, Kant, Locke, or St. Augustine reflexively, and college students outside the philosophy department will generally draw a blank to those iconic forerunners of ethical thought. A simpler strategy is required, which we will provide in the next chapter. First, however, a brief review of historical approaches to ethics can greatly inform young adults and their educators.

This chapter will describe nine classical ethical approaches with roots in moral philosophy. Some will seem more helpful or sensible to each reader, and several may be combined when thinking through decisions. In order to begin appreciating one's own ethical sensibility, a crash course in these nine approaches to moral philosophy will be helpful.

Cultural Relativism

It is always useful in considering the cultural context when making decisions. Cultural traditions, expectations, and norms often guide which behaviors are acceptable and which are not. Ethical behavior in one cultural context may be deemed patently unethical in another. For example, the use of corporal punishment may be considered appropriate and necessary for disciplining children in a particular region or culture. In others, any form of physical punishment of children may be judged offensive, inappropriate, or frankly illegal. Similarly, arranging one's son's or daughter's marriage is perfectly normative in some cultures, while in many Western traditions such practices are not accepted.

Cultural relativism can create harsh realities, many of which seem barbaric through Western eyes. For example, female circumcision is considered an appropriate practice in certain cultures, whereas to many others, it is deemed outright mutilation and misogyny. Some cultures forbid or simply overlook the education of females, and this state of affairs is largely accepted as the norm. Some women feel empowered and protected by culturally mandated garments covering their faces, while many women view this practice as demeaning. In many liberal communities, gay marriage is widely accepted and embraced, whereas in other communities the cultural ethos condemns it. While cultural relativism may not lead one to condone the norms of another culture, awareness of the power and import of such relative norms can shed light and greater understanding. Fundamentally, cultural relativism reminds us that our own personal ethics emerge in a context of larger social norms and traditions, and that each society and sub-society has developed its own view of what constitutes an ethical practice.

Egoism

This approach to ethical behavior will appeal to the hedonists among us. Egoism espouses that by doing what will make us feel the best, we are ultimately behaving ethically. While this might seem like a selfish perspective, it is possibly the approach that most people take when making ethical choices. When faced with an ethical decision, most people are likely to consider which decision is in their own best interest and will benefit them the most.

An example faced by a college student might involve their choice of careers. If a student has been under parental pressure to pursue a medical or scientific career yet feels called to study English literature, it could be argued that the most ethical choice is the one that is most authentic and true to one's self. While parents might be angry or disappointed, there is a certain integrity in honestly making a more authentic and personal career choice. This would be an example of egoism.

Egoism can also lead to surprisingly generous and positive contributions to society. For example, seemingly altruistic acts of philanthropy or volunteer service may be largely motivated by one's desire to feel good about oneself, receive public praise, or see one's name immortalized on a building. Nonetheless, this "selfish" need to feel generous or important can lead to highly positive social actions.

Sometimes, however, egoism can lead to the exploitation or mistreatment of others. For example, believing that just because people are drunk doesn't mean they should be inconvenienced by not driving their cars can clearly lead to deadly and criminal results. Or justifying a dangerous and illegal football maneuver on an opponent by viewing it as simply a means to win and help the team further illustrates the limitations of a singularly egoistic approach. Nonetheless, honest awareness of one's best interests in the context of other ethical guidelines can clarify impulses and ultimate decisions.

Utilitarianism

This approach seeks to resolve ethical dilemmas by deciding what course would be in the best interest of most people. This is a largely democratic approach to decision making that seeks to maximize the most benefit to the majority of people. Seeking a majority vote is a classic example of the utilitarian approach in action. While often very effective and ethical, this approach also has potential limitations and abuses.

For example, if the majority of people in a community voted to murder a known child molester, this is unlikely to be deemed ethical. Similarly, if the white majority of citizens in a community voted to limit the rights of its nonwhite citizens, this could also be viewed as an egregious abuse of power. Ethical dilemmas are complicated and require a complex, well-integrated decision-making process. Even the seemingly common-sense notion of a majority democratic vote can prove unethical. At other times, such a simple vote is of clear fairness and benefit to the community.

Absolute Moral Rules

This approach is every bit as black and white, right and wrong, as it sounds. In the absolute moral rules paradigm, one should always and in all circumstances abide by proscribed rules. Moral absolutism is most closely associated with Emmanuel Kant, the famous philosopher. He forwarded the ethical view that actions are intrinsically right or wrong, independent of context or consequence. Thus, in the Kantian view, stealing is always wrong, even if the theft was committed to save the life of a starving child. His most famous illustration exposes the limitations of this approach. He suggests a scene where one witnesses a man running past another man chasing him with a knife and knows exactly where he runs to hide. When the man with the knife asks where the man is hiding, Kant suggests that moral absolutism requires one to answer truthfully, knowing that it may lead to injury or even death.

The potential rigidity of this approach is evidenced in this example, yet there are some behaviors that we might believe are always right or always wrong. For example, most everyone will agree that the sexual abuse of a child is always wrong, or the law against robbing banks is always right. However, most behaviors occur in contexts and cultures that inform how a behavior is viewed and can lead to desirable outcomes justifying their ethical basis.

The Social Contract

As social animals, in order to live as harmoniously as possible within a community, we must rely on formal and informal rules for behavior. Laws and mores provide structures and guidelines for people to live as safely and orderly as possible. When someone violates a social contract, there are consequences enforced through legal or social means.

For example, damaging property or harming others represents a clear violation of the social contract in almost all communities. Arrests, fines, and other formal punishments are designed to deter such behaviors. However, many informal social contracts encourage us to behave in mutually beneficial though not legally mandated ways, for example, by waiting in line to buy a theater ticket or purchase a cup of coffee. Violating this norm by cutting to the front is likely to result in social censure in the form of angry looks, a fight, or the refusal of the salesperson to serve the violator. When evaluating an ethical dilemma, looking to the rules and standards of the community at large can provide guidance.

The Rights Approach

This approach rests on the fundamental belief that every person has rights that deserve protection. For example, in America, the right of every person to speak freely is protected. The rights of every citizen to vote, obtain a public education, and even own a legally obtained firearm are upheld. However, many behaviors are not viewed as the rights of individuals, such as harboring a criminal, selling drugs, or evading taxes. Discerning which rights a person holds is often a source of great controversy. For example, should someone who is unwilling to work or contribute to society be entitled to government-sponsored food and housing? Should someone who wishes to commit suicide be allowed to carry out that personal choice? In some countries, the rights of women to receive an education and travel freely are quite controversial, while in others, the rights of children not to be forced into labor are not upheld. In a college environment, should students of legal age have the right to consume and distribute hard liquor? Do fraternities have the right to discriminate against groups they dislike, such as gay or Jewish or disabled students? And on a more mundane note, does a college roommate have the right to have her boyfriend sleep over every night? Thus, ethical decisions based on determining an individual's rights can be complex and difficult.

The Justice Approach

Treating others fairly is the fundamental tenet of the justice approach to ethics. It posits that everyone should be treated in an essentially equally fair manner. It might seem self-evident that all people deserve to be treated with respect and equality, yet in reality, many people do not receive such justice. For example, all Americans are expected to receive equal treatment under the law, yet African Americans are arrested and imprisoned at alarmingly disproportionate rates. Similarly, while it may seem just for the best college applicants to gain acceptance, often those with legacy connections or financial wealth to wield are admitted over more qualified students. A very handsome and socially skilled man may receive a job offer over a far more experienced and capable applicant who is unattractive and shy. Is this fair, and in keeping with the justice approach to ethics? Other than in cases of clear violations of laws or mores, such outcomes can be hotly debated.

In many cases, all of us must determine what constitutes justice in our choices. For example, is it just for us to purchase fancy cars and clothing rather than donating significant funds to feed the hungry and house the poor? Or is justice at play when a Little League team aggressively recruits all the best and biggest ball players in the community, thus stacking the advantage drastically in its favor? Often, even where acting wholly within the law, we are forced to confront whether or not our choices serve justice.

The Common Good Approach

This approach advocates that what is best for the community trumps individual needs. If it is in the best interest of the health of a community to ban public urination, individuals may be fined or arrested for violating this community standard of health. Similarly, many nonsmoking zones have emerged due to the dangers of secondhand smoke, and individuals are often denied their right to smoke cigarettes in public places. Similarly, most communities view it in their best interest to imprison sex offenders or ban drunk driving.

Nonetheless, what constitutes the common good is often open to debate. Gun control advocates would argue that stricter regulations would protect society from gun violence, while others argue that it would make it less safe. Some college campuses feel it is in the overall best interest of the students to offer gender-free bathrooms, while others view this as an unwarranted option. Similarly, while the larger community may benefit from people purchasing low-emission cars, others feel that their individual freedoms should prevail in such cases.

Often, communities put controversial actions to a democratic vote, with the majority vote reflecting the community's own view of what will serve the common good. Making such determinations can be very challenging and controversial but also very useful in understanding what is at stake when confronted with an ethical dilemma.

The Virtue Approach

Most of us would like to be virtuous, or at least strive to exhibit the qualities of honesty, integrity, responsibility, compassion, and many others. In seeking to determine how to behave ethically, this model proposes that we determine which action is the most virtuous. Thus, behaving in ways characteristic of virtue is the guiding principle to behavior. As human beings, however, we often struggle to overcome selfish or pleasure-seeking instincts in order to behave according to such moral ideals. Understanding which qualities and values we may be compromising from a virtue standpoint can help illuminate the correct path.

The virtue approach requires us to put aside our impulses and personal needs to behave in a manner that would be the most devoid of self-interest to the detriment of others. Without seeking solely to satisfy our own needs, we are freer to discern a path that has a purity of goodness, or virtue, at its base. Thus, doing the right or ethical thing can be discerned through qualities encompassing honesty, integrity, and other characteristics to be highlighted in the next chapter presenting the RRICC model of ethical decision making.

A FIVE-STEP PROCESS FOR ETHICAL DECISION MAKING

It is important to mention that these moral philosophy approaches to ethics simply represent some of the diverse perspectives on the goal of making sound, reasoned ethical decisions. Reflecting on how to use these principles in ethical decision making suggests that many of these principles may in fact conflict with other principles in actual practice. For example, the egoism approach might suggest one course of action while the justice approach suggests another. The utilitarian approach may seek to please the most people while the virtue approach might not take the pleasure of others into consideration. The point is that not all approaches to moral philosophy and ethical decision making will lead to the same conclusions about how to think through and resolve ethical dilemmas. Rather, they provide various frameworks for evaluating and resolving ethical conflicts with a richer and more thoughtful lens. Think of them as tools in a toolbox. Sometimes one wants to use a hammer, or a wrench, or a screwdriver to solve a particular problem. Sometimes multiple tools are required. Familiarity and fluency with these moral philosophy approaches provide coherent structure and theory to apply when seeking to assess and resolve ethical challenges.

Along with achieving familiarity with these ethical models, it is important to have a sense of the steps and a process involved in applying them. The Markkula Center for Applied Ethics at Santa Clara University (see appendix E) offers a thoughtful way to think through ethical decisions regardless of the ethical approach one decides to use to solve an ethical challenge. They recommend progressing through the following five steps.

Recognize an Ethical Issue

Too often people don't necessarily see the ethical issues and conflicts in front of them. These ethical questions can be highly nuanced and require alertness to identify. For example, many people may attend to major ethical conflicts such as marital infidelity, fraudulent business practices, or stealing from others, but they may not be alert to the fact that ethical challenges can be quite subtle. These more nuanced issues can all too easily evade their conscious attention. Learning to become more attuned and sensitive to ethical challenges is vital to recognizing both the subtle and large ethical issues that inevitably emerge in daily decisions. For example, deciding whether to drive versus bike to work, drink a can of a roommate's beer, flirt with a friend's love interest, or order the nonsustainably farmed fish are small decisions based on one's personal ethics, conscious or not.

Get the Facts

Rather than relying on instincts, habits, and emotions, it is important to thoughtfully get the facts needed to make an informed ethical decision. Before making an important decision it would likely prove useful to consult with relevant stakeholders, secure whatever input and objective facts are available, and push aside emotional reactions while obtaining this information to make an informed and objective decision based on reason and evidence. For example, perhaps a group of protesters is yelling rudely and angrily at people. It might be easy to immediately condemn them, yell back, and dismiss their intended message. However, perhaps in learning more about what prompts their outrage one learns that they are all victims of rape. What they are yelling is not personal but a message of demand for the school to institute measures to better protect women. Talking to one of the protesters, or even informed observers, may lead one to adopt a more compassionate viewpoint and response to what felt merely rude and hostile on the surface.

Evaluate Alternative Actions

Too often people think that there is only one ethical choice to be made and alternative choices are inferior. It is often frustrating for people to hear that the "correct" ethical decision might differ based on the particular ethical model being applied. For example, while a justice approach might lead to one ethical decision, the utilitarian or common good approach to problem solving might lead to a very different conclusion. Thus, before making an ethical decision, it is advisable to consider different points of view (e.g., virtue, common good, absolute moral rules) in order to discern the pros and cons of each approach before settling on a final decision. Ethical decisions are often complex and ultimately subjective, sometimes seeming to have no truly satisfactory solution. This is where careful appraisal of various resolutions can help one arrive at a measured, well-thought-out decision.

Make a Decision and Test It

Once a decision is made, it is important to test it by consulting with others whom one respects and values. Having consultants available to

run decisions by can be enlightening, since they often may consider outcomes and implications for decisions that never occurred to the deciding
person. A consultant can be anyone from a friend or family member to
a highly experienced mentor or ethicist. As long as the person's opinions
are valued and offered thoughtfully, additional information and perspective may add to one's ability to weigh difficult decisions.

Act and Reflect on the Outcome

Once an ethical approach is decided upon and carried out, it is important to learn from the experience and thoughtfully evaluate the outcome
of the decision. How did the decision pan out? What were the upsides
and downsides? Did others feel treated fairly or provide feedback? How
does the decision maker feel about the decision in hindsight? So often
there are both intended and unforeseen outcomes that one can learn
from so that future ethical decisions are better informed and chosen.

Using these five steps to make ethical decisions, regardless of which
ethical approach or principles are used, is likely to result in more intentional and thoughtful ethical decision-making practices that will improve over time and with practice.

CONCLUSION

Colleges can do a great deal to teach and help cultivate ethical awareness in students in the context of some formal framework for understanding moral choices. While 2,500 years of moral philosophy is impossible
to convey in depth, some familiarity with these time-honored models
helps provide a structure through which students can view their choices.
We have highlighted nine classical ethical approaches: cultural relativism,
egoism, utilitarianism, absolute moral rules, the social contract, the rights
approach, the justice approach, the common good approach, and the virtue approach. Then we discussed a five-step process that can be used to
make good ethical decisions. In the next chapter, we present the RRICC
model of ethical decision making, which provides a far simpler yet extremely useful approach to teaching and evaluating moral choices.

Chapter 4

The RRICC Model: Five Ethical Principles for Decision Making

In any moment of decision, the best thing you can do is the right thing.
The worst thing you can do is nothing.

—Teddy Roosevelt

Moral philosophers have approached ethics from a great variety of perspectives. Cultural relativism, egoism, utilitarianism, absolute moral rules, the rights approach, and the common good approach are just some examples. However, when most of us mortals make daily decisions, we rarely invoke such heady philosophical concepts. Rather, we need common sense and clear and easy-to-remember guidelines for assessing our ethical choices.

In 2004, Tom Plante described such a system to enable ethical decision making. In his book, *Do the Right Thing: Living Ethically in an Unethical World*, Dr. Plante presents the RRICC model as an accessible reference point for making difficult decisions. The acronym RRICC stands for respect, responsibility, integrity, competence, and concern—five standards by which we can all assess our judgments. These five ethical principles to live by are personal and individual, but each of us can make decisions we can feel good about by using them.

These principles have been distilled from several thousand years of moral philosophy, religion, ethics, and long-held codes of conduct. For example, the Hippocratic oath, written 2,500 years ago, still remains a standard imparted to physicians graduating today. Sacred scriptures from a variety of religious traditions also emphasize these principles. The Hebrew Bible, the Muslim Koran, and the Christian New Testament are replete with consistent moral and ethical principles that are reflected in the RRICC model. For example, treating others with respect is imparted in many scriptural texts. In the Jewish Talmud, "Let the respect due to your companion be as precious to you as the respect due to yourself" (Mishna Avot 2:10) clearly reflects the importance of respecting others. Principles of concern and responsibility are seen in other Talmudic and biblical words. For example, "When the community is in trouble, a person should not say, 'I will go to my house and I will eat and drink, and my soul will be at peace.' A person must share in the concerns of the community as Moses did. Those who share in the community's troubles are worthy to see its consolation" (Babylonian Talmud, Ta'anit 11a). Integrity is represented in "The Lord detests lying lips, but he delights in men who are truthful" (Proverbs 12:22).

In the New Testament, concern for others is a frequent theme in the writings of St. Paul and the Gospel of Matthew. Respect is seen in "Be devoted to one another in brotherly love. Honor one another above yourselves" (Romans 12:10), while concern for others is heard in "Love your enemies and pray for those who persecute you" (Matthew 5:44) and "Be compassionate, as your heavenly father is compassionate" (Luke 6:36).

These examples show that the RRICC principles have withstood the test of time in both secular and religious traditions. For college students, using accessible concepts such as respect, responsibility, integrity, competence, and concern provides a ready reference for weighing decisions based on one's own immediate ethical standards. These principles have been incorporated into Dr. Plante's training seminars for psychology interns and postdoctoral fellows in child psychology and psychiatry at Stanford University Medical School. Similarly, the RRICC model has been integrated into work with clinicians and college students. These principles are neither magical nor exclusive. Many organizations present their own models, whether invoking the Ten Commandments or the Boy Scout oath of honor. The RRICC model is used here as an easy, clear, surprisingly comprehensive set of guideposts that most everyone can understand and accept.

THE FIVE RRICC PRINCIPLES: RESPECT, RESPONSIBILITY, INTEGRITY, COMPETENCE, AND CONCERN

Respect

Treating others with positive regard and consideration is fundamental to upholding the rights and dignity of others. Respect for others is akin to the Golden Rule: "Do unto others as you would have others do unto you." Making ethical choices requires that we take into consideration the rights and needs and feelings of others. We all know people who think only of themselves and often neglect or even abuse others in the course of satisfying their own goals. When facing an ethical dilemma, it is fundamentally important that we ask ourselves if our choice will ultimately respect the rights and needs of others.

In college, young adults are thrust into a world of great social complexity. It may not always be possible to simultaneously take care of oneself and acquiesce to the desires of others. Still, how we communicate and operate while asserting our personal choices goes a great distance toward enabling an ethical outcome. For example, let's say it's 2:00 a.m. and you have a huge paper due in the morning. Your roommate wants you to turn off the light so she can sleep better, but you need to continue writing and don't have another viable place to safely study. Clearly, it wouldn't be ethical to reject your roommate's need for sleep by telling her, "Sorry, not my problem." However, it may be ethical to apologize to your roommate, explain your dilemma, and ask if she will allow you to make it up to her in some way. In this fashion, you are communicating that your roommate's rights and needs are valid and respected, even though you can't (or choose not to) acquiesce to her request.

In 2015, video was taken of a fraternity exuberantly singing a horrible racist chant at the University of Oklahoma. In the moment, the fraternity brothers were only thinking of their immediate circle of friends and likely assumed the chant was acceptable to all present. However, if the group of chanters had taken even a nanosecond to ask, "Is this respectful of African Americans or outrageously disrespectful?" a blessed silence likely would have followed. Also in 2015, photos were posted online of Penn State female students in compromising sexual situations and humiliating states of intoxication. Before taking these photos, or failing to intervene on the women's behalf, a brief reflection on the principle of respect for others may have helped stave off such horrible behavior.

We don't always put others' needs before our own. However, thoughtfully considering how our actions may disrespect others affords us the opportunity to seek other options, compromises, or ways of communicating our regard for the rights of others. Respect is a fundamental component of ethical behavior, and therefore central to the RRICC model of decision making.

Responsibility

There are various ways to define responsibility. Accountable, dependable, trustworthy, and reliable are all terms we apply to those we regard as responsible. Do you fulfill the promises you make? Do you deny your role or shirk your commitments? Can others trust you to perform your duties, fulfill your commitments, and accept accountability? Clearly, in order to behave in an ethical manner, one must follow through on obligations and remain accountable.

For example, imagine a college student agreeing with her parents that she will retain a 3.0 grade point average in order to continue to receive financial support. Does she make a genuine and diligent effort to fulfill her responsibility in this agreement? If her GPA slips below the minimum 3.0, does she make excuses and blame her parents for being unreasonable, or does she accept responsibility, and the consequences, for the choices that led to these grades? Similarly, if a student agrees to water his roommate's plants while he's away and forgets, resulting in the plants' demise, will he be viewed as responsible? No, but if the student accepts responsibility for his failure, apologizes, and offers to purchase new plants for the roommate, an ethical outcome ultimately can be achieved.

Responsibility is an ethical concern in serious issues that place college students' safety at risk. Choosing to drink shots until one passes out may not seem like an ethical issue on the surface. A student might simply view it as a personal choice with only personal consequences. However, when other students need to revive and carry the student to his or her room and then help clean up the next day from all the vomiting, this "personal choice" will be seen as neither responsible nor ethical. Furthermore, if the student had needed admission to a hospital for medical care, what is the personal responsibility, and ethical implication, of placing one's life and health at risk and imposing on the medical system for care? Thus, ethical behavior requires responsible behavior.

Integrity

If asked, virtually all college students would say that they would like to be persons of integrity. Integrity constitutes qualities of honesty, fairness, and morality, and a consistent adherence to one's values. It also connotes a wholeness, an image of a solid individual who can be counted upon. In order to make ethical decisions, it is always helpful to ask if a choice upholds one's sense of integrity.

Here is a classic example that involves choosing to either uphold or diminish one's integrity. Joe has been in a monogamous relationship with Margarita for two years. While on a spring break trip, Joe finds himself in a mutual flirtation with another woman. He believes that there is no way Margarita could ever find out about it. Joe considers whether to have sex with this woman, thinking that if Margarita never knows about the infidelity, it can't hurt her. Then Joe reflects on the concept of integrity. Will having an illicit encounter, however secret, enable him to maintain his own sense of integrity? What would it feel like to know he has cheated on a woman he loves? Would it damage him, as well as the relationship? Joe decides that his own sense of personal integrity is ultimately more valuable to him than a fleeting sexual encounter, and, with great restraint, ends the flirtation.

Another classic college example involves the many opportunities to cheat in academic work. Integrity is choosing to do the right thing even when no one is looking, and in spite of whether or not one will be caught. This is a very difficult standard to uphold when students see their classmates gaining unfair advantage through academic cheating, thus bolstering their sense of justice, or even necessity, in also cheating. Yet being a person of integrity involves sacrificing short-term gains or forgoing immediate temptations in order to live with an enduring sense of honesty and uprightness. It is an ongoing challenge to confront such choices and resist gratification in the service of a more abstract concept such as character or integrity. No one always makes the right decision, and, in fact, by making poor choices and feeling the hangover of shame or lowered self-regard, young adults learn through experience how much their integrity means to them.

Competence

At first blush, it may not seem obvious how competence relates to ethics. After all, people have all kinds of skills and abilities, as well as weaknesses, yet everyone has the capacity to behave ethically. In the RRICC model, competence refers to having the necessary skills and knowledge to carry out one's responsibilities. Competence means knowing the extent, as well as the limits, of your abilities, and knowing when you can handle a job and when you need to seek assistance. Some competencies are obvious: a surgeon must have the necessary training and skills to successfully perform a heart bypass in order to be an ethical physician. On the contrary, a physician whose judgment is impaired by drug abuse, or whose manual dexterity is compromised by injury or illness, could not practice ethically and puts her patients' welfare at great risk.

Many ethical dilemmas involving competence are far more murky. Let's say you have volunteered to lead a backpacking trip for incoming freshmen. You have backpacked a lot but have always relied on others for map reading and trail finding. You think you have the general hang of it—after all, you've been on many hikes—but can't say you feel confident interpreting topographical maps. Also, you've had a lot of knee pain lately and hope it'll ease up soon. Given these challenges to your potential competence as a trip leader, how can you most ethically fulfill your responsibility? Clearly, it would not be ethical leadership to begin the trip without great familiarity with the route and maps. Seeking input from another experienced hiker can help bolster your knowledge of the trail and help problem solve some potential route complications on the way. Making sure that you have the necessary familiarity with the relevant maps and trails is fundamental to proceeding as a competent leader.

Similarly, just hoping that your knee will be fine leaves the other hikers vulnerable should it render you unable to hike. Being unable to carry your own pack or hike out to safety without assistance would neutralize much of your competence and in fact greatly burden the participants. An ethical approach to assessing and ensuring your competence might involve being examined by a physician. If the doctor says it's a minor problem that will respond rapidly to ibuprofen, you can proceed with more confidence. Similarly, you can alert your supervisor to this issue and seek his or her guidance and a possible backup. Assessing and assuring one's competence to carry out a job or responsibility is fundamental to performing ethically.

Concern

Concern is caring for and having compassion for others. It involves showing concern not only for those close to us but even for those people unknown to us who might be affected by our choices. Often, concern involves caring for those less fortunate than ourselves and being willing to feel and act on behalf of those who are suffering or deprived. Few of us can emulate Mother Teresa, but we can expand our range of social consciousness beyond our immediate sphere.

Many colleges today emphasize in their mission statements the goal of educating students who strive to make the world a better place. University immersion programs, social outreach efforts, international opportunities, and human rights groups on campuses speak to these values. In small and large ways, pausing to determine if one's choices demonstrate concern for others can greatly expand one's character, humanity, and, yes, ethical decisions.

Here are three small examples of demonstrating concern. First, let's say you have an empty bottle that would be most convenient to throw away. Choosing to make the effort to place it in a recycling bin shows concern for the planet and world's population over your own immediate convenience. Second, you have no intention of ever traveling to the Philippines, nor have you ever known anyone of Filipino descent. But a student organization is collecting donations for relief efforts following a major hurricane in the Philippines that has recently taken many lives and displaced thousands. Showing concern can involve having compassion for the victims of this natural disaster and demonstrating it through your sympathy or active support. Third, some guy is stumbling around drunk and heads toward his car. You are disgusted by this person's sloppy intoxication and think he's a jerk but realize that his driving is a really bad idea. You can show concern by trying to prevent him from driving, either by intervening directly, enlisting his friends, or contacting the police. All of these actions demonstrate the ethical principle of concern for others, even strangers and the unseen.

Here is another example often encountered in college life. You have a friend who seems very depressed. Increasingly, she's been missing classes, staying in her room, and not really taking care of herself. You talk to her and she says just to leave her alone; she's not worth caring about and might as well be dead. You encourage her to go to the counseling center, and she says she'll think about it. During the next week she seems even more despondent and is irritable and uncommunicative when you try to express your concern. Should you just drop it at this point, since, after all, you have plenty of your own worries? Or should you consider going the extra mile and alerting the resident advisor of your concerns? While no rule states that you must get involved, it may be the best ethical decision if you have genuine concern.

PUTTING IT ALL TOGETHER: ETHICAL DECISION MAKING IN PRACTICE

It is easy to feel like an ethical person in theory. However, when faced with adversity, sacrifice, and real challenge, that is when the true test of one's character, honor, and ethics comes into play. You may not truly know what you are made of ethically until tested. Furthermore, many decisions and actions proceed without any awareness whatsoever that an ethical issue is at stake. The first step to making ethical choices is recognizing them in the first place.

This is where college faculty and staff come in. Young adults finding their way in the excitement and freedom and varied challenges of college life need frank instruction, modeling, and ongoing reflection to truly integrate an ability to thoughtfully recognize and resolve ethical conflicts. As we will discuss in chapter 6, universities can make huge contributions to a mindset of ethical alertness and intentional decision making in their students. These issues of formal instruction, student life programming, and faculty and administrative modeling will be further discussed later. For now, let's examine how to adapt the RRICC model to the ever-present array of ethical dilemmas.

True ethical conflicts are murky and complicated. Not all five of the RRICC elements may point to the same unified conclusion. This is where personal values and life choices are examined in the full knowledge of what's at stake. Here is an example that many students will face when applying to internship programs.

Jiao has applied to five internships in marketing and management for the summer. She's an ambitious person and wants to develop skills and networks that will facilitate her career development. Her top choice is a Facebook internship, but any of the five programs will be better than being unproductive over the summer. She hears first from her second and fourth choices, but Facebook won't make offers for another two weeks. Her second choice, Tesla, wants an answer by the end of the week in order to seek other candidates if necessary. Tesla asks that she sign a commitment letter if she accepts the internship, promising not to back out or take other offers.

Jiao is terrified of losing the Tesla opportunity if Facebook doesn't accept her. She doesn't even want to ask Tesla for an extra week to decide for fear that they'll revoke her offer. She wonders if she should just grab the Tesla offer, sign the agreement, and if Facebook does come through, just back out of Tesla. Jiao wisely recognizes this as an ethical, as well as a career, dilemma and reviews the RRICC guidelines one by one.

First, she considers whether her plan demonstrates responsibility. She knows that backing out of an agreement would be irresponsible, but if Facebook falls through, it would save her. She also has a responsibility to her long-term career goals. Nonetheless, she knows deep down that to back out of an agreement would not be ethical.

Second, Jiao reflects on how best to show respect in this situation. Perhaps the most respectful option would be to tell Tesla straight up that she very much wants the internship but is waiting to hear back from Facebook. Hopefully they'd allow her an extra week to decide, but then again, she could risk losing the offer. Again, she knows that it wouldn't be respectful to knowingly renege on a promise.

Third, how can she handle this conflict with integrity? In no way can she justify making a false promise and preserve her integrity, but can she be straightforward, persuasive, and assertive in asking Tesla to wait another week? Perhaps they'd appreciate her honesty and integrity and be willing to wait. Then again, they might just move on down the list.

Fourth, in terms of concern, Jiao isn't genuinely worried about Tesla filling their intern slots. However, she is genuinely concerned about her own career, and while she wouldn't intentionally want to harm another candidate, it's hard for her to feel concerned about some hypothetical other. Jiao feels conflicted over whether failing to show concern is a compelling ethical deal breaker in this case, and feels more hesitation over the integrity issue most of all.

Fifth, Jiao considers which course will exhibit competence. Jiao truly believes that she has the necessary skills to handle either the internship at Tesla or Facebook. She believes she'll do a great job at either. Nonetheless, how she handles the application and acceptance process also reveals a certain aspect of her professional competence. Does she want to be the kind of employee who can be counted on to directly and honestly appraise her employer of her level of commitment, or the type who finesses employers solely for her own gain? Does being a competent professional also require complete transparency in employment agreements, or is that a separate issue altogether? Again, Jiao is conflicted about this particular ethical criterion.

Taken together, Jiao realizes that she'd ultimately feel most comfortable with her decision if she could avoid compromising her integrity and being professionally regarded as irresponsible. She can't get around the conclusion that it would not be ethical, nor can she feel at peace with herself, if she signed a deceptive agreement with Tesla. Instead, she calls the contact person at Tesla and explains her situation. Jiao emphasizes how excited she would be to train at Tesla and asks if they could wait for her to hear from another company prior to making a commitment. She's told that, unfortunately, they do need to know by the end of the week. Jiao contacts Facebook and tells them that she was given another offer but they are her top choice. Would they be able to let her know by the end of the week if she's been accepted? Again, she's told that their process is not flexible and she'll have to wait the two weeks. Jiao decides to accept the sure bet of the Tesla internship, signs the commitment agreement, and does not back out even when Facebook makes her an offer two weeks later.

In this scenario, Jiao had to make a very difficult choice. Her sense of integrity and ethical values feel strengthened by her placement of honesty over deception, in spite of the sacrifice she makes. She resolves to explore Facebook again next summer, and invests herself fully in the opportunity available to her at Tesla.

Here is another example of a very common and highly complex campus situation that has major social and ethical implications. Anders is a third-year student living in campus housing with three roommates. His college has suffered numerous alcohol-related tragedies in the past decade, including deaths, sexual assaults, hazing abuses, and vandalism. Anders resents the college's ban, believing it impinges paternalistically on the autonomy of students. He doesn't even drink hard alcohol, only the occasional beer, since he's a competitive miler on the track team.

One afternoon, two of his roommates charge in with two cases of vodka. They ask him to hide it in his car until the party they plan to have on Friday night. It is, of course, "illegal" to possess hard liquor on campus, but Anders doesn't want to let down his roommates or come across as supporting a policy he doesn't even accept. Even more, he hates to be a buzzkill. Nonetheless, Anders is uncomfortable harboring the alcohol given that violators face suspension, which would also result in the loss of his athletic eligibility for the year.

Anders's college has integrated the awareness and teaching of ethical decision making into classrooms and throughout student life. He's heard plenty about the RRICC model, and here is a relevant time to use it. First, Anders considers how hiding the liquor upholds the standard of responsibility. Yikes, he can't get very far before acknowledging that anyone in the administration, as well as his parents, would view the rule violation as flagrantly irresponsible. But is it respectful, he wonders? It certainly respects his friends and the concept of student autonomy, but it pretty clearly violates and defies the rules set by the administration.

The integrity criterion for ethical behavior proves trickier and raises complicated questions for Anders. On the one hand, he feels that by violating the alcohol ban, he is demonstrating the integrity of his beliefs. Yet on the other hand, the powers that be would undoubtedly be unsympathetic to this view and would condemn his holding of alcohol as showing a lack of integrity vis-à-vis the college rules. Anders is conflicted; should he defy the rules, risk the consequences, and stand up for his belief that the ban is insulting? Or should he uphold the college rule and in that sense behave as an upstanding student and policy-abiding member of the campus community?

Concern is also a complicated standard. He's immediately concerned for his roommates' well-being should they be caught with the vodka, and concerned that they succeed in throwing a party that apparently means a lot to them. However, Anders can concede that there is some truth to the risks posed by hard liquor for the kids he knows. They will drink whatever's available until they're no longer standing, if history is any indication. How would he feel if someone gets assaulted, drives while drunk, causes the police to intervene, or becomes so incapacitated they need medical care? What if someone dies? Anders wonders if he should value concern for the physical safety of other students more than the infantilizing implication of the rule or the intended fun of his roommates. The risk of being partly culpable for anyone being harmed genuinely gives him pause.

Finally, would hiding the alcohol in his car fulfill his value on competence? Well, he certainly could make every effort to keep it safely hidden for his friends, but it probably isn't an act that would be viewed as an indication of sound judgment or maturity by many—especially those in a position to issue consequences.

After spending the time to think through these ethical standards, Anders concludes that he doesn't want to have anything to do with the alcohol and its potentially high risks. Nonetheless, he doesn't want his friends to view him as a chump or a coward. He sits down with his roommates and has an honest heart-to-heart with them, explaining all his reservations and conflicting emotions. By the end of the conversation, his roommates are also feeling uneasy about their plan and consider how they now want to proceed, fully aware of the larger ethical and safety implications.

CONCLUSION

This chapter presents the RRICC model for ethical decision making in the college context. The fundamental criteria for evaluating the ethics of decisions, which include responsibility, respect, integrity, concern, and competence, are discussed in full, and examples are provided to illustrate their relevance for young adults. Scenarios depicting complex ethical conundrums are presented, and the process of utilizing the RRICC model in decision making is delineated. The pervasive nature of ethics in so many aspects of college life are discussed as demanding alert awareness to their presence and an intentional, structured process for their personal and deliberate resolution.

Part II

What Colleges, Parents, and Students Can Do to Nurture Ethical Development

Chapter 5

Creating an Organizational Culture of Ethics

In this age of moral autonomy, each individual is told to come up with his or her own worldview. If your name is Aristotle, maybe you can do that. But if it isn't, you probably can't.
—David Brooks, *The Road to Character*, p. 258

There are many things that colleges can do to create a campus culture that supports and nurtures ethics. In fact, it is likely that the principles for creating a culture that supports and nurtures ethics might be similar for most any organization and not only limited to colleges and universities. Other educational institutions, such as primary and secondary schools, as well as corporations, nonprofit organizations, governmental agencies, and many others could all benefit from incorporating policies and strategies that contribute to ethical climates in the workplace. Closely attending to just a few important and easy to remember strategies to help create and sustain a culture of ethics could potentially enhance many organizations. The purpose of this chapter is to introduce several important approaches and principles to help create and sustain an atmosphere where ethics are fully integrated, nurtured, and supported. Educational as well as noneducational institutions could be well served by focusing their attention on these principles to create more ethical environments for all involved with their organizations.

SET CLEAR EXPECTATIONS FOR WHAT IS AND IS NOT OKAY

All organizations have both spoken and unspoken rules and guidelines about how to act within their environments. This includes everything from attire, attitudes expressed, and behavior toward colleagues, consumers, and the public. For anyone who has worked at several organizations, even within the same sector as corporations or universities, they can likely describe how the cultures of these organizations differ, and sometimes differ quite radically. For example, in our case, going from the University of Kansas (for graduate school) to Yale University (for clinical internships) and then to Stanford University and Palo Alto (for our first jobs out of our training years) exposed us to very clear and distinct differences in culture and expectations for behavior and attitudes as psychology professionals.

Many of the cultural norms and expectations of an organization are never expressed in writing but can be inferred once one closely observes and participates in the environment of the organization for some duration. Some organizations highlight ethical values and decision making more than others. Many may pay lip service to following ethical guidelines but don't practice what they preach. Some are more utilitarian than others. Others are more hospitable and gracious than others. Yet all organizations, including colleges and universities, could be more thoughtful and intentional about both their expressed and more ambiguous cultural norms and expectations when it comes to ethical behavior and expectations. For example, some colleges have a culture of excessive drinking on weekend evenings or before and after major campus athletic events such as football games. Alumni returning to campus for homecoming and other major alumni events such as reunions may relish reliving the behaviors of their youth while on campus and, for example, drink to excess as they did during their college days. A culture of heavy drinking is thus maintained by both the current and past student population, and, further that, reinforced by various campus traditions and activities (e.g., tailgating before big sporting events, attending frat parties, playing drinking games).

Regardless of the expressed campus rules about behavior on campus by students, faculty, staff, and even alumni, each organization creates certain expectations about acceptable and unacceptable behavior. Organizational leaders could pay very close attention to the culture that has evolved on their campuses and spend some time examining and contrasting campus cultures elsewhere to determine precisely where the points of intervention might be to better nurture ethical behavior and expectations. Campus cultures can drift in both welcome and unwelcome directions over time. Like the popular example of a frog dying while submerged in very gradually heated water, so too can campus leaders fail to recognize the slowly shifting cultures of their campuses without thoughtful and close attention, and actively comparing and contrasting their campus environments with those of others.

Outside observers sensitive to ethical issues can be a helpful resource to assess the ethical culture of an institution. Site visits from those who specialize in organizational ethics could be helpful for all organizations to engage in their attempts to constantly improve the ethical climates of their institutions.

MODEL DESIRED BEHAVIOR (ESPECIALLY FROM ORGANIZATIONAL LEADERS)

Research conducted by well-known Stanford psychologist Al Bandura (1986), among others, has made clear that people tend to model or copy the behavior of others (especially well-thought-of and desirable others), and that leaders within any organization act as models for those below them in the organizational chart. Thus, any organizational leaders must be mindful that they are being watched and observed very closely and that others in the organization will likely follow their lead when it comes to ethical behavior and attitudes.

This important insight and empirical evidence about modeling the behavior of others is nothing new. While research in psychology and group behavior may have quality data to support this phenomenon, it has been well known for centuries and even millennia. For example, at the end of the Good Samaritan parable in the Gospel of Luke, Jesus states to his listeners, "Go and do likewise." This famous quote well articulates the desired result of observing leaders. In more contemporary times, Bandura defines the specific stages of observational learning to include attention, retention, reproduction, and motivation. Thus, for observational modeling to occur, one needs to observe or attend to the model, remember the model's behavior, reproduce the model's behavior, and be motivated by some form of reinforcement to do it again and again (Bandura, 1986).

Thus, organizational leaders, whether they be university presidents, deans, student leaders, or company CEOs, must practice what they preach and be sure that they model for others the desired behaviors that they wish to nurture within their organizations. If the highest standards of ethics are desired within an organization, then high-profile leaders in that organization must demonstrate these standards and be beyond reproach in this regard. Key leaders throughout campus communities must make clear their engagement with desired ethical behaviors at all times. Their actions often will speak louder than their words when it comes to helping to create a more ethical environment within their organizations and, ultimately, their students.

REINFORCE DESIRABLE BEHAVIOR AND DON'T REINFORCE UNDESIRABLE BEHAVIOR

This is a very simple truth from basic operant conditioning that any college freshman would learn about in an introductory psychology course. Also, it is a truth that has been known for generations. If one wants a behavior to continue, then it should be reinforced. If one wants a behavior to discontinue, it should not be reinforced. This is a pretty simple truth, yet it is often hard to thoughtfully and consistently implement in many organizations and individuals alike. And it is certainly easier said than done. Organizations must be mindful and intentional about what behaviors they want to reinforce and what behaviors they do not want to reinforce, and invest in the staff and resources necessary to carry out these goals. Ethical behavior must be clearly reinforced so that it will continue to occur. Problematic unethical behavior should not be reinforced if the organization wishes to extinguish these undesirable behaviors.

Thus, when people engage in unethical behaviors, it would be best if they didn't get any reinforcement or advantage for doing so. For example, getting away with cheating and thus earning a top grade or an award in class, or winning kudos on the athletic playing field, shouldn't be tolerated and certainly not reinforced. Unethical behavior among faculty, staff, and administrators should be consistently and swiftly corrected. For example, being deceptive or dishonest or exploitive should be quickly condemned and corrected. Treating others with disrespect or contempt should not be tolerated if the organization values honesty and respectfulness throughout the university.

Often it takes careful evaluation to best determine what behaviors are or are not reinforced. For example, while excellence in the classroom is always desired on a college campus, giving easy As to get good teaching evaluations for tenure and promotion review becomes an ethical problem. While meeting budget expectations is important for any organization, skimping on quality products and services or finding ways to fire staff without adequate merit or warning may involve undesirable unethical behaviors.

Offering opportunities for recognition, awards, and social reinforcements for desirable ethical behaviors can go a long way to promote the type of ethical culture desired in any organization. Certainly, these rewards or reinforcements must be thoughtfully considered and delivered with carefully articulated educational value.

FOCUS ON SKILL BUILDING AND PROBLEM SOLVING

Organizations, especially educational ones, can do a great deal to focus their attention on developing ethical skills and problem-solving techniques. After all, educational institutions are in the business of education and of using the latest research and best practices to teach students and employees alike meaningful ways to think through ethical challenges and solve ethical dilemmas. Rather than only stating what kinds of behaviors are expected or not, institutions must help explicate practical step-by-step strategies for developing effective ethical decision making, behavior skills, and strategies for resolving ethical conflicts. Workshops, easy to use reference materials, consistent messaging, and ongoing and readily available consultation from peers or mentors are just some of the many ways institutions can assist in training students and staff to best use these tools to achieve better and more thoughtful ethical decision making.

Additionally, organizations can have someone act as CEO (i.e., chief ethics officer) who may help individuals and groups throughout the organization think through ethical decisions. Many organizations do this already through some kind of compliance office. However, these professions tend to be primarily concerned with legal standards and ramifications, and are often staffed with attorneys. A chief ethics officer is very different from a compliance officer in that ethical decision making is aspirational—trying to be and become our best selves rather than merely being sure to "cross the t's and dot the i's" in order to follow rules and stay out of trouble. If confidentiality is ensured, then a chief ethics officer can have a powerful and very helpful role in an organization, assisting the university community in thoughtful and collaborative consultation about ethical issues both small and large.

Skill-building opportunities can also be enhanced by ongoing supervision and consultation with both peers and supervisors. Providing opportunities for staff, faculty, students, and others to discuss ways to better integrate ethical approaches into their activities in an intentional manner can further strengthen the ethical fabric of the university.

PROVIDE THE TOOLS PEOPLE NEED TO ACT ETHICALLY

If an organization wants to create a culture of ethics, it must be sure that members have the tools that they need to do so. These include adequate and appropriate training, consultation, modeling, and supervision. These tools also include being able to bring internal and external scholars and experts into the campus dialogue, engaging staff and students at all levels of training in problem solving as well.

Having an ethics ombudsman or point person for an organization can be especially valuable. They or their staff can provide a focal point for getting tools and resources to better help with ethical consultation.

Tools can include implementing established best practices in processing ethical decisions. This can include the use of the RRICC model as well as other organization-specific models of ethics. Additionally, having a framework for organizations to discuss and reflect on ethical challenges can be essential in providing a common, consistent language and set of values for ethical decision making. One example of a helpful framework for ethical decision making includes what we call the "Four Ds." These are defined as discovery, detachment, discernment, and direction. It is an easy to remember set of guidelines that can be employed for a wide variety of decision-making challenges, including ethical decision making. This model is an adaptation of one outlined and made famous by St. Ignatius of Loyola, the founder of the Jesuits in the 16th century, and is discussed in detail in his well-known project called the *Spiritual Exercises* (Mottola, 1964). Although originally used for religious reflection and direction, the Four Ds have proven to be a useful tool in contemporary secular decision making and are easily adaptable for ethical reflection in college students and others.

Discovery refers to making efforts to get the information one needs to make good decisions. It might include some research on decision-making options; consultation with others, including experts; or an assessment of one's own goals and skills. Discovery reminds us to be sure that we have the facts and any additional information we need to be sure that we are fully informed before making important decisions.

Detachment refers to trying to think in a neutral manner without attaching decisions to particular needs, wants, or judgments. Detachment reminds us to avoid being overly invested in a particular outcome that might color or warp our decision-making process. Poor decisions are more likely a result of not thinking in a rational, logical, and detached manner.

Discernment refers to the thoughtful reflection needed to make good decisions and paying attention to what actions result in *consolation* versus *desolation*. Consolation is the sense of peace, contentment, and solace one experiences when decisions are made in congruence with one's values and principles for living, while desolation refers to the disconnection or dissonance that is experienced when decisions are made and ultimately clash with our values and principles. Discernment is the process of thinking through ethical problems while paying close attention to how possible decisions may prove congruent with how we want to feel and act as ethical beings.

Direction refers to the decisions made and actions taken once the discovery, detachment, and discernment processes have occurred. Direction is the movement toward implementing ethical decisions while carefully considering both intended and unintended outcomes. Alertness to the lessons learned in evaluating the success of one's decision can be put to good use in improving future ethical decisions.

PROVIDE CORRECTIVE FEEDBACK

Another basic and important set of principles borrowed from introductory psychology is the notion of immediate corrective feedback. Unless leaders offer timely and thoughtful corrective feedback to individuals and departments throughout their organizations, they are unlikely to create and maintain a culture of ethics. Reinforcement for behavior that is desired, and corrective feedback for behavior that is not desired, is fundamentally critical to help create and sustain a culture of ethical mindfulness and behavior.

This corrective feedback needs to be conducted in the spirit of collaboration and education rather than in terms of punishment or chastisement. Collaboration and education allow for more openness and less defensiveness when feedback is provided. Immediate feedback is critical to maximize a fuller understanding of the problem behavior as well. Additionally, confidentiality with corrective feedback hopefully maximizes the chances that a nondefensive response to the feedback will be attained.

CONCLUSION

These six principles can be very helpful to a wide variety of organizations that desire to create a more ethical culture. Whether they be educational institutions, such as colleges and universities, or other organizations, these principles provide an easy to remember and straightforward set of suggestions that are aspirational in nature yet offer a clearer focus on ways to maximize ethical behaviors within diverse organizational climates. Having these important principles well understood and frequently used and discussed within organizational life hopefully will allow all members of these organizations to be much more attentive to how their work and learning environments can be more ethically sound.

Chapter 6

How Universities Can Teach and Embody Ethical Thought

The first step in the evolution of ethics is a sense of solidarity with other human beings.

—Albert Schweitzer

Universities possess both enormous influence and weighty responsibility in the education of their students. Many schools embrace the dual opportunity and responsibility of value-based education, actively integrating educational paths toward graduating ethical, socially conscious students with a strong personal sense of honor. For example, the mission statement of Santa Clara University includes an emphasis on developing future leaders of "conscience, competence, and compassion." Most colleges at least advocate a similar goal, but differentiating lip service from genuine educational programming separates the schools that truly make ethical formation a priority. While students enter college as products of their family values and larger social influences, universities can make an enormous impact by doing what they do best: educating. Education in ethical awareness and decision making is ultimately no different from teaching students to think critically, sharpen habits of the mind, and develop other academic skills.

It is important here to distinguish between imparting preconceived notions of morality and teaching the critical thinking skills necessary for students to thoughtfully define their own code of ethics. It is not the job of colleges to tell students how to live their personal lives, but it is the job of colleges to teach high-level cognitive skills in all subjects. Just as important as it is to teach students how to reflect carefully about social constructs, scientific theories, and political ideas, students need some structure and foundation for learning critical thinking skills around their own ethical decision making. Thus, we make a clear distinction in this book between universities seeking to impart particular moral judgments and instead imparting the concepts and foundational thinking skills necessary for students to become aware of and resolve their own ethical choices.

Why should colleges be motivated to invest time, resources, staff, and money into so seemingly abstract a concept as ethical formation? What is the payoff for the institution and its students? First and foremost, university trustees and leaders must believe in the fundamental value of educating ethically equipped individuals to contribute to the betterment of the world. This ideal will not be embraced by every institution. Second, colleges should be motivated to lower the incidence of destructive behaviors on campus. By nurturing thoughtful, ethically based decision-making skills, impulsive and antisocial incidents will decline. Third, colleges are increasingly sensitive to negative publicity, and headlines about cheating, rape, alcohol poisoning, racism, and the like are highly damaging to university reputations. As a result of such negative publicity, college application rates tend to fall, and the prestige of the college takes an unwelcome bruising. Perhaps even more threatening, alumni and donors frequently voice their dismay by withholding donations. Finally, colleges are not simply diploma mills, which teach facts and crank out employment-ready students. Colleges are responsible for the education and guidance of young adults in highly formative years and therefore cannot neglect to help students discern and make choices based on their own personal ethics.

There are a variety of levels at which colleges can implement programming. The more comprehensive and integrated the value on ethical formation, the more influential such programs can be. In this chapter, programs colleges can institute are described at six levels: (1) pre-orientation materials and on-campus orientation programs, (2) curricular requirements and opportunities and cocurricular programming through student life services, (3) student ethical leaders and models, (4) faculty and administrative modeling, (5) emphasis on restorative justice models of restitution and reconciliation instead of punishment, and (6) enhancing the fun and status of ethics events. Only by prioritizing, integrating, and modeling ethical decision making into all aspects of education, athletics, and student life will such concepts be developed and genuinely embraced by students.

PRE-ORIENTATION AND ORIENTATION OF NEW STUDENTS

Entering students are eager to learn about the culture and values of their college. They want to know what is valued, rewarded, and deemed critical for success. By emphasizing the role of ethical thinking throughout their college education, colleges can orient new students to their expectations and opportunities regarding ethical priorities. Even before setting foot on campus, pre-orientation materials can spell out the school's committed programming and emphasis on ethical development. Having a common model—be it the RRICC model; the Three Cs of conscience, compassion, and competence; or a variety of other ethically centered visions—can help students be exposed early on to the language and culture of their university. Pre-orientation materials can serve several purposes. First, they can explicate the campus vision and programming for ethical development, along with their specific "common language" model. For example, with the RRICC model, a brief description and summary can provide students and their parents with a common means of discussing and resolving ethical dilemmas. Second, high-risk aspects of student life and their ethical underpinnings can further alert students and families to the college's priorities of minimizing excessive alcohol and drug use, sexual assault, noninclusion, and dishonest academic practices. Some schools provide videos and other educational materials for students to review even prior to arriving on campus.

Third, outlining the specific programming designed to teach ethical decision making and behavior can provide an overview of the arc and depth of the school's commitment to this aspect of their education. Describing curricular requirements and opportunities; residential training around sexual assault, alcohol abuse, and other detrimental behaviors; and ongoing lecture series and other cocurricular events further help students anticipate and appreciate their opportunities. Fourth, highlighting ethical student leaders on campus, and the awards and recognitions they have received, provides a real-life model of the school's values, shining a bright light on the types of ethically oriented students the college hopes new students will strive to emulate. Similarly, faculty mentors and educators in ethical development can be introduced. Fifth, spelling out the university's adjudication procedures that model and emphasize ethical treatment of others provides a further glimpse into these institutionalized values.

Once students arrive on campus for orientation, these programs and values can be brought to life. In each dorm and residence hall, workshops introducing the RRICC or other ethical model adopted by the school can be introduced, and common ethical conflicts with roommates and other students anticipated and discussed. Student life services can bring in speakers to discuss alcohol and drug use, sexual assault and high-risk sexual behavior, and academic integrity. These conversations ideally should continue in weekly or monthly check-in meetings where incidents around ethical conflicts and dangerous behaviors can be brought to light, and students can discuss their dilemmas in a safe and supportive environment.

Orientation can also introduce students to any mandatory ethics curriculum; many schools require that students take at least one ethics course related to their field of study for graduation. Many schools also offer an array of ethics-oriented courses, some even offering a major or a minor in ethics. Faculty and staff representatives can be highlighted and made accessible, and student leaders introduced.

Freshman orientation (or new transfer student orientation) is an ideal time to reach enthusiastic and open new students eager to learn about and embrace the campus culture and values. Introducing real programming in ethical decision making can alert students to the expectation and emphasis placed by their college on this educational goal.

CURRICULAR AND COCURRICULAR EDUCATION IN ETHICS

If a college does not require and offer educational instruction emphasizing ethical concepts and decision making, it is in many ways unfair for them to expect their students to behave and strive in thoughtfully ethical modes. Teaching by example involves dedicated coursework and cocurricular programming. Colleges can offer ethics courses ranging from moral philosophy, business ethics, medical ethics, science ethics, sports ethics, religious ethics, and professional ethics, to name a mere few. Similarly, offering forums and lectures where ethical principles are discussed further underscores their importance and normalizes their complexity and ongoing presence in all of our lives. Bringing in noted speakers, offering a weekly college-wide ethics discussion group led by a faculty member, having ethics reflection groups in dorms focusing on issues in residential life, and designating ethical leaders and committees for assistance in school governance and adjudication procedures are a few examples of cocurricular offerings. Similarly, athletic programs can formally discuss sportsmanship and ethics in collegiate sports. Through a relatively small dedication of funds and staff time, tremendous inroads can be achieved.

ETHICAL STUDENT LEADERS AND MODELS

On many campuses, the star athletes, musicians, politicians, artists, scholars, and other "winners" are often celebrated and rewarded. Awards, contests, and publicity all convey our society's admiration of such high-achieving individuals. Rarely is the same respect and attention afforded those individuals who dedicate themselves to providing ethical and moral leadership and inspiration on campus. Yet these individuals abound, and quietly pursue their beliefs and activities. By rewarding and highlighting students who model and fight for ethical objectives, students perceive that the college, and society at large, values these less visible "champions" or moral leadership. Developing university awards and grants for such individuals, and publicizing their achievements and examples, visibly demonstrates that ethically inspired pursuits are valued by their college right along with football stars and outstanding scholars. This form of clear modeling and honoring of ethical student leaders speaks volumes.

FACULTY AND STAFF LEADERSHIP

Academic faculty sometimes complain that they are rewarded and valued for their scholarship in particular and their teaching and service only to a secondary degree. In order to attract quality faculty to ethical leadership, mentoring, and reflection, colleges need to provide incentives. When faculty feel appreciated, recognized, and rewarded for their contribution to the ethical development of students, they perceive its worth and respect within the administration. Therefore, in order to develop faculty who can serve as ethical instructors, mentors, and models, colleges need to prioritize and incentivize ethical education.

There is no simple formula for nurturing and designating ethics leaders among the faculty and staff. Colleges may determine that assigning specific individuals to serve as mentors, group discussants, or instructors for ethics courses plays a central role in reaching students. Some schools will develop dedicated ethics institutes and academic ethics departments to carry on the ongoing work. Students need to know how this notion of ethical choice plays out in real life, and putting forth professors who can speak from their own experience and professional work provides examples of ethics in action, grounded in intellectual understanding. Endowed professorships, institute directors, award recipients, grant awards, and other mantles of leadership and achievement help to highlight these individuals and their work to the larger student body. Highlighting such leaders in college materials and magazines and other publications also helps to emphasize their importance to the university.

Staff employed in student life can also be highlighted to students through similar means. Carving out clear ethical development roles and recognizing outstanding individuals and programs further illustrates the value of ethics. By embedding these leaders and models throughout the university, and paying more than lip service to their importance, the lived application of ethics is demonstrably highlighted and admired.

ENHANCING THE FUN AND STATUS OF ETHICS EVENTS

Everyone on a college campus knows which events are the most fun and receive the most investment and attention. Events that feature generous offerings of food and beverages, are set in attractive venues, receive publicity, and welcome attendees with warmth and enthusiasm all enjoy popularity and good attendance. Lectures, discussion groups, awards ceremonies, and workshops held in drab classrooms without food or fanfare, music, or comfort lack a sense of hospitality, enjoyment, and importance. A small but visible investment in amenities that can add enjoyment and status to ethics-oriented events can make an enormous impact on the message the university sends and the response from participating, engaged students.

STUDENT GOVERNANCE AND ADJUDICATION

Student government exists to influence policy, procedures, resource allocation, and program development, all representing the interests of the student body. The priorities and values of the student leadership are reflected in their support for certain decisions and in their words and actions. Student leaders can help make decisions of moral and ethical consequence, and articulating these as important helps to further model and support ethical thinking on campus.

Many colleges have highly active student senates that weigh in on issues large and small. From divestment to tuition fees to planning the spring concert, student leadership leaves its fingerprints throughout the school. Again, by propping up and highlighting student leaders who embody ethical awareness, colleges can underscore the value placed on ethical decision making.

When a student violates a campus rule or code of conduct, an adjudication process begins. Typically, a student panel or representative, in addition to faculty and administrative representatives, weighs in on deciding the appropriate consequence for misbehavior. Punishment in the form of fines, suspension, probation, and even outright banishment can be determined. However, we would argue that even in these situations, universities should do what they do best: teach. Thus, helping to educate and remediate transgressors, along with providing opportunities for restoration and reconciliation with victims, is far more effective and ethical. In chapter 15, we discuss in detail how colleges and parents can respond to the invariable mistakes of young adults, providing restitution, education, and a road to redemption.

DEVELOPMENTAL CONSIDERATIONS

Integral to the modeling, teaching, and oversight of ethical behavior on college campuses is a fundamental understanding and appreciation for the unique developmental status that defines young adulthood. Youth entering university are hungry for the tools and resources that will enable them to define personal and career goals, develop increased self-discipline, grow socially, develop enhanced independence, and consolidate a realistic identity of which they can be proud. Colleges are in the unique position of providing benevolent authority and instruction to a largely homogenously aged group of individuals. Understanding the motivations, conflicts, and age-appropriate strengths and weaknesses of their charges serves to bolster opportunities to influence students positively and sensitively in the development of ethical awareness, problem solving, and intentional decision making that aligns with their personal beliefs.

The Four I's are helpful to faculty and staff seeking an informed understanding of students poised at this particular time in their rapidly changing lives. Colleges must ask: (1) How able is this student to make independent choices versus needing structure and support for optimal functioning? (2) How does this student define their identity; what is important to them about their values, personalities, goals, relationships, and codes of conduct? (3) Interpersonally, how are they best equipped and most challenged in their social and intimate relationships? and (4) How well are they containing negative impulses as evidenced by their ability to focus academically, engage in safe and healthy relationships, and contend with a host of temptations? Seeking to discern students' developmental challenges and strengths can assist faculty in guiding, modeling, teaching, assisting, and sometimes disciplining them humanely and ethically and with an eye toward enhancing their positive growth and development.

CONCLUSION

Colleges can readily create a culture and intellectual forum for building ethical thought and behavior in students. In this chapter, we reviewed aspects of ethical integration into colleges through a number of routes: pre-orientation and orientation of new students, curricular and cocurricular education, ethical models and student leaders, faculty and staff leadership, elevation of the status and positive perspective on ethics, and ethical integration into student governance and adjudication procedures. Taking this multipronged approach to fully embodying ethical principles through modeling and teaching can convey a powerful and consistent message. Importantly, sound understanding of the developmental challenges and strivings of college students will greatly enhance the effectiveness of all ethical programming.

Chapter 7

What the Faith Communities Can Do to Promote Student Ethics

Non-violence leads to the highest ethics, which is the goal of all evolution. Until we stop harming all other living beings, we are still savages.
—Thomas A. Edison

While ethical principles discussed in this book and elsewhere have mostly emerged from the influence of centuries of moral philosophy, all of the major religious and spiritual traditions have posited over millennia their own strategies for ethical living. These great wisdom traditions have provided thoughtful and detailed guidance about how their adherents should live their lives. Regardless of the religious tradition or branch within each tradition, practical and aspirational strategies for living life and making challenging ethical decisions are nurtured among these faith traditions. Furthermore, religious services, community-based volunteer and service opportunities, sacred scripture reading groups, and both ongoing clerical and peer support (including counseling and spiritual direction) are available to religious followers, all of which can be helpful in facilitating ethical behavior among spiritually oriented college students.

While secular colleges and universities may not endorse any particular religious tradition or spiritual group, they typically allow religious traditions to offer a wide range of services to their students either on or closely off campus. Many secular colleges and universities even have chapels on their campuses and often provide office space to religious groups located in central campus locations such as within their student unions or student activity centers. Colleges and universities who do maintain a religious affiliation also typically provide offices, meeting spaces, and other support and services to religious traditions that differ from their own. For example, Catholic colleges and universities usually have a campus ministry office that has representatives employed by the school from Protestant, Jewish, Muslim, and other non-Catholic groups with space available for nondenominational as well as denominational worship services and meeting spaces for all of the diverse religious traditions and groups.

A brief review of the Stanford University Office of Religious Life Web site, for example, lists an impressive array of campus religious organizations represented at this secular university. These include numerous faith traditions: Baha'i, Buddhist, atheist and humanist, Catholic, Evangelical Christian, Orthodox Christian, Latter-Day Saint, Episcopalian, Presbyterian, Christian Science, Hindu, interfaith, Muslim, Jewish, Sikh, and Zoroastrian. All of these faith communities stand ready to embrace students and nurture their college experience and ethical development through the values and spiritual teachings of their respective religions.

By virtue of their immersive work with college-age students, clergy and staff in campus religious programs are well steeped in the developmental nuances of young adults. Familiarity and compassion for young adult challenges with intimacy, independence strivings, identity, and impulse control greatly enhance the ability to both connect with and communicate relevantly to this special population of young people. Campus-based religious programs are likely to be highly attuned to ethical and moral lapses en route to attaining the Four I's, and therefore well positioned to advise, teach, and counsel college students in making personal choices according to their own personal code of ethics.

Religious groups often play an important and perhaps even critical role in the ethical formation of their affiliates, and in an ongoing way with college students as well. These traditions certainly do not support unethical behavior or encourage their members to lie, cheat, steal, engage in substance abuse, or participate in sexual assaults, just for example. In fact, they do the opposite. They not only encourage their members to maintain high ethical and moral standards but also provide ongoing support to do so. For example, worship services often include scriptural readings about how to live a better life as well as offering models of admirable and virtuous behavior (e.g., the lives of religious figures). These groups also provide alternative activities for weekend evenings and semester breaks that tend to be wholesome, engaging, and often community-service minded. Thus, religious groups on campus can be a critical tool in helping to provide an environment where ethical principles and behavior are encouraged, modeled, and supported among those who choose to participate.

Many religious groups encourage responsible behavior in the hot-button realms of alcohol and drug use, sexual engagement, and acceptance and respect toward others. These groups often provide corrective feedback, encouragement, and support to young adults seeking to behave in an ethical manner. Of course, many members of these faith traditions may struggle with problematic behavior even if they are highly engaged with their faith tradition, but they can be supported and encouraged by peers and faith leaders to avoid problematic behaviors and act in a manner more congruent with their aspirational sense of honor. Peer support and pressure can be powerful influences in dissuading group members from acting in unethical ways.

We hope to emphasize that no particular faith has the edge in the pursuit of ethical ideals. Rather, each of the major faith communities upholds many values in common, while understanding and practicing these values in their unique manner and theology. A good example of the power of nondenominational and egalitarian approaches to moral and ethical ideals through faith is seen at Florida State University, a huge, regional, secular state school. FSU has developed an interfaith program titled the Spiritual Life Project. Led by an interdisciplinary group of student-elected professors, the project seeks to provide forums for the teaching, discussion, reflection, and promotion of "the whole person." As they state on their Web site, "The FSU not only focuses on intellectual development, but as a community of moral discourse" it seeks to help develop in students a "sense of commitment to higher ideals." Participants "reflect on their meaning and purpose in life," "come to a clearer understanding of the complex moral issues inherent to life," "develop the knowledge and skills for effective, ethical and responsible participation in the world," and "engage in critical thinking through open dialogue among diverse individuals within, across and outside of religious contexts" (Florida State University, 2016). Monthly meetings are organized toward these ends, demonstrating the value of interfaith perspectives in contributing to students' development of more ethical and meaningful lives.

Perhaps some common examples that demonstrate how religious groups on campus encourage and support ethical behavior and activities may be of value. The following is not an exhaustive list by any means, but it does provide common examples of how religious groups and traditions help to guide their members on campus toward ethical and prosocial behavior while discouraging problematic and destructive behavior.

ALTERNATIVE SPRING AND SEMESTER BREAKS

College term breaks, especially spring break, have too often become an opportunity for students to find a sunny beach location where they can engage in a great deal of alcohol consumption and sexual indiscretion. Spring break partygoers in Florida, South Texas, and other warm beach locations have become legendary for their sometimes shocking and over-the-top misbehavior. So well known are these traditions of reckless spring break party going that notorious television shows and films have capitalized on the spectacle of college students abusing alcohol, drugs, and each other. *Girls Gone Wild*, for example, focuses on these college break activities telecast from popular spring break locations in order to take advantage of viewers' appetites for observing outlandish and unabashed alcohol-fueled behavior. Other shows and television channels, such as MTV and more mainstream network television shows such as the *Today Show*, *Good Morning America*, and CNN, also often report with amusement from spring break locations showing scantily dressed students partying and cavorting sexually in warm climates. To many students, this looks like the pinnacle of the college experience, especially as so few more worthwhile and in fact edifying options are offered.

Yet one new and popular way for colleges to address this spring break tradition of sun, fun, beer, and sex is the proliferation of "alternative spring breaks." While they are not always hosted by campus ministry or religious groups on campus, they often are organized and spearheaded by them. At Santa Clara University, for example, many students spend their spring (or winter) break in warm climates such as Mexico, El Salvador, the Southwest, South Florida, and elsewhere, but rather than endeavoring to party and overindulge in alcohol and casual sex, they work with the poor and marginalized within these communities. Experiencing active solidarity and contributing positively to disadvantaged groups while living and working alongside them has been seen to provide greatly positive, inspiring, and lasting benefits to the participants. While engagement in social service and community-building activities are laudable, it is the experience of connecting and identifying closely with other groups that can prove transformative. Some of these trips might be organized around building a school or home, building a water system for a community that doesn't have one, tutoring young children in English or in other academic topics, or learning about income inequality or slave labor practices in the powerful context of solidarity and community with the citizens. Organizations such as Habitat for Humanity, among many others, work collaboratively with college groups to work out the details of these service-related vacation trips.

Research has found that students who participate in these community service, or social immersion, alternative spring breaks actually return to campus with higher levels of compassion as well as better stress management skills relative to students who do not participate in these programs (e.g., Mills, Bersamina, & T. Plante, 2007; T. Plante, Lackey, & Hwang, 2009). And these trips provide a healthy alternative to the more common spring breaks that highlight sun, fun, alcohol, and casual sexual behavior, often referred to as the classic "debauchery spring break."

Thus, religious groups on campus typically help to spearhead meaningful alternative spring breaks and other term break programs (e.g., Thanksgiving break, summer break, long weekends) that help to offer students ethical and engaging activities with the added bonus of avoiding the more problematic and stereotypical spring breaks that highlight alcohol abuse and casual sex in warm climates.

SHABBAT DINNERS

In the Jewish tradition, Shabbat begins at sundown on Friday evening and lasts until sundown on Saturday evening. Jewish communities on college campuses, typically called Hillel Centers, usually offer a fun and mostly student-led service on Friday evenings preceded or followed by a festive group dinner. These services and dinners provide an enjoyable Friday night activity with time to consider meaningful issues and socialize with peers in a healthy, wholesome, and usually alcohol-free environment. Since Friday and Saturday evenings tend to be the most high-risk times for abusing alcohol and getting into compromising sexual situations, these alternative Jewish activities on Friday evenings assist students in sidestepping the pressure and peer influence of more problematic evening activities on campus. Thus, Jewish groups on campus offer regularly scheduled wholesome and uplifting alternative activities during the prime partying times on most college campuses. The Jewish community is not alone, in that other religious groups have perhaps taken a page from their playbook in offering similar alternative activities during the prime partying times of Friday or Saturday evenings. Evangelical Christian groups, such as Campus Crusade for Christ, are another good example typically offering fun and community-building group events on weekend evenings. Additional religious groups on campus also typically provide special services, dinners, and activities during Friday and/or Saturday evenings, as well as throughout the week.

Importantly, these gatherings are not merely a means of helping students avoid problematic situations. Rather, the values, ethics, and camaraderie imparted within most religious groups directly uphold the principles of RRICC discussed earlier: respect, responsibility, integrity, competence, and concern.

COUNSELING SERVICES

Campus ministry and religious groups typically offer free counseling services to members of their faith tradition with on-site clerics or lay ministers. Many students who struggle with emotional, behavioral, and relational challenges, as well as ethical conflicts, often feel more comfortable having counseling or discussion sessions with leaders or peers who share their faith or religious background. Rather than going to an unknown professional mental health staff member at the college's student health services on campus, or to off-campus professionals, entering into a counseling relationship with a spiritually oriented therapist can be especially helpful for some students. Conversations after a religious service or event or perhaps during a retreat, community-service activity, or after a meal offer the opportunity for discussion and counseling that may be more comfortable, casual, and organic to college students rather than making a formal appointment with a licensed professional at the university health facility. As students struggle with ethical and other concerns, having easy and regular access to clerical or lay pastoral counselors or peer mentors at no charge to them is a very helpful resource. Additionally, these religious leaders and peer mentors may keep a thoughtful and careful eye on these students, developing ongoing relationships through regular contact at services and religious events in order to help prevent problems from getting too serious. Religious groups on campus are a natural and convenient way to get spontaneous or structured counseling experiences and to keep a benevolent eye on troubled students as well.

SPEAKERS AND DISCUSSION GROUPS

Most campus religious organizations offer regular speaker series and discussion groups. On- or off-campus speakers make presentations on a wide range of topics that might be of interest to college students and that typically overlap with ethical living. Additionally, various discussion groups, which may or may not be closely associated with on- or off-campus speakers, often cover numerous topics of likely interest for students. These forums provide excellent opportunities for ethical topics to be presented and discussed. For example, the Catholic community at Stanford, as well as many other top secular universities such as Yale and the University of Michigan, offer the Esteem Program to students on their campuses. The Esteem Program is a national Catholic university program that provides guidance on speakers and includes regular discussion group meetings and mentoring of Catholic students on campus. Volunteer mentors are often university faculty, staff, or local leaders in the Catholic community who meet regularly with students to discuss personal and career development, faith formation, and other matters. The Esteem Program is free for students and is extended to both undergraduate and graduate-level participants. The Esteem Program also has a peer-mentoring element, with older students serving as big brothers and sisters to the younger students. These ongoing speaker series, discussion groups, and mentoring meetings all provide rich opportunities for discussing and reflecting on ethical decision making and behavior. A combination of casual socializing as well as structured discussions and speakers on a regular basis can be helpful to support ethical decision-making conversations, provide positive models, and further nurture close relationships for private consultations.

Religious groups on campus provide a unique and special place for students who share an affinity to a religious and spiritual tradition. The opportunity to gather and reflect upon issues of the day, personal and professional conflicts, and ethical challenges integrates thoughtful decision making in keeping with personally chosen values and ethics. Religiously affiliated and secular institutions attempt to assist students with their religious and spiritual needs while on campus by allowing religious groups, clerics, and campus ministers to host a wide variety of campus programming. Since religious and spiritual traditions inevitably are interested in ethical decision making and behavior, they provide a ready-made opportunity to assist college students in appraising their own ethical approaches to their lives. They are often one of the few realms in campus life that provide clear goals and guidance for ethical behavior with resources to support students in their efforts to live more ethically.

Examples of such rich programming at colleges abound. At the University of Georgia, campus ministries offer weekly small group discussions where "the message is made practical and applied to your unique life situation." One recent year's programmatic theme was "Living a Hall of Fame Life." Also available are numerous specialized ministry programs (e.g., freshman ministry, separate men's and women's ministries, and hearing impaired ministry). Outreach programs encourage participation, and one year's spring trip mission will involve trail building on the Appalachian Trail. Virtually every college campus has the capability of offering faith-based programming aimed at supporting the character and ethical development of students drawn toward spiritual approaches.

CONCLUSION

While religion and faith may be neither necessary nor sufficient factors in the development and enhancement of character and ethical values, they surely can help foster and nurture such ideals when attentive to this goal. The rich array of spiritual communities on college campuses provides yet another ready resource for championing and supporting the personal ethical values students seek and require to function as successful, gratified, responsible citizens of the world. By taking the common values evident in the world's great faith traditions, ethical and moral development can be further incorporated through students' existing religious affinities.

Chapter 8

How Parents Can Help Young Adults Prepare Ethically for College

Many of us have instincts about right and wrong, about how goodness and character are built, but everything is fuzzy. Many of us have no clear idea how to build character, no rigorous way to think about such things.

—David Brooks, *The Road to Character*, p. 256

Parenting, of course, is a deeply personal endeavor. There is no right way, wrong way, or one-size-fits-all guide to raising ethical children. Parents must follow their own personal moral code in imparting ethical standards and imperatives to their children. Therefore, colleges are initially dependent on parents to perform the lion's share of ethical formation for their incoming students. Colleges can help, however, to prepare both parents and students for their own ethical expectations and models. Parents can benefit greatly from encouragement and concrete recommendations for defining their own codes of ethics, and develop in tandem with their teenagers an intentional process for spotting and resolving ethical conflicts. With personal clarity enhanced, parents are better equipped to actively prepare teenagers for coping in a healthy manner with the upcoming challenges of college life.

While parents model and teach ethical behavior from early childhood on, the year leading up to college provides a critical window for colleges to partner with parents to impart skills necessary to negotiate the young adult challenges confronted by college students. During senior year, parents can contribute mightily to their teen's preparedness through a series of open dialogues. This chapter presents steps that parents can take to be in sync with their teenager's education into their college's ethical model. In conjunction with guidelines from schools, this chapter will discuss how to (1) build a foundation of trust and respect around sensitive topics, (2) generate open, nonauthoritarian dialogue around the topic of personal ethics, (3) utilize the Four I's in normalizing and enhancing a more informed understanding of teen behavior, (4) review and reinforce college materials related to codes of conduct and ethical guidelines, (5) help instill familiarity with the RRICC model, and (6) discuss potential flash points during college that demand ethical awareness and a usable structure for decision making.

BUILD A FOUNDATION OF TRUST AND RESPECT AROUND SENSITIVE TOPICS

High school seniors are not renowned for their openness to parental advice and probing. In fact, developmentally, seniors need to push away from parents to soften the eventual challenge of separation and practice their necessary budding independence. It is no simple task to engage teenagers in heady discussions of personal morality, ethics, and high-risk behavior, at least not without resistance and eye rolling. So how can parents broach these imperatives in a manner that invites their high school seniors to reflect upon and voice their own viewpoints on such complex matters? The first step involves a simple skill that evades many parents: listen.

In order to explore these topics with older adolescents, parents need to *ask*, not *tell*. After all, college students will be resolving dilemmas on their own and in ways consistent with their own goals and values. Helping teens begin the delicate process of self-reflection required for active decision making involves gently drawing them out with curiosity about their maturing beliefs. For example, a parent can ask, "What are your thoughts about college drinking?" rather than providing their own views and prohibitions. Similarly, asking their views on the principles of RRICC and their views on college temptations are likely to yield more self-examination and information than parental lectures or instruction. If teens are encouraged, or better yet, required, to review and participate in ethical exercises provided by their colleges prior to beginning school, parents can actively engage, reinforce, and acquire a common language with their students.

GENERATE OPEN, NONAUTHORITARIAN DIALOGUE AROUND THE TOPIC OF PERSONAL ETHICS

When teenagers detect judgment and disapproval, they are unlikely to expose their true struggles and beliefs. As difficult as it may seem, focusing on listening and asking about their thoughts will enhance their willingness to communicate honestly in the future. Realizing that a high school senior is a work in progress, not a finished product, can help parents better tolerate their teenager's less than fully formed beliefs and decisions. Bracing one's self to listen and respectfully explore their teen's views, even when they differ from one's own, and without judgment, is a valuable investment in their future willingness to open up with parents around sensitive situations and topics.

UTILIZE THE FOUR I'S IN NORMALIZING AND ENHANCING A MORE INFORMED UNDERSTANDING OF TEEN BEHAVIOR

In order to genuinely listen and truly appreciate the views of adolescents, it is extremely important to keep in mind their developmental imperatives at this age. Effective parenting requires alertness to the developmental demands impinging on children through all phases of their lives. With college-age students, staying attuned to the Four I's, which invariably drive and confound them, provides a simple shorthand for better appreciating the healthy strivings and current limitations underlying their decisions. It's important to keep in mind where the goals of independence, identity, intimacy, and impulse control are being served in the choices and views of young adults.

Reflecting on one's own young adulthood can help to bring the Four I's into sharper focus in appreciating the teenage and young adult minds. Parents would do well to write a paragraph about their behaviors, triumphs, and errors in the realms of their own strivings toward independence, defining identity, seeking intimacy, and controlling impulses during the college years. Writing an honest reflection of these four hallmarks of development can heighten awareness of the complexities involved and humanize their own teen's often messy process of development. If colleges can provide the impetus and structure for families to commence this undertaking, an extremely beneficial process can begin to unfold.

Don is a 49-year-old engineer. His eldest son, Joey, is planning on attending college away from home in the fall. In reflecting on his 18-year-old self long ago, Don is amused and startled to revisit his own early struggles with the Four I's. In terms of independence, Don wanted to get as far away as possible from his parents' strict control. Entering college initially felt like utopia, as Don could do whatever he wanted without his parents' knowledge or inevitable disapproval. Don embraced this liberation to the hilt, and dove headfirst into the party scene on campus. His first quarter was a disaster. He was drinking so much, getting so little sleep, and missing so many classes that he was placed on academic probation. His parents threatened to remove him from school. Looking back, Don can see that in wanting to be independent, he neglected to monitor himself and evaluate his impulses, and without supervision he wasn't yet prepared to make all his own decisions.

REVIEW AND REINFORCE COLLEGE MATERIALS RELATED TO CODES OF CONDUCT AND ETHICAL GUIDELINES

Identity was another memorable developmental hurdle. Don, a two-sport high school athlete, wasn't outstanding enough to play baseball or basketball at the college level. He had always viewed himself as an athlete first and foremost, savoring both the attention and camaraderie of being "a jock." In college, Don was uncertain of his new role and identity, feeling anonymous and unexceptional among the swarms of students. He had few other interests than sports, and being only an average club athlete at college felt almost embarrassing. Don started to party excessively and flamboyantly in order to garner the attention and companionship he enjoyed in athletics. If he couldn't be a star athlete, he could be a championship drinker and mischief-maker. This false identity proved fragile and ultimately detrimental to his health, his academics, and his pursuit of a realistic and positive identity.

Intimacy became a compelling refuge for Don. During most of his freshman year, Don did a lot of hooking up and had many sexual partners. These encounters were both a solace and a point of pride, compensating for his feelings of inadequacy in athletics and academics. In his sophomore year, he met a young woman, Kate, who meant a lot to him, and they developed a close and meaningful relationship. He felt like his best self with her and didn't have to be a star in anything to earn her respect and affection. At the same time, he began to develop more authentic friendships and engage in recreational activities that didn't involve alcohol. He found his relationships deeply and increasingly important, stabilizing, and rewarding.

Don's impulse control improved after many hard lessons were learned, including terrible hangovers, a couple of fights, embarrassingly memorable nights of out-of-control behavior, and a series of unpleasant, acrimonious entanglements with women. As he became more secure in his independent functioning, intimate relationships, and realistic identity, his impulses became easier to prioritize and control.

After engaging in this Four I's exercise, Don had a lot more empathy for the path his son was about to embark upon. He resolved to withhold judgment and criticism as much as possible, and both hear and discuss his son's choices in the context of normal developmental struggles with the Four I's. His appreciation for the healthy longings underlying his own missteps as a young adult braced him for his son's potentially rocky journey.

HELP INSTILL FAMILIARITY WITH THE RRICC MODEL INTO EVERYDAY FAMILY LIFE

Parents can help prepare their teens for college by first familiarizing themselves with the RRICC model of ethical decision making. Colleges have an opportunity at this juncture to supply them with these educational materials. After all, ethical behavior is important for everyone, not just college students. Learning first to recognize ethical situations and then to think instinctively in terms of respect, responsibility, integrity, competence, and concern when making even everyday decisions will allow parents to model and raise ethical challenges within the family context.

Where might these commonplace ethical challenges emerge? Here are some common but ethically nuanced daily family decisions:

1. Do I really need to recycle this smelly tuna can?
2. I know there's a drought, but I really want to take a long, hot shower.
3. My son left his phone on the kitchen table. Would it be so wrong to sneak a peek at his recent text messages?
4. My daughter does not want me to intervene with her basketball coach's harsh and critical treatment of her. Maybe I'll just send him a confidential e-mail?
5. I know that my son copied his friend's math homework. Should I just ignore it since so many of the kids do that?
6. My younger daughter feels that she has more chores than her older siblings. She has more time and is so much more cooperative than her brothers. Should we discuss this as a family?

7. My son has taken "creative license" with his résumé on college applications. He's not really lying, but he's definitely exaggerating his accomplishments and distorting some of the facts. Since colleges are so competitive, maybe he needs to do this and perhaps I shouldn't intervene.

8. My daughter went to a party last night where the parents were away and unaware of the 30 or so teenagers drinking at their home. I found this out by eavesdropping on her phone conversation with a friend. What should I do?

9. Our family dog was diagnosed with advanced cancer. Should we pay for expensive, painful medical procedures or consider palliative care or even putting her down?

10. My husband had an affair, and my daughter suspects it. Should I be honest with her?

Needless to say, a vast array of such situations arise often in daily life, and the ethical implications are endless and challenging to resolve. Learning to recognize the ethical aspects of everyday decisions is the first step toward making ethically informed choices. Pointing out and discussing these choices with teenagers can gradually orient them toward automatically thinking in similar terms.

Not many teens, however, want to listen to their parents, or their universities, pontificate on moral rights and wrongs. It is imperative that parents raise these questions from a genuine position of open engagement. Just encouraging teens to voice their own thinking, conflicts, and personal morality is a huge victory, even when their choices may differ from those of their parents. Respecting their right to make their own *informed* and *thoughtful* ethical choices is critical to encouraging them to utilize the RRICC model toward that end. It is also important for parents to realize that ethically charged choices are often fraught with ambivalence and sacrifice, and no one can always make the right call. Nonetheless, even recognizing when parents' own needs trump their ethical values can afford opportunities to compensate and repair any wrongs they may have done, teaching teenagers that even where they choose selfishly or disrespectfully, there is always opportunity to lessen any harm or hurt.

Joey is conflicted about whom to take to his senior prom. Back in March, he told Gabriela that he'd take her, and she's been clearly looking forward to their big date. However, in the meantime, he's developed a crush on Donna and really, really wants to invite her. He thinks of the RRICC model and knows immediately that honoring his commitment to Gabriela would be the most responsible, respectful, integrity-filled, concerned, and competent decision. Still, he only gets to go to one senior prom.

Joey decides to invite Donna, as his heart calls him to do. However, mindful of the RRICC principles, he problem solves how he can still tell Gabriela in as respectful, caring, and responsible a manner as possible. He asks her to meet up after school and tells her that he has something hard to discuss with her. He tells Gabriela how much he likes and respects her and hopes not to hurt her feelings. He says it may be hard for her to accept his decision but he is trying to be honest. In revealing his choice to take someone else to the prom, Joey listens to Gabriela's hurt and anger and seeks to reconcile with her over time. He offers to help her arrange another date and still pay for her ticket to the prom. While hurt and angry, Gabriela has to at least respect Joey's efforts toward honesty, responsibility, and caring and emerges from the conversation still feeling valued and treated with respect.

This example illustrates that people can't always make the "right" decision, and that ultimately there may be more than one "right" outcome. How one steps up to the plate in honestly confronting and seeking to repair the ethical fallout from one's choices is completely consistent with the RRICC model. Discussing with teens one's own complex and imperfect choices, and how one could have resolved them more ethically, goes a long way toward humanizing their own complex decisions.

Ideally, high school seniors will receive materials from their college of choice regarding the school's official codes of conduct and mission and identity statement. Encouraging families to review these documents together and understand where RRICC principles pervade the ideals of their college can help to reinforce and prepare students for inevitable complications of college life.

DISCUSS POTENTIAL ETHICAL FLASH POINTS AND CONUNDRUMS

Difficult choices await teenagers in college, and most will not revolve around the more sensationalized flash points of alcohol/drugs, sexual conduct, or cheating. Many will involve simple conflicts with roommates, competing demands as a recruited student-athlete, work/study responsibilities, or financial accountability. While the potential examples are limitless, here are a few of the categories that colleges and parents will find fertile for discussion:

1. Interpersonal Relationships. This fundamental human realm constantly requires us to ask, "Who do I want to be in the world?" How we treat others,

make compromises, convey acceptance, and display honesty and the overall principles of RRICC define us daily in our interactions. Peers, parents, professors, community members, and administrators will all test our character and potentially confront us with difficult choices that require the steady application of ethical intelligence.

2. Asserting Autonomy and Independence. While rules might not be made to be broken, it can be a lot of fun doing so. Thus, young adults seeking to celebrate their sense of freedom and independence can run awry of institutional rules, trampling over boundaries imposed by authorities with audacity and glee. Often, the very authorities seeking to contain them become perceived as the enemy, and autonomy is misdirected toward simply opposing those in power. It is so very difficult for young people to differentiate between genuine independence and mere counterreaction to perceived controls. Sometimes these misdirected strivings result in some of the most egregious mistakes and even crimes: violent hazing rituals, cheating, excessive drug and alcohol consumption, assaultive sexual behavior, and financial fraud and deceit. Discussing with teenagers how to express their beliefs and opinions and newfound rights as adults within safe and healthy bounds can help them learn to differentiate reactive acting out from mature acts of independence.

3. Self-Regulation. Eating, sleeping, studying, exercising, and socializing all seem like the most natural, straightforward requirements in college. Nonetheless, absent parental oversight, college students are often unskilled in regulating their own basic needs and responsibilities. The powerful draws toward socializing, partying, creative expression, sexual exploration, and other wonders of college life can be hard to self-monitor and manage. Classically, college freshmen are the most notorious for all-nighters, missed classes, poor eating habits, excessive use of drugs and alcohol, and academic problems. Learning to manage one's basic health needs and athletic, academic, and work responsibilities amid the sheer excitement of college life is a learning curve for virtually every student.

4. Sexuality. Suddenly, for probably the first time in their lives, college students are living and sleeping in the immediate proximity of prospective sexual partners of both sexes. No more "open door" or "four feet on the floor" policies. No more nighttime curfews. No need to surreptitiously hide condoms and other forms of sexually-transmitted-disease and birth control. No more harsh judgments and guilty consciences with parents. Most students will remain careful and selective regarding their sexual choices and behavior. Many, though, will be impulsive and too easily tempted by various attractions and opportunities, resulting in unwanted pregnancy, sexually transmitted diseases, or, most commonly, heartbreak and emotional harm. All too often, excessive alcohol impairs judgment and leaves students vulnerable to unwanted sexual engagements or even assaults. As much as parents and young adults can tolerate, discussing these impending decisions

openly and without judgment can greatly enhance their propensity to think through their choices and invoke RRICC principles.

5. Academic Demands and Challenges. Many college students find themselves falling behind or even failing classes. Finding oneself endangered academically causes many students to feel deeply inadequate, scared, and panicked. Sometimes students seek shortcuts, and sometimes these shortcuts involve cheating or hiding the truth from parents. Families need to discuss the possibility of such difficulties arising during college and how they can respond. If students feel safe to discuss their fears and failures with their parents, they are far more likely to remain aboveboard and seek productive solutions. Colleges are also charged with providing emotional and academic support during crises, and students who seek out such help are far less likely to resort to dishonest academic practices.

CONCLUSION

At the heart of all the learning, reflecting, and discussing is the implicit message that maintaining one's ethics, character, and values is highly valued by both colleges and families. Ethical achievements are all too infrequently acknowledged and celebrated in our world, as athletic prowess, academic achievement, financial success, and celebrity tend to take center stage. The stakes are high, however, in neglecting this critical aspect of human development. Parents and colleges that give mere lip service to ethical decision making without truly providing ethical forums, models, and didactics are failing to fully educate and equip young adults to function successfully and positively with ethical intelligence in society. Colleges and families can partner effectively with young adults in this invaluable process of ongoing, structured, ethical discernment and decision making.

Chapter 9

What Students Can Do to Nurture Their Own Character Development in College

It's because I work in ethics, and, more specifically, applied ethics, that I think it's important that if you have things to say that you think are right and you think could make the world a better place, it's important that many people read about them.

—Peter Singer

While colleges, parents, and communities can do a great deal to nurture ethics among young people, ultimately students themselves bear the lion's share of responsibility for their own ethical IQ. For students to benefit personally and meaningfully from the teaching and modeling provided by diligent universities, they must make the active effort to integrate ethical principles into their own personal mindsets and decisions. All the combined efforts of faculty, staff, and parents to help students appreciate the value of ethical choices will be wasted if students aren't convinced of that value and motivated to engage in improving their ethical thinking and behavior. All of the efforts of the university environment, both in and out of the classroom setting, can only go so far if students are not willing to engage in ethical reflection and formation.

Therefore, students must be active and engaged partners when it comes to ethical formation during their college years. They must see the value to themselves and their communities, both now and in the future, of attending to ethical decision making and formation on a personal basis. College students can begin this process by asking themselves one fundamental question: "Who do I want to be in the world?"

While college students are notorious for acting as if they have the world by the tail and have all the answers, few feel anywhere near that level of confidence or clarity. Understanding one's own developmental challenges throughout life can help provide insight into all sorts of needs, conflicts, and struggles. During college, if students can begin to appreciate their relationship to the core imperatives of identity, independence, intimacy, and impulse control, they can better understand what drives them, derails them, and confounds them and learn how to make healthy decisions in the service of these goals. Students who avail themselves of insight into their own age-related strivings, and where they most struggle or thrive, can much more consciously and intelligently make good judgments about their choices.

For example, many college freshmen find themselves feeling homesick and unhappy at school. They may withdraw from others and have difficulty staying motivated or focused academically. If students can grasp that they are confronting the developmentally normal challenge of independence in their first time away from home, they may be better able to problem solve how to seek the support and connection they need, from both parents at home and resources at school. If students merely feel that their longing to leave school and return home should be quickly heeded, or that there is something horribly wrong with them for experiencing these normative struggles, poor outcomes are more than likely. Understanding their own developmental trajectory, and having compassion for themselves and a context for self-understanding, enhances the chances of forward progress.

If colleges provide instruction into the Four I's, students can learn a structure around which they can process and understand their own strengths and vulnerabilities in the areas of identity, independence, intimacy, and impulse control. This knowledge empowers young adults to humanize their struggles, make healthier personal choices, and accept ongoing responsibility for their intentional decision making. Then they are more personally equipped to answer this fundamental question.

WHO DO I WANT TO BE IN THE WORLD?

This is a fundamental question we should all ask ourselves at many points during our lifetimes. This question does not pertain to career, success, or other tangible goals one might have. Rather, this question addresses character, personal conduct, and traits of integrity and humanity that define us through small and large choices and actions. Do I want to be someone who is unfailingly competitive and oriented toward maximizing self-gain in all contexts? Do I want to be someone who balances the desire to help others with my own self-interests? Do I want to be someone who is seen as responsible, compassionate, and respectful of others, or do I not really care how others are affected or what they think or feel about me? Do I want to be someone who seeks immediate, optimal gratification, or am I a person with larger priorities? Do I want to have self-discipline, or would I prefer simply to worry about outcomes later? These are just a few of the types of questions young adults can benefit from pondering in order to live with intention and a stable framework for resolving the litany of choices that will confront them.

College freshmen are often painfully aware of how they present themselves as new students. They are constantly being asked where they're from, what their interests are, and how they're being perceived through their dress, peers, affiliations, and all forms of behavior. Young adults may often want to be known as successful, popular, attractive, articulate, fun, lovable, creative, or other identities. More subtly, if young adults can also understand that they will constantly be declaring their core selves by virtue of their characters, they can better understand how important their ethical choices can be. Do they want to be the guy caught in a cheating scandal? Or the gal that can party hard and get the most crazy? Or the friend that others can count on and trust? Or the leader who does the right thing? Or the person whose word is as good as gold? Or the person who will compete ruthlessly to "win"? All these questions of how others view us and how we view ourselves ultimately reveal our values and ethics.

Students need to grasp the value of tending to their ethical choices and personal character. Not only is an individual's good character a source of enormous pride and self-respect, but it's also critical to how they are viewed by others. Having a strong sense of personal morality and ethics also pays off in terms of helping students to avoid making some of the destructive choices that can derail their path, relationships, and successes. If colleges have active and engaged partners for ongoing ethical conversations, with students motivated by understanding the huge benefits of charting their own paths to ethical clarity, successful outcomes are dramatically enhanced.

THE CHARACTER OLYMPICS: IF ONLY

Everything seems to be a competition these days. The race to get into a college of one's choice drives home to students the need to develop talents, rack up achievements, stand out, and otherwise demonstrate special abilities that can differentiate them from the crowd. Alas, not everyone can be a champion swimmer, a debate team captain, a star in the musical, or a National Merit Scholar. Most of us are limited by virtue of our innate abilities to become exceptional athletes, musicians, or scholars, no matter how much effort and commitment we devote to improvement. However, *everyone* has the capacity to be a person of stellar ethical standards and character. Certainly, character and its related virtues are difficult to quantify and are rarely highlighted by awards and attention. Yet we know such people when we meet them or when we're touched by their example, their integrity, their generosity, or their steadfast reliability and trustworthiness. While the rewards of character may be less celebrated in many societies than competitive talents, they are profoundly grounding and gratifying and, it could be argued, of ultimate importance in living a meaningful and rewarding life.

College students don't realize it, but they can be leaders and distinguish themselves as individuals of sound character. Importantly, when we describe character and ethics we are not ascribing to any particular morality guidelines. Rather, young adults must decide for themselves whether they want to feel good about living and behaving. The particular moral choices may differ vastly between individuals of equally good character. Thus again, anyone can step up and be an exemplar of character, perhaps not on a grand Olympian stage, but in their everyday small and large interactions, priorities, decisions, relationships, and actions. It is the responsibility of all students to assume ownership of their ethical paths and accept agency over their ethically charged decisions and overall characters. The notion that "stuff just happens" is too immature and passive a posture in life, and students need to see themselves as the stewards of their own manner of living and choosing in the world. In short, students need to feel responsible for developing their critical thinking skills regarding their own personal ethical choices and take advantage of the resources colleges can provide to develop their sense of agency and facility with these high-priority decisions.

WHAT STUDENTS STAND TO GAIN

When a college requires a course on ethical decision making, or requires attendance at ethics discussions and workshops within the residence halls, students are apt to dismiss the topic and the agenda as a box the college has to check. In mandatory sessions, students are often more prone to simply show up, snooze through, and otherwise not participate in any meaningful way. Therefore, it's critical that students understand the potential personal benefits of ethical knowledge and skills in achieving their career, lifestyle, health, and relational goals. Understanding that an admirable character is a precious commodity—their precious commodity—students can become genuinely motivated to attend thoughtfully and intentionally to how their choices reflect their characters.

We all know people whom we trust. We all know people whom we respect, not just for their achievements, but even more viscerally for their humanity. Referring to someone as a person of integrity, exhibiting honesty, compassion, and other traits that reveal them as having strong character, we are praising them with an ultimate compliment. Who wouldn't like to be viewed by others in such a manner? Who wouldn't want others to trust their word, value their leadership, and otherwise regard them as someone of high character? In the short and long run of life, individuals who earn such a reputation with others will undoubtedly benefit in their career success, their interpersonal satisfaction, their physical and emotional well-being, and their abidingly strong self-regard.

Increasingly, as our technological society chips away at privacy and secrecy, our newsfeeds are rife with reports of people being exposed for their unethical and often illegal behavior. Whether it's an online "have a secret affair" Web site, an attempt at financial deception, embarrassing behavior captured in Facebook photos, or hacked accounts revealing the wide range of human improprieties, it is naive to believe that our choices are invisible and will remain secret. Similarly, academic integrity programs such as Turn.it.in.com allow professors to screen out plagiarism and confront cheaters. Web cams, video cameras, online sleuths, law enforcement officers, and other tools of surveillance should also alert us to the improbability of "getting away with" unethical behavior. While avoiding embarrassment, humiliation, job termination, and even arrest is not the loftiest of reasons for knowing how to make ethical choices, they are still worth avoiding!

All we have at the end of the day is our reputation and our good character. Misfortune can strike, we can be treated unfairly, we can be hurt by a loved one, and we can even get an F on an exam. However, if in the face of these setbacks we can take heart in our sound character and continue to comport ourselves with integrity, a certain salvation is achieved in our unwavering and uncompromised sense of selves as individuals whose character itself is a source of pride and strength. As stated by Sami El Okaily, a student at American University in Dubai, "Unethical actions may lead to success but ethical actions will lead to a longer lasting success."

A CEO once commented that when hiring employees, anyone who is an Eagle Scout will always get an interview with him. Why? In his view, an Eagle Scout embodies the quintessential character ideals of the well-known Boy Scout law, "A Scout is trustworthy, loyal, helpful, friendly, courteous, kind, obedient, cheerful, thrifty, brave, clean and reverent." While a rather tall order, in this CEO's view, someone who has achieved the rank of Eagle Scout is likely to have many of the fine character traits he would like to see in his employees. We can't all be Eagle Scouts, but we can all have characteristics of which we're proud and which others view with high regard.

CONCLUSION

Erroneously, young adults may enter college with the expectation that the university is accountable for how well and how much they learn. The more adult revelation is that education is not a static, passive process dispensed by others but a call to active and ongoing reflection, effort, cultivation, and integration. It is not uncommon for professors and administrators to feel that they are working harder to provide teaching and resources than students are willing to expend their own efforts. Each college student begins to grow up when they take active accountability for ethical choices and the type of character these choices reflect. Young adults intensely crave independence and freedom but can often lose sight of their responsibility and agency in exercising that freedom productively. Gaining genuine insight into their unique developmental strengths and challenges while learning effective problem-solving skills grounded in their own ethical values can lead to empowering students to make choices that are consistent with who they want to be in the world.

Chapter 10

In Their Own Words: Students Offer Their Views on Ethics Development at College

Bad company ruins good morals.

—1 Corinthians 15:33

A book dedicated to the ethics formation of college students without including the direct voices of students is incomplete. What do students themselves think about ethics on campus and how to help create campus environments that nurture and develop ethical formation? We asked students taking an ethics class at Santa Clara University to chime in by offering their perspectives. With their permission, we have included some of their thoughts about ethics on campus and what they think could be the most fruitful directions for ethical formation and development. Of course, their views are not necessarily those of the authors but represent their perspective on ethical and other challenges on campus. Students were enrolled in an Ethics in Psychology course in 2015 (note that the syllabus for the course is included in appendix A of this volume). Their quotes have been used with their express written permission.

BUILDING ETHICAL MUSCLES

One student highlighted the importance of building ethical skills over time with a helpful analogy to physical fitness (i.e., push-ups). He underscored that we can't expect college students to make challenging ethical decisions without adequate preparation and ongoing practice. He makes a good point. Expecting college students to arrive on campus, typically directly from their parents' home and the confines of their local high school, and then behave with good ethical decision-making capabilities when confronted with a great deal of independence and little adult supervision is unrealistic. This student made the point that one has to be mindful that ethical decision making is a practice that needs foundational support. He states:

In the same way that one cannot expect a layman to do 100 push-ups with no practice, one cannot expect the college student population to act more ethically with little to no practice. To have our college students conduct themselves in a more ethical fashion, we must give them the opportunity to flex and work their ethical muscles. Initially, students should go over the most common ethical perspectives. The second stage would involve placing students in scenarios where they would most likely confront decisions that are likely to face them and guide them through the right course of action. The key point to note with the model that I am proposing is that students need to understand how exactly their own actions and ethical choices affect them as well as affect the world around them. Unless you have students connect to the material and understand the sheer magnitude of their decisions, they will not understand why it is so important. Over time, this will not only make them ethically sound and well-grounded, it should make them understand that ethics related discussions have a very vital and real role in our day to day lives.

—Zach Hines

ACADEMIC PRESSURE

Several students offered thoughtful comments on the intensity of academic pressure for current college students. Increased pressure and competition likely creates an environment that can lead to unethical behavior related to academic integrity. Additionally, a student from China offered a unique perspective about diversity and cultural factors that impact ethical decision making on campuses, especially as it relates to cheating.

The issue here lies in between these two very important foundations of college education. On one hand there is the ideal mission of fostering learning. In the ideal world, students would enter into university programs with an eagerness and enthusiasm for learning, ready to delve into all that a school has to offer in terms of classes, extracurricular activities, and other programs and services. Students would all have an equal opportunity to become that perfect competent student who discovers their passion and vocation, who is self-motivated and thus takes pride in his or her work, who collaborates well with others, and who isn't afraid to ask tough questions. Yet on the other hand, there are the two enemies of this idyllic education system: time and money. With the pressure for students to graduate in a timely manner, higher education systems have somewhat lost this highly esteemed value of intellectual growth. A student's college career is less fluid and more structured than in the past. There is a list of requirements, of classes to take, and alongside that there is the pressure to finish a class with high marks. Within their major, students trudge through the same required classes, turning in assignments because they need to in order to get a grade. In many cases, students must resort to cheating because each class demands so much time and effort that it seems impossible to get it all done on time and with the standard of excellence required to get the A.

If students were given the freedom to choose from a wide selection of these types of courses, they could essentially create their own roadmap through college or pathway that suits them best. Again, rather than taking required classes to receive the mandatory number of credits to graduate, students can explore the many options the school has to offer.

Overall, there are a few major points to take home. College students need a way to demonstrate adequate levels of competency in various fields as they graduate and venture off into work life. Rather than following a list of requirements to fulfill a number of credits and graduate on time, students should learn at their own pace using online or blended class structures to be able to sit with the material at a time when is most convenient for them. Using a pass/fail assessment system would relieve pressure of competition, and re-center the focus of classes from course completion and grades to obtaining knowledge and understanding of a subject. Higher education is meant to provide students with a foundation of knowledge to prepare them to graduate and enter into a career of their choice. College is supposed to challenge students and allow them to grow. It's time to bring back the core of what education is about. Education is empowering and students should be in control of how and when they learn. Thus, students will leave college more competent, knowledgeable, and ready to live up to the highest standards of ethics.

—Megan Schiel

Megan offers a thoughtful reflection on the tensions between the ideals of higher education and the reality that creates temptations for cheating and other ethical challenges. Her concerns have been debated and considered across campuses over many years and even decades. A tension exists between the ideals and the reality of higher education within the context of our culture. She hopes that educational ideals can bring back the need for students to be in charge of their education and to learn for learning's sake using competency-based models. In doing so, ethical decision making perhaps appears a bit easier and more clear.

A student from China, Evangeline, offers a very thoughtful and unique perspective on the challenges that international students often have, especially from an Asian culture such as China, where they seek their higher education from colleges in the United States. The attention to cultural differences offered by Evangeline's personal perspectives and insights can help to better appreciate the special concerns that international students might have and the challenges they may experience.

Chinese students are often compelled to engage in academically dishonest behaviors because of unique family dynamics. Almost all current Chinese students are only children as a result of China's one child policy. They are loved by two parents and four grandparents who all have great expectations, including an elite education. Such expectations can be very burdensome, and Chinese students may feel obligated to do well at school, which then leads to academic dishonesty. Furthermore, some Chinese students choose to study abroad in the United States to escape the Chinese educational system, possibly because they do not do well. They often have false perceptions of classes in U.S. universities being easier; thus they may not put enough effort into studying and have to cheat to pass the class, or they may intend to cheat from the outset and not study at all. In order to avoid the ethical obstacles of academic integrity, Chinese students should balance their families' expectations with their own expectations and fulfill the responsibility of studying as students.

Psychological distress may increase the likelihood of unethical behaviors performed by Chinese students. Studying abroad in the U.S. is not easy, especially at an age vulnerable to the psychiatric disorders. Language difficulties, lack of social connection, homesickness, etc., all contribute to psychological distress, and Chinese students, especially those who are unfamiliar with western cultures, often find themselves stunned by the availability of alcohol and drugs. Therefore, distressed Chinese students may be tempted to use psychoactive substances to escape from reality. Moreover, behaviors such as substance abuse are treated less seriously in the U.S. than in China, which may mislead Chinese students into thinking that drug use is okay. For example, marijuana becomes legal in several states in the U.S., while famous Kung Fu movie star Jackie Chan's son was arrested and jailed for six months in Beijing for marijuana use and possession. People in China criticized his behavior harshly and demanded him to quit the entertainment industry, but his fans defended him by referring to the legality of marijuana in the United States. Substance abuse is unethical, in that drugs are harmful not only to abusers, but also people around abusers. Instead of escaping from reality temporarily, Chinese students can use resources on campus or off-campus to help their depression and anxieties.

U.S. universities should be well prepared to prevent potential unethical behaviors committed by Chinese students. First, issues including plagiarism, academic integrity, [and] bullying need to be addressed in international student orientations. Plagiarism is not taken seriously in China, which results in the majority of Chinese students knowing little about plagiarism. Ouyang Huhua, a English professor at Guandong University of Foreign Studies in China, illustrates that "the notion of plagiarism is alien to Chinese culture . . . and it is hard for Chinese students to conceptualize the idea . . . students coming here to study are suddenly supposed to write a paper in this new system. It is hard for them" (Gill, 2008). Chinese students need to be properly educated about plagiarism and other unfamiliar topics before school starts. Second, advisors who are knowledgeable about Chinese culture can enhance students' performances. Cultural differences frequently lead to misunderstanding. For example, it may seem confusing to some advisors that many of their Chinese advisees are business majors. However, if they know the family backgrounds of most Chinese students whose parents are mostly in business industry, they can better assist and guide them on the path to a successful career. Advisors can also use cultural relativism and subjectivism to better understand advisees' behaviors. Third, professors who are teaching Chinese freshmen should allow them time to adapt. A poor grade in the very first academic term of studying abroad life can be stressful. Professors should take students' language proficiencies and familiarity with American grading system into consideration. Although grades are hard to justify, it is best to base evaluations on both performance and efforts. Finally, universities should host support groups within the international student body for students to connect and support each other, as well as school events for them to meet more local students. Many ethical controversies can be prevented if universities put efforts into educating Chinese students and faculties.

—Evangeline Yang

Evangeline expresses her personal opinions based on her own experience, and certainly Chinese students each have their own unique experiences of culture, family, and the transition to living abroad, which may differ widely from Evangeline's. She makes clear that faculty, staff, and fellow students better understanding international students' unique challenges, expectations, and experiences, and helping those students assimilate into the American educational system, needs to be made a high priority for higher education administrators and communities.

ALCOHOL

Several students highlight the importance of efforts to better manage alcohol consumption on campus. Ian highlights the importance of more graded exposure to alcohol before having the opportunity to do great damage to self and others with poor decision making in a brand new alcohol-pervaded college. He believes, as do many others, that those students who have the most trouble with alcohol at college are those who have little understanding and experience with negotiating their own personal relationship to alcohol before arriving on campus. While he is thoughtful about laws and policies regarding drinking by minors, he endorses more thoughtful exposure to the challenging issues of alcohol use and both cultural and peer pressures as early as possible before potential damage and poor decisions are made.

In an ideal world, there would be one solution that could be applied to all of the ethical dilemmas found on a college campus, but this is not the case. I believe that the best solution in this case is also the simplest solution: exposure. Ethical issues seem to arise when students are experiencing a new sense of independence, and are subsequently bombarded with new people and experiences that they've never encountered before. It is easy to see how these people may act unethically simply because they have not experienced similar situations in their lives.

Unfortunately, in many colleges, the issues of sexual harassment and assault are often intertwined with alcohol abuse. I believe that a large part of this problem is due to the fact that many students have never consumed alcohol before coming to college. While I am not advocating for excessive imbibing of alcohol for minors, I do think it is important that they get some exposure before they come to college. Alcohol can often be an uncomfortable thing to talk about with minors, but it is very important that they are at least informed of the basics of alcohol, how it can affect someone, and it can affect different people in many different ways. In my experience, the people who abuse alcohol the most are the ones who never drank alcohol before they came to school, and in part, never gained a sense of what their limits are.

—Ian Maltzer

Teresa highlights the need to have alcohol-free events for students so that socialization and fun on campus isn't always connected to alcohol consumption.

All students should participate in sober events in general to help lower the feeling that alcohol needs to be involved in order to have fun. These events should be exciting and involve socialization so that they can lead to more ethical decision making in the future. For example, students could go on hikes or play friendly sports games and make it open to all students. If students enjoy these activities, then they are more likely to continue to participate in them over choosing to drink. These activities not only help foster social relationships, but they also encourage good health and physical activity. Some other ideas could be going to the movies, attending sporting events, having baking competitions, or playing board games. The idea is to meet new people and make new friends, because socializing in a safe and fun environment is a more ethical, healthy, and overall a better decision than binge drinking.

—Teresa Wickstron

GREEK LIFE

Several students focused their attention specifically on the Greek system. Allison thoughtfully points out that the mission statements of many Greek houses for both men and women do, in fact, highlight ethical behavior and formation. By coming back to these ideals and principles, Allison is suggesting that the Greek system could actually align productively and inspiringly with ethical formation on campus rather than be an obstacle to it.

Colleges and Greek organizations alike profess important mission statements and statements of purpose that drive their actions and decision making. All statements differ to varying degrees in their wording and purpose, but Greek organizations excel at developing missions focused on moral and ethical responsibilities. The Santa Clara vision of "competence, conscience, and compassion" is well embodied in the ten Greek organizations bordering its campus. Sororities profess virtues of "social responsibility" (Delta Gamma Fraternity), "justice and right" (Alpha Phi International), "values and ethics" (Alpha Delta Pi), "allegiance to strong ethical principles" (Kappa Kappa Gamma), and a "lifetime opportunity for moral growth" (Kappa Alpha Theta Fraternity). Fraternities encourage "standards of morality" (Sigma Pi Fraternity), "friendship, justice, and learning" (Sigma Chi Fraternity), "the importance of virtue" (The Pi Kappa Alpha Fraternity), "ethical behavior and decision making" (Kappa Sigma Fraternity), and "mental, moral, and social development" (Tau Kappa Epsilon Fraternity). Regardless of one's personal views on Greek life, it is nearly impossible to disagree with the virtues and ideals set forth by these organizations. Further examination of these ideals pushes administrators and non-affiliates to reexamine the beneficial role active on campus Greek life could play in any institution of higher education.

—Allison Byrne

Another student, Christian, offers suggestions that highlight respect for diversity and giving back to the local community in Greek life on campus. In this way, he echoes Allison's suggestions regarding ways that the Greek system could be part of the solution and not part of the problem in ethical formation of students on campus.

One way to ethically diversify Greek Life would be to blindfold active members during the interview process of potential pledges as a way to select member unbiasedly. Fraternities and sororities should also actively seek ethnically different students, not because it would be nice to have a diverse institution, but [because] studies have illustrated that "interracial interactions are positively and significantly related to gains in leadership skills, psychological well-being, intellectual engagement, and intercultural effectiveness during the first year of college,"

(Bowman, 2013, p. 875). This perfectly blends into what Greek Life has histori-
cally wanted to uphold—develop leadership. Another method to ethically avoid
intentional or unintentional discrimination is to use the acronym S.H.R.E.D,
which will prompt people to be open to sexual orientation, heritage, religion,
ethnicity, and disabilities. Using different tactics to recruit potential pledges
while keeping an open mind to benefits of diversity will ensure an ethical process
of selecting new members to be more inclusive and rich.

It is also important for Greek Life to give back to the community at large
as many well-established institutions ethically do so today. One way for Greek
Life to engage with its community is to mandate that all incoming and outgoing
members of a chapter take a civic engagement course or to record a certain
number of hours doing volunteer work for others in need. If this requirement is
not done by the end of the school year, a fine and suspension will occur.

—Christian Deamer

CHEATING

Several students discuss how to combat academic cheating on campus
by changing the way we think about and respond to cheating behavior,
and altering how we design the classroom environment to minimize the
desire and perhaps the need for cheating as well.

Tackling the issue of cheating on college campuses as an ethical problem, rather
than looking to reduce the ways in which it can occur, can potentially yield bet-
ter results and prove more valuable for the student.

Students can unfortunately find ways to engage in unethical behaviors in aca-
demia despite rules and restrictions. Thus, it is crucial to view this as an issue of
integrity, honesty, and ethics in order to successfully encourage college students
to behave more ethically throughout their college career.

There is obvious value in focusing on ethics behind all decision-making and
behaviors. Keeping this in mind, it can potentially be very beneficial to address
cheating in academia in light of the different ethical frameworks.

—Jessica Olhausen

The changes required at academic institutions will undoubtedly take time to
implement, however small shifts in grading policies and course objectives are
steps in the right direction. As a Biology and Psychology double major at
Santa Clara University, I have experienced two completely different academic
environments; while one focuses solely on achievement and earning the maxi-
mum number of points, the other encourages growth and true learning. Needless
to say, courses in which professors stressed effort over excellence were signifi-
cantly more enjoyable and engaging. Though I have not participated in aca-
demic dishonesty, the temptation to do so was something I and other classmates

experienced in achievement oriented classes. At an institution that stresses values and moral development, the culture of competition and cutthroat assessments promotes enmity between students and a drive to win at the expense of learning; this culture does not inspire adherence to what is right. I believe that more courses should adopt a course evaluation similar to my Ethics in Psychology lecture; providing students with a competency based approach eliminates the fear of failure; effort rather than excellence guides the grade. Another great example of growth oriented course evaluation is providing students with the opportunity to earn points back on assessments if they choose to complete Securing an E for effort over excellence. Students willing to return to old assignments and improve their understanding of challenging concepts will gain more from the class; ultimately effort will once again guide the grade. Shifting the focus away from point tallying to actual understanding of academic concepts eliminates students' fear of failure, rather encouraging learning from failure.

Establishing this new academic culture will combat the top four reasons students resort to cheating. Firstly, students will recognize that hard work and effort is all that is required to secure rewarding careers; the pressure to forgo ethics to move oneself forward disappears. Second, if academic institutions stress growth over achievement, students will feel accomplished if they present their best work and thus will not feel pressure to impress parents with top grades. Furthermore, passing a class will not be judged by scoring the highest marks, but rather by taking the time to achieve competency in a course; cheating will not aid in personal understanding of the material. And lastly, if professors establish opportunities for students to demonstrate their improvement in the course and academic competency, students will rarely feel as though the professor is acting unfairly–eliminating the temptation to earn more points unethically. By presenting a culture of effort over excellence, the role of ethics will return to academic work in undergraduate institutions.

—Sonya Chalaka

In fact, the nature of academia really seems to incentivise [sic] academic dishonesty. Many students find themselves in massive, quite difficult classes that are graded on a curve, meaning that their performance depends on how well they do relative to others in the class. The students at large institutions hardly ever meet the professor, and whether or not they pass the class depends on beating others in the class on a handful of exams. Furthermore, students' entire futures are often dependent on how well they do in intro level classes, and these classes are often designed to "weed out" those in the class that are unfit to continue. But for students who have wanted to be a doctor since they were 3 years old (or at least their parents wanted them to), cheating on a midterm sounds a lot better than relinquishing your entire life goal based on the results of one test.

In response to this pervasive academic dishonesty, many universities enforce very strict consequences; at Santa Clara University, the usual punishment for cheating, whether it was copying homework from another student or copying answers on a final exam, is at minimum failing the particular assignment, and often leads to failing the entire course and being reported to the office of student integrity. These consequences can be disastrous for students, as it hurts their GPA, means they often have to retake classes, could make them lose their scholarship, and follows them on transcripts for the rest of their lives. Yet, the punishment has not really deterred the crime.

—Michael Turgeon

When asked to make ethical decisions and given the tools to do so, students offer a wide variety of perspectives on how to help create more ethical communities and cultures on college campuses. Their voices are perhaps the most valuable to hear when trying to design policies, procedures, and programs to support ethical formation on campus. Including their direct quotes, with permission, provides a sampling of how thoughtful students can offer much to the discussion of campus ethics formation.

In addition to student voices at Santa Clara, we also interviewed students at Dartmouth College, an elite and secular Ivy League school that does not require ethics in its core curriculum. With their express permission, we quote these students below about building a more ethical climate on campus.

I think that an enhanced ethical climate is best done through the emphasis of "awareness" throughout our core curriculum. The College attempts to do this by requiring classes in the "Systems and Traditions of Thought, Meaning," and "Value and International or Comparative Studies," but these classes rarely discuss ethical awareness. One may be required to read, for example, Aristotle's Politics, *which has a significant ethical agenda. However, class discussion and subsequent course material is usually based on raw information rather than the relation of the work to practical, everyday life. I think this is the key to a more ethically minded campus. By relating the information to how you go about your day, you become aware of ethics in your observations and decisions.*

—Phil Gomez

I think that Dartmouth's ethical climate could benefit from some kind of formal ethics training or class incorporated into one's major—an econ major too often comes and goes in four years without discussing the morality of capitalism or Wall Street misconduct. I see the new residential housing system as a way to form communities in a more academic setting, which is likely to embody ethical principles and norms.

—James Fair

. . . the best option would be to include ethics within our core requirements for graduation.

—Noah Goldstein

These thoughtful students, among others we interviewed, seek ethical guidance through their university curriculum, hoping for practical and applied applications.

CONCLUSION

Respecting and harnessing the wisdom and best instincts of students is critical to a partnership around ethics on campus. Students need to be included and their voices heard when designing and implementing strategies to integrate character development and thoughtful ethical decisions into campus policies and programs. This chapter highlighted a number of student insights in their own words, underscoring the need to channel the invaluable contributions of students into the ethical college culture.

Part III

Best Practices in Ethical Development on Campus

Chapter 11

Best Practices: Curricular

[Emerging adults] have had withheld from them something that every person deserves to have a chance to learn: how to think, speak, and act well on matters of good and bad, right and wrong.
—Christian Smith, *Lost in Transition*, p. 69

One way to better enhance, nurture, and encourage ethical reflection and development among college students is to integrate ethics education into the academic curriculum. Certainly those who study or major in philosophy, religious studies, and a number of other academic disciplines would likely be required to take courses in ethics as part of their academic major, minor, or distribution requirements. Additionally, many liberal arts colleges and faith-based colleges require all students to enroll in philosophy and/or religious studies classes that include some attention to ethics education. In most colleges and universities, ethics is usually taught in the philosophy department, and the majority of these courses focus on moral philosophy in particular. Often, these courses take a historical and theoretical approach to the subject matter of ethics rather than an applied approach. Thus, students may learn a great deal about ancient Greek philosophers, as well as more contemporary philosophers such as Immanuel Kant, John Locke, and so forth, but they may learn rather little about the practical application of ethics and ethical decision making in their current personal and professional lives.

Two best practices that can assist college students to develop skills in ethical decision making include (1) asking all students, regardless of their academic major or minor, to take at least one applied ethics course prior to graduation and (2) using an applied ethics approach that is specifically relevant to their academic major or primary field(s) of study. In this way, students have the opportunity to develop critical, ethical decision-making skills in an academic environment for course credit that is geared toward their major field of study and likely their future career.

At Santa Clara University, for example, all students throughout the college must take at least one approved ethics class, regardless of their academic major, as part of a university-wide core curriculum requirement. Thus, students in any of the departments and divisions within the College of Arts and Sciences (i.e., social sciences, natural sciences, arts, and humanities), as well as those students in the business and engineering schools, must take at least one ethics course. While most of the approved ethics courses happen to be offered through the university's philosophy department, an emphasis on applied ethics allows all academic departments to develop and offer their own ethics courses designed specifically for students who choose to major in these departments. In so doing, departments can create ethics courses that are relevant, creative, modern, and applied in the spirit of engaging students with practical and compelling contemporary ethical challenges rather than, for example, only studying the influence and wisdom of ancient Greeks and other moral philosophers in a purely theoretical and historical manner.

The wisdom of asking all college students to take at least one approved class in ethics and allowing individual academic departments to develop classes that fulfill this requirement is a best practice in terms of encouraging ethics education, formation, and development among college students, and likely serves as a fundamental way to develop and nurture ethical skills during the college years. It provides students with an opportunity to develop a foundation in moral philosophy yet apply these general principles to their particular areas of greatest personal, academic, and career interest.

Colleges and universities can freely adopt this model of ethics training if desired. Of course, many colleges and universities are reluctant to add more courses to their standard core curriculum or general distribution requirements without taking other requirements away. In addition, some faculty must see the value and therefore be willing to teach a departmental ethics course even where none has been previously offered. Thus, thoughtful consideration must be given before adding more requirements to an often overloaded curriculum at many institutions. Colleges and universities must therefore reflect on their strategic priorities in educating their students before making any significant changes to their academic requirements.

Those institutions that desire to offer this particular best practice approach to ethics education for all students may wish to ensure that several key elements are included in their required ethics courses. These elements are in many ways mandatory to accomplish the goal of quality applied ethical formation at the college level. Still, they need to be adapted to fit the needs and desires of a wide range of diverse (i.e., public, private, secular, faith-based, and two-year community college) educational institutions. These key elements are briefly detailed below.

FOUNDATIONS IN MORAL PHILOSOPHY

The first part of the ethics course, regardless of the academic department where the course is offered, is to provide students with a solid, yet concise, foundation in moral philosophy. Asking students to read and discuss general approaches to ethics and ethical decision making, as discussed in chapter 3 of this book, can be accomplished within a few weeks of an academic term. Of course, colleges on the quarter system who offer 10- to 11-week terms must be more efficient and streamlined relative to institutions on a more leisurely 15- to 16-week semester schedule. Thus, the foundations in moral philosophy and ethical systems portion of the course could be longer and presented in more depth for institutions using a semester system.

Thoughtful discussion, presentation, and readings on the history of moral philosophy, as well as the different approaches to ethical decision making (e.g., utilitarian, social contract, justice, virtue, absolute moral rules), can be completed during the first part of the course to provide students with not only the foundation but also a set of tools to frame their ethical conversations and applied ethical problem solving later in the term. Having an understanding of these different approaches to ethical decision making and an appreciation for the intellectual and historical wisdom of these approaches provides the much needed foundation for application of these principles in more applied and contemporary ethical dilemmas.

APPLICATION TO SPECIFIC ACADEMIC DISCIPLINES

The second part of the ethics course involves examining the key ethical conflicts and ethical decision-making approaches particular to individual academic fields of study. For example, students who major in health-care related fields (e.g., psychology, public health, pre-medical or nursing, social work) would likely be interested in how ethics is applied to their future fields of study. Medicine, psychology, social work, nursing, and so forth all have their particular professional codes of ethics that their respective professional organizations have endorsed, as well as various resources for ethical reflection and decision making. Business, engineering, and other fields also have their own strategies and expectations regarding ethics and ethical decision making. Thus, the second part of the ethics course helps student to better understand and appreciate how ethical issues, dilemmas, and concerns are addressed within the broader context of their academic area of interest. Students then become aware of and more facile in employing the tools and knowledge that are available to them from their respective professional organizations and career-relevant academic literature.

It is often customary in many fields to use case studies to help students discern ethical issues and approaches to challenging situations within their chosen fields. Using case studies that are interesting and relevant to students in health care, business, engineering, education, and so forth helps to maximize engagement as well as provide an opportunity for serious reflection about the types of real-life issues they may likely face in their professional lives after graduation.

APPLICATION TO EVERYDAY LIFE

The third part of the course is to expand ethical reflection and decision making beyond the academic discipline of choice and the norms of any given profession to the everyday life of students. This is an important and perhaps critical step toward minimizing the compartmentalization of ethical decision making that often happens in keeping personal and professional lives separate. For example, this approach addresses the challenge of students integrating their ethical values and problem-solving strategies into both their work lives and personal lives. Incorporating emphases on both personal and job related professional ethics is a more holistic educational approach that integrates the way students proceed to live ethically and consistently in all realms of their lives.

In this part of the course students are asked to read, discuss, and reflect upon the ethical challenges that they face in their personal lives, including observations of ethical situations they witness among their peers on campus. While the course remains an academic one (and not group therapy, for example), a focus on personal ethics using real case examples of ethical challenges helps to solidify the kinds of thoughtful reflections that they hopefully acquired during the earlier parts of the course. Certainly, confidentiality concerns must be considered if students are asked to discuss personal ethics in class. A respectful appreciation for the public versus private nature of ethical decision making is critical for students to feel comfortable and safely share any personal ethical concerns and issues in the classroom setting.

Students are asked to engage in problem-solving discussions using the principles learned from moral philosophy in the first part of the course as well as the discipline-specific ethical guidelines from the second part of the course to assist them in their reflections about the many personal, professional, and ongoing ethical concerns they will inevitably confront.

ANOTHER APPROACH TO ETHICS TRAINING: THE FRESHMAN 101 COURSE

The course described above involves a typical academic class offered for graded credit within typical discipline-specific departments. This course would look and feel like any other academic class on campus. However, another way to approach ethical training within the academic curricular setting could utilize a very different model. This approach could have a more relaxed student life feel to it that may have some important advantages relative to the traditional classroom-setting type of course discussed earlier in this chapter. This alternative and best practices approach to ethics training would include a mandatory first-year student, pass/no pass course (let's call it "Freshman 101" here, but other names for the course could be suggested as well) that is offered and taught through the residence halls rather than in traditional academic departments and classrooms. In this way, students would be required to attend the class during their first term or first year at college and have the benefit of achieving academic course credit. Yet the class could offer the advantages of a low-pressure and relaxed environment with grades assigned as pass/no pass and perhaps the credits provided might be fewer (e.g., one or two credits) than earned in a traditional full-credit academic course. Offering a small seminar-like class in a comfortable residence hall environment with 20 students or less meeting perhaps once or twice per week in the evening could create a more reflective, engaging, and open environment. Commuting students could also participate in this experience by either joining groups in the residence halls or meeting in the student union or student activity center on campus during the day or in the evening if preferred.

In most college and university settings, academic course work for credit needs to be taught by, or at least monitored by, faculty members. However, using this Freshman 101 model, student life staff members as well as graduate students and advanced undergraduates could all be part of the teaching and learning team, perhaps supervised by an academic faculty member. Thus, while faculty would be ultimately responsible for the academic content and pass/fail grading of the students, advanced undergraduate and graduate students, as well as student life staff, could provide much of the hand-on teaching and learning experiences for these new college students.

Topics for reading and class discussions would include ethical decision making around important and relevant college topics such as academic cheating, sexual behavior and misbehavior, alcohol and drug consumption, diversity issues, roommate conflicts, and so forth. Academic materials and research on these topics from psychology, public health, sociology, law, and other academic fields could be provided to ensure that the class was well grounded in quality research, best practices, and state-of-the-art understanding of these important areas. Case studies, ongoing and current research on these topics, and problem-solving strategies to cope with particular issues on campus could all be integrated into the course as well. Additionally, reflection on their own personal ethical values and principles for behavior could be discussed throughout the class.

The goal of this style of class would be to have an ongoing, for-credit academic class that would be casual yet rigorous enough to ensure that new freshmen have the opportunity to reflect, discuss, and learn about typical ethical challenges for new college students. While faculty must ensure that adequate academic rigor is provided, student life professionals can ensure that the material is relevant to the actual lived experience of college students. Graduate and advanced undergraduate students can also act as peer mentors and models for quality ethical decision making and discernment.

Colleges could adapt this model to fit their needs and purposes. For example, some may choose to offer the course on a pass/fail basis, while others might prefer offering the class for a grade. Some might choose to include additional college student survival topics such as time management and study skill suggestions, while others might wish to focus on ethical decision making only. Certainly, colleges can stay true to the spirit of these class suggestions yet make a variety of accommodations to fit their needs.

CONCLUSION

Ethics formation in college students can be supported and nurtured through academic course work that could be made available to all students, regardless of academic major or field of study. Offering appropriate readings and instruction in basic moral philosophy, discipline-specific ethics, and personal ethics in an integrated and engaging manner may prove useful for all students. A positive consequence of a mandated applied ethics course for all students may be an ongoing effort to create an ethically informed campus community that hopefully would translate to other classes, extracurricular activities, and residence halls as well. Beginning these thought processes and conversations early, and thus building them into the student mindset from the outset, can help create a campus culture where ethical decisions become conscious and intentional.

Appendix A offers two sample syllabi, the first from a course described in this chapter that is used in the psychology department at Santa Clara University with students who tend to major in psychology, liberal studies, and public health. The syllabus can be adapted in ways that make sense for other academic disciplines, as well as altered to fit the needs of individual faculty in diverse educational institutions and environments. Appendix A also includes a second applied ethics course offered in the philosophy department that can also be adapted to best suit other departments and disciplines.

Appendix B offers several syllabi from quality Freshman 101 courses used with permission from faculty at the University of South Carolina and at George Mason University. Again, these syllabi can be altered as desired by individual faculty and institutions to fit their specific goals and needs.

Chapter 12

Best Practices: Extracurricular

In just about every area of society, there's nothing more important than ethics.

—Henry Paulson

Ethics formation can also be supported on college campuses outside of the traditional classroom experience. While academic courses on ethics are an important and perhaps crucial step to help students develop the framework and solid foundation for ethical decision making, applying their academic and classroom learning to extracurricular activities throughout the college, as well as off campus, helps to solidify their learning through application in real world settings. This can be accomplished in a variety of ways.

COMMUNITY SERVICE VOLUNTEER ACTIVITIES

Most college campuses provide students with opportunities for community service, volunteerism, and engagement. While some of these activities may be integrated into their academic course work (e.g., working at a homeless shelter for mentally ill clients while taking an abnormal psychology course, working in a daycare or preschool program while taking a child development class), many of these opportunities are offered to students as part of their extracurricular student activities. Often students are motivated to volunteer in the community to get a break from their studies, learn important skills, make connections to others, and so forth.

Volunteer activities in the community provide a rich environment for ethical reflection and formation. The key is to have structured periodic or ongoing reflection built into the experience. This allows students to discuss and process ethical issues, dilemmas, questions, and concerns while engaging in their community volunteering activities. For example, students might question the ethics of chronic homelessness while working in a shelter, and further question the ethics of some shelters denying access to homeless individuals engaging in ongoing substance abuse. They might also consider the pros and cons of allowing homeless clients with mental illness to make their own choices about their treatment and care. Students working in low-income schools might wonder about ethical principles associated with allocation of funds to gifted students, confidentiality between students and parents, or issues associated with ameliorating the lack of food availability in certain homes. Having structured opportunities to discuss their experiences with peers, mentors, and supervisors allows for deep reflection and consideration of ethical issues and dilemmas.

STUDENT CLUBS AND ORGANIZATIONS

Students can easily feel lost and anonymous within a large campus community. Student clubs are a way to affiliate with smaller groups of like-minded individuals, allowing for a stronger sense of inclusion and connection. Many student groups focus on diversity by bringing together particular ethnic, religious, language, political, sexual, and other target groups of individuals. These clubs might range from groups of Latinos, Muslims, Francophiles, Zionists, Palestinians, lesbian-gay-bisexual-transgendered, libertarians, social outreachers, computer gamers, and an almost endless variety of clubs. Some of these clubs engage in political and rights-oriented activities, and some may attract the animosity of other groups or individuals on campus. By virtue of their opinions or minority status, it is incumbent upon universities to provide ethical guidelines to campus clubs and organizations in order to promote safety and civility as well as respect, responsibility, integrity, concern, and competence (RRICC).

Each club can design its own charter and mission statement specifying the ethical comportment expected of members. For example, clubs should demand that their members show respect for other individuals and groups, even when advocating strong positions or beliefs. Encouraging each college club to enforce its own RRICC standards can help focus the leaders and participants on maintaining these qualities within all of their activities and communications. Thus, while a group might advocate against the right to obtain an abortion, the employment of harassment, denigration, hate-mongering, provocation, sabotage, and other more subtle forms of disrespect and insensitivity should be clearly forbidden.

Historically, college campuses have been hotbeds of protest, social rebellion, and confrontational stances on numerous sociopolitical issues. Fights have erupted between competing interests, and harassment has at times escalated to vandalism and violence. Student groups advocating divestment from Israel have clashed with Jewish groups; anti–gay marriage sentiments within fundamentalist religious groups have clashed with supporters; anti-war groups have clashed with hawkish political groups. Just as the university must protect its campus and students from harm, it is also necessary to ensure that student organizations abide by the principles of RRICC. While leaders within each student group must take responsibility for the behavior of its members, the university must provide ultimate oversight in ensuring that all organizations are behaving ethically toward the entire college population.

By including ethical decision making as an integral part of the education, ethos, and ongoing dialogue of each campus, the value placed on RRICC is readily extended to clubs who are themselves responsible for providing necessary supervision, intervention, and corrective feedback to members. The importance of comporting oneself with integrity and relating to others of diverse beliefs and backgrounds respectfully on campus is a necessary requisite to students' ability to succeed personally and professionally during college and long beyond.

FRATERNITIES AND SORORITIES . . . BUT MOSTLY FRATERNITIES

Those in the know do not need to think twice if asked where on campus the most frequent and serious violation of laws, ethics, and campus standards occur: fraternities. Alcohol abuse in a highly charged sexual environment vastly increases the probability of dangerous behaviors, resulting in alcohol poisoning, malicious hazing, sexual assault, vandalism, and the like. Campuses have a long road ahead in creating safer, more inclusive, and more respectable cultures within the often raucous, alcohol-centric, hypersocial fraternity and sorority cultures, yet embarking on that journey is critical to student safety, integrity, health, and, ultimately, character and education.

Ethics are not inherently fun or sexy endeavors in the minds of many, and certainly this extends easily to fraternity members. Parties, yes. Hypermasculine displays, yes. Alcohol-fueled hooking up, yes. Intense bonding and brotherhood through long-held traditions and rituals, yes. But contemplating and discussing ethics? Not so much. Universities will have better success in this realm not only by setting rules and restrictions with strict consequences for violations, but also by promoting and recognizing ethical citizenship as a celebrated and rewarded status. Thus, providing meaningful recognition and even tangible rewards to fraternities that best demonstrate the principles of RRICC can create incentives while highlighting the often invisible ideals of ethics by holding up exemplars for praise.

Fraternities are not all bastions of decadence and bad behavior. In fact, many fraternities are highly committed to both campus and community service, contributing their skills, time, and energy toward helping others. Fraternities also promote fellowship, loyalty, leadership, mutual support, and other laudable qualities. Harnessing the positive aspirations within these groups of young men both to elevate their personal characters as well as to contribute meaningfully to the larger community can focus on what is right, rather than what is wrong, within fraternity life.

ETHICS BOWLS

Many campuses throughout the country are engaged in the Ethics Bowl program. Students debate ethical issues and dilemmas and then compete in local, regional, and national competitions. These events are similar to other college debate-team events, yet focus on ethically complex issues and events. Students learn to reflect upon ethical issues and fine tune their thinking, speaking, and debate skills with peers on and off campus in a fun, engaging, and team-building experience. This annual competition can receive enhanced publicity and attention at schools that wish to highlight ethics among their top priorities and values.

PUBLIC ETHICS CHALKBOARDS

At Santa Clara University, there is a large Ethics Board located near the primary cafeteria in the student union on campus. This large chalkboard poses an ethics question and asks students to provide brief answers to the weekly question in an anonymous manner. Students coming and going to their meals pass by the Ethics Board and can choose to participate by weighing in on the ethics question of the week or simply by reading what others have written. The Ethics Board provides an opportunity for students to regularly consider ethical questions of the day and participate by weighing in on their views about the issues presented to the campus community for consideration.

STUDENT ACTIVISM AND PROTESTS

Across college and university campuses nationwide, for hundreds of years, protests have been synonymous with student life. Protests have been sparked by issues ranging from the mundane, such as unacceptable cafeteria fare, to the monumental, such as large-scale social controversy: war, racism, politics, social injustice, gender inequality, and a vast range of sociopolitical-economic concerns. Student protests are so notorious on college campuses because they are synonymous with the energy and rebelliousness of youth at this particular developmental stage of life. By virtue of the developmental imperatives that propel youthful energies during those young adult years—such as the need to express oneself, affiliate with like-minded others, and push back against authority— protests are a natural outgrowth of many thoughtful and engaged students. Truly, the Four I's are spectacularly evident in the phenomenon of activism, as youth seek to claim their identity, bond and develop intimacy, assert their independence, express passionately held beliefs, and stage public actions that often challenge their emerging impulse controls. Thus, the college protests that routinely garner national attention are vivid microcosms of the larger developmental yearnings and struggles predominating at this age.

Furthermore, protests are held in the name of strong ethical beliefs. Stop investing in gas and oil! Pull our troops out of Afghanistan! Intervene in genocides! Protect women from rape and assault! Ban abortion! Black lives matter! The list of fervent causes in which protesters believe they hold the higher moral ground is long and contentious. Often, they pit one campus group against another, or students against the administration or government. As a result, campus protests are rife for opportunities to meaningfully and civilly engage and persuade other students toward their cause. They are also rife for conflict, aggression, violence, and righteous outrage and disregard for the rights of others.

Thus, student protests also provide an ideal forum for encouraging, teaching, and demonstrating the values of RRICC that can only better elevate the student cause and the level of student communication with opposing groups. The fundamental RRICC principles can guide colleges as they seek to instruct and oversee student protests as ethical exercises in keeping with certain key guidelines and expectations accompanying them.

An example of a typical college protest can best illustrate how the Four I's and the RRICC principles come into play. A highly charged example involves Palestinian students protesting against Israeli policies in which students sought to demand that the university divest from companies and products that support Israel. First, let us view such a protest from the developmental pulls of the Four I's. Clearly, in aligning with any group—be it in favor of Palestinian rights, Israeli rights, or administrative autonomy—students are declaring a passionate aspect of their identity. Not only are they aligning with a specific group or belief, but they are also expressing their degree of passion and willingness to confront conflict and disruption in the service of their beliefs. Second, emerging adults are powerfully driven to attain intimacy and the closeness of camaraderie. The joining together of fellow students in a common cause invariably strengths bonds and enhances feelings of loyalty and connection. Similarly, battling against a common "enemy" further unites groups, albeit with obvious dangers of polarization and animosity. Third, by defying authority and asserting strong beliefs in opposition to prevailing norms or powers, students enact a clear demonstration of independence, a hugely imperative developmental aspect of the college years. Finally, the power, protection, and passion of groups and their sense of righteousness in their, and only their, beliefs can easily fuel uncharacteristic aggression, hate speech, acts of vandalism, and even violence. These impulses must be kept in check lest the protesters (a) harm others or property, (b) stray outside the bounds of their legal rights, and (c) fail to convey their message and earn attention or respect in a cauldron of anger, shouting, and unchecked acting out.

Spectators in protests also express their identities and personal boundaries, as well as their RRICC principles. Do bystanders shout their disapproval, tear down banners, give thumbs-up signals, or enter into meaningful conversations with the protesters? All students—those protesting, those opposing the protesting, and those with no preconceived "skin in the game"—should be expected by colleges to behave ethically, civilly, and in keeping with standards of conduct spelled out by the school's policies. Protests can be inspiring and productive forms of communication and defiance, yet they can often devolve into antagonistic, disrespectful, vitriolic, counterproductive, and even violent conflicts. Educating *all* students in the ethical protest conduct required of them within their free speech rights provides immensely educational opportunities. Universities should use these forums as opportunities to convey and teach a range of ethical decisions and beliefs.

One example of a college protest that generated terrific questions of what constitutes ethical protest behavior is the Dartmouth College Black Lives Matter action of November 2015. The majority of the protest was conducted with a large interracial coalition of students representing both black and nonblack student supporters in a civil yet powerful expression of outrage against perceived systemic racism. Banners and signs were carried, passionate speeches delivered, engaged dialogue conducted, black clothing donned, and symbols of racial oppression displayed. By all reports, this phase of the demonstration was powerful, positive, and inspiring. Unfortunately, following this central demonstration, a smaller group of students decided to move their protest into the student library where a number of students were studying, personally confronting and disrupting students they condemned as being "complacent" and demanding that they stand if they were in support of their message. Students who did not stand were reportedly berated, called "Privileged white——," told to "F—— off," and otherwise yelled at with obscenities and antiwhite racist language. Those who did stand were told, "We don't care about you." Some students began to cry and were told, "F—— your white tears," while others reported feeling intimidated and trapped. This library protest became the topic of fervent outrage, by both protesters and nonprotesters, and generated an extensive conversation about free speech rights and the ethical implications of protest behavior both on and off campus.

This example is fertile for examination through the RRICC model, and involves complex discernment and ethical assessment. When conveying feelings of victimhood, anger, and demands for institutional change, when do the free speech and valid feelings of the protesters cross into violations of the rights of others? Where should one draw the parameters of responsibility, respect, integrity, concern, and competence in the endeavor to decry the belief that one's own humanity has been violated? Where does conduct violate the honor code and other standards set by the college, and how can these be addressed and resolved in these most charged and heated of climates? These and many other questions are generated by such protests, and colleges have both an opportunity and an educational duty to engage all parties in these discussions toward a consistent resolution, and even more so toward an edifying educational exercise in examining the intellectually and emotionally complex issues at stake.

In a letter to the Dartmouth community following these events, President Hanlon issued this statement on November 23, 2015:

1. *Each Dartmouth student is a full-fledged citizen of this community, with all the rights and responsibilities that citizenship entails.*
2. *We strive to balance freedom of speech with strong community values of civil discourse—though we recognize that at times these principles conflict.*
3. *At their core, institutions of higher education are places where open inquiry and the free debate about difficult and sometimes uncomfortable ideas must thrive.*

On Thursday evening, Nov. 12, a large demonstration by members of the Dartmouth and Upper Valley communities culminated in a moment of silence in front of Dartmouth Hall. This demonstration was a powerful expression of unity in support of social justice—Dartmouth at its strongest.

I cannot say the same about events that transpired in Baker Library immediately afterward. I have heard reports of vulgar epithets, personal insults, and intimidating actions used both by students who entered the library and students who were already in the library. We are actively investigating all reports of violations of College policy, and will enforce appropriate sanctions. Such behavior is antithetical to our values and goals as an institution. As one of the great institutions of higher learning, we are committed to the open and energetic exchange of ideas. And as Dartmouth's citizenship pledge reminds us, we must treat each person with dignity and respect. Abusive language aimed at community members—by any group, at any time, in any place—is not acceptable.

This incident and administrative response is an example of reiterating RRICC principles and encouraging ongoing discussion, assessment, and enforcement. In subsequently offering students individual attention and a safe place to voice their concerns, administrators sought to engage these young adults in a process whereby their youthful Four I's could be respected in the context of the values laid out in the RRICC model. While colleges use their own terms, models, and language, the principles of the Four I's and RRICC provide a shorthand that is easily conveyed.

CONCLUSION

Ethics formation can also be supported on college campuses outside of the traditional classroom experience. While academic courses on ethics are an important and perhaps crucial step to help students develop the framework and solid foundation for ethical decision making, applying their academic and classroom learning to extracurricular activities both on and off campus helps to solidify learning through application in real-world settings. This can be accomplished in a variety of ways in preexisting and easy to introduce forums. This chapter presented the fertile ethical realms of community service, student clubs and organizations, Greek life, Ethics Bowl competitions, public ethics chalkboards, and university policies in mining the ethically rich terrain of student activism. Highlighting the Four I's and the five RRICC principles throughout the university dialogue helps solidify and model their applicability and value.

Chapter 13

Best Practices: Residential Life

Educating the mind without educating the heart is no education at all.
—Aristotle

Perhaps one of the most important places where students can practice and learn about ethics during the college years occurs through daily living in the residence halls. Of course, not all college students live on campus. Many are commuting students living with their families of origin or on their own with or without roommates, intimate partners, or others. Yet, depending on the college or university setting, many students across the country live in campus residence halls, including both large and small dormitory or apartment campus settings as well as on- or off-campus fraternities and sororities. These living environments force students to live in close quarters and be attentive to and mindful of many rules, regulations, and policies of the house, creating important opportunities for quality ethical formation and reflection on how to meaningfully engage and interact with peers.

Even under the very best of circumstances, numerous ethical challenges will emerge while living in various types of residence halls on campus. Possessions get broken or stolen, arguments and fights occur, students may disrespect others by making noise while others are sleeping or studying, individuals may undervalue the possessions and needs of their roommates, hall mates, and dorm mates. It is inevitable that many students living closely together sharing bedrooms, bathrooms, and common living space will develop various tensions and problems that create important and rich learning opportunities for ethical reflection and development.

Being mindful of the RRICC model described earlier, many of these daily living challenges in close proximity to peers involve issues of respect and concern for others in particular. Learning to respect the needs and desires of others who share close living quarters can be a challenge for those who have never before lived in tight living arrangements with strangers or acquaintances. Respecting the property, sleep-wake cycles, and behavioral habits and preferences of others whose views and behaviors differ from one's own is a challenge for any new college student. And doing so with peers who may come from all over the country and the world, representing a wide variety of cultures and traditions, can make getting along even more difficult. Additionally, during the all-important and often stressful freshman year, roommates are often matched in a largely random fashion, with minimal attention to compatibility on many large campuses. Thus, successfully sharing a very small, perhaps 12-foot by 10-foot, living space with a total stranger who was randomly assigned is rarely easy, even under the very best of conditions.

Concern for others is a challenge living in large dorm environments in that at any given time, at least some students will be highly stressed, in crisis, and experiencing emotional, financial, relational, academic, mental health, and other critical needs. Of course, ethical students should have compassion and express concern for fellow students in need, yet they also must do so thoughtfully and carefully so as not to get overwhelmed by the stressors of their many peers. This can be a difficult tightrope to walk, and requires the ability to set appropriate boundaries, engaging with compassion and integrity the needs and desires of peers while balancing one's own needs and responsibilities.

Dorm rules and regulations, including a wide range of policies and procedures for living together, are inevitably needed to ensure adequate order and safety. The rights of all students need to be respected, and specific rules about quiet hours, overnight guests, fire safety, contraband such as firearms and drugs, and so forth need to be carefully considered with the interest of all parties involved.

Reminding students of these rules and policies, as well as enforcing them, is often left to resident assistants (typically older students, or sometimes employed faculty or staff) who also live within the residence hall environments. Young students often need gentle (and sometimes frequent) reminders that these policies and procedures are needed for everyone's safety, security, and happiness. But in addition to having a list of rules to follow, these policies can easily be viewed through the lens of ethics and relational character. Being attentive to the developmental stage of young college students and using the RRICC model can assist new students in enlarging their view of rules for dorm living into ethical guidelines and challenges rather than just ordained rules and proscriptions. Thus, framing the policies and procedures for residence hall living through the lens of ethical guidelines can go a long way to assist students in understanding their personal stake in their complex relational worlds. Rarely are the subtle choices involved in friendships enlightened by standard rules, and the RRICC principles underlying interactions can enhance the success and dignity of residential relationships.

For example, an emphasis on respecting the rights of all is highlighted through regulations about noise, as well as rules about overnight guests. An emphasis on concern for the welfare of everyone is highlighted in rules about locking the living space, reporting alcohol and drug violations, and prohibiting electrical devices (such as hot plates and burners) that may result in fires. Ethical principles that highlight competence are noted in the careful selection and extensive training of resident assistants.

When conflicts inevitably arise, an educational ethical approach can be used for intervention. Rules and regulations will be violated, fights and arguments will occur, and people will feel that they have been treated poorly and unjustly by peers. Interventions by peers, resident assistants, and others should occur quickly with immediate corrective feedback, and always be explored with a compassionate and educational approach. Of course, a punitive response may be necessary at times when violations are severe or actual crimes are committed, such as when others are harmed, laws are broken, or property is significantly damaged. Mechanisms and procedures for intervention should be developed that underscore restorative justice principles wherever possible.

Most students can readily grasp the mostly standard rules and regulations involved with campus living. Unfortunately, the more nuanced aspects of interacting with others may not be recognized as important ethical and character-based challenges. For example, what should a student do if they hear another student make a racist comment? How should someone proceed when a roommate is severely intoxicated and a choice involves alerting staff to ensure safety while exposing the student to possible discipline? What is the right thing to do regarding a fellow student who is teased and largely marginalized by the dorm community? How can one contend with a dorm friend who is losing weight rapidly and severely compromising his or her health? Or with a friend who has boasted about cheating on a term paper? These decisions are frequently encountered by students, and reframing them as opportunities to behave with character and ethically informed decisions can greatly enhance the value students place on carefully making such choices.

INTEGRATING ETHICAL VALUES INTO RESIDENTIAL LIFE

Teenagers arrive on campus eager to simultaneously fit in and define themselves. They are alert to the prevailing ethos of the university and are influenced both consciously and unconsciously by the values and messages they perceive around them. Colleges vary in their highlighted goals and values, some emphasizing academic excellence, others social justice and making the world better, while others encompass the prevailing vibes of partying, athletic competition, or uniqueness and diversity. Whatever the prevailing ethos, it assuredly trickles down through the culture and fabric of the institution to influence the values, goals, and thinking of its staff, faculty, and students. Thus, beginning the conversation and emphasizing ethical decision making and strong character from the day students arrive is important to setting expectations and conveying the values of the campus community.

Institutional culture is powerful. People behave differently within varying contexts, such as a cutthroat corporate culture or a prosocial nonprofit. Individuals largely adapt to the prevailing culture and often adopt the values, goals, and methods advanced within the organization. The same is true of educational institutions. Since residential life serves as a powerful microcosm of the university culture, integrating education, conversation, and a heightened value on ethical behavior can impact students immediately and powerfully from the day they arrive.

Providing a written document

Students entering dorms should be provided with a written statement describing the ethical goals above and beyond the simple regulations of residential life. Ethical behavior and the RRICC (or other) strategy for ethical decision making should be introduced and examples provided for application in day-to-day dorm life. The benefits of living ethically for personal pride, relational success, and both academic and professional integrity can be highlighted, and the university's commitment to ethical development underscored. This document alerts new students that more than conventional rules prevail on campus, and an overarching value on behaving with respect, responsibility, integrity, concern, and competence are part of the ultimate mission of the university.

Initial Dorm (or Floor) Meetings

So much needs to be covered during those initial meetings students have with their residential advisors and fellow new students. Resources available to students, activities and events within and outside the dorm, safety requirements, and rules regarding drugs, alcohol, and noise all need to be defined and discussed. Furthermore, students are eager to get to know one another and need to alleviate anxieties and quickly form bonds. Introducing ethics in the midst of all these imperatives might seem superfluous but, we would argue, both important and comforting to students longing to feel safe in a new environment and community. Knowing that fellow students are expected to behave with integrity and that their own better instincts are encouraged assists young adults to feel safely held within a caring, thoughtful, edifying environment.

During these early gatherings within the dorm, the complexity of residential life can be discussed. None of the students have previously had hundreds of housemates, and knowing that some strategies and guidelines exist to help them think through challenging relational and stressful academic situations can greatly assist these young adults. Empowering new students with the tools and agency to realize their own personal code of ethics will serve them well throughout college and beyond.

Monthly "Ethics in the Dorms" Conversations

Each month, at a regular time convenient for the majority of students, a casual group conversation led by a staff advisor can raise and resolve ethical challenges confronted by students. Being asked to help a friend cheat on a test, confronting a roommate for her inconsiderate messiness, rallying around a troubled or marginalized student, and other issues related to fairness and individual responsibility in groups may all arise. The staff advisor can help to facilitate students' questions and the dilemmas they raise while helping them use the RRICC model to make their own decisions.

Bulletin Board Use

Bulletin boards posted either physically or online visually alert students to important events and opportunities but also signal the ethos of the community. On most college campuses, one need only to review the postings on various bulletin boards to pick up a sense of the predominant cultures and subcultures on campus. Similarly, in dorms, utilizing bulletin boards to highlight ethical issues helps to communicate these ethics-related issues, speakers, courses, awards, and opportunities on campus. The visual reminders of this important mission of the university serve to underscore the verbal messages students have received.

In summary, ethics are not the sexiest of campus themes. Issues related to academic opportunities, parties, concerts, athletic events, and other activities central to campus life are more likely to garner interest and attention. Nonetheless, by emphasizing how ethical decisions and character pervade all aspects of one's life during and after college, and providing these with the same high status afforded other realms, students become attuned to their responsibility in deliberately and intelligently addressing these challenges. Residential life, as a form of subfamily and community within the larger campus, is an ideal center for imparting and emphasizing ethical decision-making skills.

GREEK LIFE: FRATERNITIES AND SORORITIES

Greek life presents both unique challenges and opportunities for ethical development and behavior on campus. Notorious for excessive drinking, hazing, sexual promiscuity, sexual assault, exclusivity, and cheating schemes, sororities and particularly fraternities often represent the most reckless and unethical behavior on college campuses. Under the banner of belonging and loyalty to their sisterhood or brotherhood of pledges, the power of the group can influence individual members in extremely negative or positive ways.

Greek organizations first emerged in America with the founding of Phi Beta Kappa at William and Mary College in 1776. Similar to today's Greek organizations, Phi Beta Kappa held defined objectives of scholarship, inspiration, and fraternity. Many common objectives exist within current Greek organizations, such as the goals of fostering community, integrity, intellectual advancement, civic engagement, and fellowship. Yet despite these laudable goals and the often clear contributions that fraternities and sororities can offer to campuses, too often these ideals and potentials become overshadowed by flagrant and dangerous misbehavior. Similarly, during recruitment and initiation into Greek houses, often the good character of pledges and the stated ideals of the chapter become lost in the power dynamics that result in hazing and loyalty rituals that ultimately bully and demean.

Data suggests that members of sororities and fraternities consume significantly more alcohol than nonaffiliated students, and engage more often in academic dishonesty (Park, Sher, & Krull, 2008; Williams & Janosik, 2007). Similarly, researchers have reported higher incidences of alcohol-use disorders and associated negative consequences in Greek members (Park et al., 2008) and found that residence in a Greek house was the strongest correlate of binge drinking in college (Wechsler, Davenport, Dowdall, Moeykens, & Castillo, 1994). Similarly alarming are the findings by Kingree and Thompson (2013) that "males who joined a fraternity between their first and second years of college showed increases in their perceptions of peer approval of forced sex and peer pressure to have sex, as well as increased high risk drinking and number of sexual partners compared with men who did not join a fraternity" (p. 219). In short, Greek life, and fraternities in particular, can be hotbeds of alcohol and substance abuse, sexual misconduct, and academic dishonesty.

Discrimination and racially isolating behavior have also been noted in Greek life. Largely homogeneous in race, these exclusive fraternities have been linked to overtly racist behavior. According to J. J. Park and Kim: "Greek life was the most racially isolating environment for White students. Of White members of sororities or fraternities, 97.1 percent stated that their organizations were majority White" (2013, p. 22). Conversely, racial diversity has been found to provide significant benefits to college students: "Interracial interactions are positively and significantly related to gains in leadership skills, psychological well-being, intellectual engagement, and intercultural effectiveness during the first year of college" (Bowman, 2013, p. 888). Discrimination in Greek organizations can also extend to sexual orientation, ethnicity, religion, economic status, and disability, mirroring the larger social prejudices in society.

Yet, importantly, Greek organizations almost universally maintain mission statements that emphasize moral and ethical values. For example, Greek houses extoll values of "social responsibility" (Delta Gamma Fraternity), "values and ethics" (Alpha Delta Pi), "lifetime opportunity for moral growth" (Kappa Alpha Theta Fraternity), "ethical behavior and decision making" (Kappa Sigma Fraternity), and values of "justice and right" (Alpha Phi International), to name just a few. Thus, Greek organizations espouse laudable virtues and are uniquely poised to promote superb ethical leadership and citizenship on college campuses. It is incumbent upon institutions and Greek houses to work hand in hand to maximize the positive actions and behaviors that conform to the ethical mission goals of both. Harnessing the positive aspirations and teeming resources within Greek life, and both promoting and rewarding them, may well have a greater benefit than simply issuing threats and punishments for bad behavior.

How can colleges harness this positive potential inherent to Greek life? By partnering qualified faculty and administrative leaders with student representatives to discuss, instill, promote, and reward implementation of positive ethical mission statements, students and colleges can work together to honestly voice concerns, seek support, and engage in collaborative strategies toward similar goals. Focused attention on the philanthropic and leadership instincts of many Greek organizations can help to nurture and channel these potentials into rewarding and edifying actions. Too often Greek houses feel marginalized by their colleges and stained with a stigma their institutions provide few resources to help them overcome. As stated by a Santa Clara University undergraduate, "If true change is going to occur, universities need to accept and own their Greek system, using it to its full potential rather than letting it simmer in its current precarious state" (Allison Byrne, December 2015).

First and foremost, it would behoove colleges to provide on-site ethics workshops to teach a process for ethical decision making with all Greek affiliates. As stated by Mayhew, Seifert, and Pascarella (2010), through introductory ethics courses, by "critically examining issues relating to justice and fairness, these students may greatly benefit from engaging in deliberate learning environments planned to help them develop their capacities for moral reasoning" (p. 379). They further stress that by challenging students to apply moral reasoning to the situations in their daily lives, they gain practical and integrated capacities to act in more ethically thoughtful ways. In particular, helping Greek leaders communicate and frame choices related to alcohol use and sexual behavior within an ethical construct consistent with the house mission statement and their own genuine ethical aspirations can develop a common cause, language, and culture for bettering one's conscious choices.

Research has consistently supported the benefits of community-service learning both for the communities being assisted and for the volunteers themselves. According to Lih-Juan (2015), "Service learning can be used in virtually any discipline and course as a tool to allow students to discover the connection between the academics of the class and the political and community issues related to that academic discipline." In other words, intellectual learning is enhanced by experiential learning, and if colleges partner with Greek leaders to organize and reward community-service learning, many positive goals can be achieved. Furthermore, such immersion learning yields tremendous benefits in allowing students to experience solidarity with the humanity of other groups, particularly those that have been stigmatized or disadvantaged. In one study examining racial perceptions and community-service learning, the findings revealed highly positive results in reducing college students' "stereotypical perceptions of individuals contending with poverty" and making it less likely for students to "blame social service clients for their struggles." Ultimately, these students became "more knowledgeable about complex social problems" (Seider, Huguley, & Novick, 2013), a vital tool in enhancing Greek life inclusion, acceptance, and diversity.

Recruitment and hazing procedures need to be self-governed but also overseen by universities. Again, creating a culture that places the mission statement virtues as the prime objective is only attainable through modeling and enforcement by senior members, and through the support, oversight, and incentivization offered by the administration. Therefore, it is only of benefit to universities to develop partnerships between valued faculty and Greek leaders to devise, organize, and reward healthy pledging. Colleges that ban Greek life on campus, forcing them off campus and outside the administration's purview, only casts a blind eye and denies a potential guiding hand to these young adult groups who deserve and can benefit from constructive adult support.

Reinforcing and incentivizing desirable Greek behavior rely on the time-honored principle of operant conditioning. Students who have both internal and external rewards for engaging in desirable behavior and desisting from undesirable behavior are prone to make better choices. Rewarding house members for "blowing" low blood-alcohol levels at parties, intervening with others making unwanted sexual advances, exemplifying academic integrity, and engaging in positive community service is the "psychology 101" of influencing behavior. Too often punishment is the only tool wielded by colleges to control negative behavior, when positive reinforcement has been shown to be more effective in creating desired behavior.

Fraternities and sororities, as the social vortex of many colleges, can make invaluable contributions, adding indelible bonds, traditions, activities, and services to the community. At their core, these organizations strive to enhance both the experience and character of their members, describing within their mission statements many laudable ethical goals. However, given that these Greek organizations are populated by emerging adults, still contending unsteadily with their developmental Four I's in a context of intense social demands and drives, behavior often goes awry. It is incumbent upon universities to harness the positive potentials inherent to Greek life through intentional partnership while also working in concert to minimize negative behaviors rather than turning a blind or merely critical eye. These collaborative efforts can be accomplished in many ways, and universities can fruitfully direct some of their considerable educational resources toward the optimization of ethical Greek life on campus.

CONCLUSION

Residential life often forms the social and emotional core of students' college experiences, especially early on. The challenges and lessons they encounter in the course of living closely with others in community provide ready opportunity for identifying and resolving real-life ethical problems. Whether in dorms, fraternities, sororities, or other living environments, integrating the concepts and tools of ethical decision making into everyday circumstances provides a fertile source of character development when wisely utilized. When ethical discussions, leaders, guidelines, forums, and emphases are brought into their "homes," students learn to incorporate the ethical skills and values modeled by their school.

Chapter 14

Best Practices: Athletics

Always do right. This will gratify some people and astonish the rest.
—Mark Twain

Athletics have become a major part of the college experience for both athletes and spectators alike. College basketball and football have essentially become the minor leagues of their respective professional sports, and colleges reap enormous financial and reputational benefits from their athletic programs and successes. In fact, according to a report in the *Wall Street Journal* (Sauter, Stebbins, Frohlich, & Comen, 2015), the highest paid public employee of every state in America is either a college basketball or football coach. Students, even nonathletes, often choose their college based on the success and excitement surrounding the school's sports teams.

Universities around the country experience enormous pressure from alumni, donors, students, and the local community to excel on the playing field. The pressure to perform and to win games can readily lead to problems in ethical conduct on the part of coaches, administrators, athletes, faculty, and even fans. Furthermore, some star student athletes who struggle with academics may risk their eligibility to play if grades are not maintained. This can create intense threats to the athletes and coaches, sometimes resulting in coercive pressure being exerted on faculty and administrators to violate their integrity by ensuring that top performers fraudulently pass their classes (Powell, 2016). Wealthy donors and athletic boosters are often all too happy to bend the rules to provide star recruits and athletes with a variety of perks to keep them happy and willing to stay on campus rather than seeking greener pastures elsewhere. Thus, ethical challenges are common in college athletics, especially (but certainly not exclusively) at the highly competitive NCAA Division I level in football and basketball.

More beneficially, for the average college athlete spanning Divisions I, II, and III who may have no prospect of playing professionally after college, sports provide a rich opportunity to develop character and sound ethical decision making. Quality sportsmanship is often highlighted in athletics even among the very young child athlete. Being part of a team, being honest, having self-discipline, engaging in fair play, being a good winner as well as a good loser, and handling oneself with integrity both on and off the field are all highlighted in sports from the youngest ages. Thus, athletics is an important and natural place for ethical formation to be nurtured in college. While a chapter on ethical issues and formation in extracurricular activities has already been provided in this volume, since college athletics are such a major part of college and university life, the topic deserves its own separate chapter and focused attention.

The NCAA offers highly detailed rules about college athletics. The rules and regulations are so detailed and extensive that most universities have no choice but to hire full-time compliance officers to attend to these details. Many of these professionals are highly educated and often attorneys. Even in lower stakes athletics, the competitive drive is strong, and it is incumbent on coaches and administrators to ensure that their athletes understand and exemplify the principles of sportsmanship. Toward this end, the NCAA has instituted policies regarding fairness and integrity geared toward "establishing a positive competitive environment for student-athletes across the country." Specifically, sportsmanship is conveyed through "values such as respect, caring, fairness, civility, honesty, integrity and responsibility . . . on and off the field" (NCAA, n.d. a). Clearly, the RRICC criteria are embedded in these ideals.

However, the NCAA tends to function as more of a stick than a carrot in that rather than focusing on aspirational ethical principles, they tend to highlight rules that need careful compliance in order for the college or university to remain in good standing and eligible to compete with other institutions on the playing field. Violations of rules place programs at serious risk for harsh sanctions, ineligibility for conference play, and the loss of potential financial and reputational gain for the college or university's athletic program.

Much of the NCAA approach in dealing with ethical issues is about academic integrity. Cheating in the classroom is a focus of NCAA rules, and thus being attentive to honesty and integrity in academic course work appears to be the main thrust of ethics for the NCAA. Little is specifically demanded in other areas of life outside of the classroom environment (see article 10 of the *NCAA Division One Manual*, 2005). Of course, regulations regarding recruitment and financial assistance are also covered in detail.

Colleges and universities, however, can do much to nurture ethical formation in athletes regardless of what the NCAA rules demand. There are many best practices to consider when colleges and universities sincerely wish to use athletics as a way to help develop and nurture ethical formation among college athletes. Fortunately, there are many colleges that do emphasize and value character and ethics in their athletes.

MODELING BY COACHES AND TEAM LEADERS

Perhaps no one is more influential for athletes in nurturing character and ethical behavior than coaches and team leaders. If coaches value and emphasize character and sportsmanship, these interests will likely influence the entire team. If a coach disregards ethics and perhaps only cares about winning at all costs, this perspective will likely also trickle down to the entire staff and team as well. Thus, if colleges and universities are interested in and serious about nurturing character development and ethical formation among their athletes, they have no choice but to start with their coaching staff. Certainly coaches want to win and compete at the highest level of performance, but they also must do so with sound ethical values and expectations. Coaches who take ethics seriously, and view character as an integral part of what makes an athlete great, will create a culture that upholds these values. Athletes know when their coach or program is ethically corrupt or cavalier.

Team leaders, such as star players and team captains, are also critical models for nurturing character development and ethics. Teammates will look to their star performers and captains as models of behavior, for good or for bad. Thus, valuing and nurturing ethical behavior can occur when student athletes have models for doing so among the coaching staff and team leaders.

COMMUNITY SERVICE

One way to help college athletes nurture and develop ethical reflection and behavior is to encourage community-service engagement. As mentioned earlier in this volume, research and best practices suggest that active engagement with community service and volunteerism has many advantages when it comes to character development, also acting as a foil to the often narcissistic and entitled culture that can develop around big time college sports. Asking college athletes to spend some time working with disabled children, battered women, homeless individuals and families, soup kitchens, and so forth can be very helpful for students to step out of the highly privileged world of college athletics and into the larger world where people struggle with a variety of life stressors and circumstances. Many athletes at the collegiate as well as professional level do in fact engage the community for the greater good, and it is important that perhaps a great many more athletes participate in these activities, and do so with some regularity. Genuine empathy with those who struggle, in a mutual learning and engagement partnership, enriches students in valuing humanity. Doing community service as a photo opportunity or simply to display on a Web site is certainly not the intent or value of these activities. A sincere and mutually beneficial partnership is needed to help athletes improve upon their character development and ethical decision making while engaging with community service and action.

ALUMNI BOOSTERS

Alumni often enjoy interaction with college athletics. They attend athletic games and performances, donate to athletic booster funds, and enjoy mentoring student athletes. Alumni can be enlisted to model character and ethical behavior as well. Certainly alumni enjoy seeing their team win and succeed, but they also can be enlisted to be proud of and support the character development of young collegiate athletes. University administrators can provide clear guidance to alumni donors and boosters about expectations regarding ethical and character development among athletes and how they can be enlisted to assist in these goals. Awards or other forms of recognition can also emphasize the value placed on athletic integrity.

STUDENTS AS AVID FANS

The heady, vibrant atmosphere at collegiate games reflects the youthful enthusiasm and pride of students cheering for their home team. Young adults in large groups can feel emboldened to behave in overly enthusiastic and even aggressive behavior in the stands, taunting opponents, hurling objects, and booing loudly. Add alcohol to the mix, and fan behavior has the potential to get out of control. (The NFL, for this reason, has banned the sale of alcohol at all games.) Universities are ultimately responsible for conveying, celebrating, and maintaining the value of sportsmanship by fans. Delineating expectations, and actively enforcing them, underscores the college's seriousness about sportsmanship among all students. The NCAA has even released a best practices model in the form of their "NCAA Game Day Environment and Fan Code of Conduct" statement. This document lists the expectations for a "safe, comfortable and enjoyable game day experience" (NCAA, n.d. b), highlighting the objectives of both fan support and RRICC-like behavior. In addition, the document takes a clear stand against behavior that is reckless, disruptive, disrespectful and vulgar, harassing, and the like. Violations of the FCOC are expected to be met with clear consequences such as ejection, loss of future attendance at games, and even arrest when laws are violated. Again, the NCAA seeks to encourage colleges to provide more than lip service to sportsmanship by publicizing fan expectations and the consequences of misbehavior in violation of these standards.

BALANCING THE CARROT AND STICK

University administrators and coaches can thoughtfully encourage collegiate athletes to nurture ethical behavior and character development with a careful mix of reinforcements and punishments, or balancing the proverbial carrot and stick. They can use reinforcements of various kinds to encourage and support ethical behavior, and they can also punish by benching, putting on probation, and offering good corrective feedback to students who violate the desired rules and expected behaviors on and off the playing field. Reflecting on the right balance of rewards and punishments is not easy and is always an ongoing struggle in athletics, and perhaps any organization. Consultation with a variety of relevant parties within the university environment—such as coaches, administrators, compliance officers, student services, and so forth—can be helpful in determining the correct balance for each institution and each student.

Highlighting student athletes who exemplify the ideals of character valued by the university can further model and reward such behavior. Awards for sportsmanship, leadership, community service, and the demonstration of exemplary character on and off the field go a long way toward promoting these values. For example, in 2014 the National Football League created a Sportsmanship Award that is voted on by players and presented in the highly publicized Associated Press NFL Honors show. The NFL states that "The award will be presented each year to an NFL player who best demonstrates the qualities of on-field sportsmanship, including fair play, respect for the game and opponents, and integrity in competition." (National Football League, 2014). These types of athletic awards highlight ethics and integrity as quintessential and laudable aspects of competition.

CONTROVERSIAL ETHICAL ISSUES IN TODAY'S COLLEGE ATHLETICS

Do college athletics exploit students by failing to pay them? This question has been more seriously debated in recent years, especially as the financial proceeds from college sports have escalated. Is it fair for universities to acquire millions of dollars of revenue on the backs of their unpaid athletes? Are full rides and scholarships adequate compensation considering the financial stakes? As coaches are earning literally millions and television and marketing revenues soar, should the student athlete share in the profits?

Underlying these concerns is the prospect of colleges exploiting their athletes ultimately for their own gain, overlooking the student's best physical, mental, or academic interests. In high-level college sports, academics are often shortchanged and students deprived of a meaningful and marketable education. The overemphasis on sports can easily make academics a mere nuisance, and coaches may even actively encourage their athletes to take easy classes and put in minimal effort. Of course, not all universities treat their student athletes so exploitatively. However, many students do suffer academically, supporting the belief that financial payment is a more just compensation for their efforts.

Another area of ethical concern is that colleges sometimes fail to protect the health and safety of their athletes in the fervor to win at all costs. Despite opportunities for injured players to petition for redshirt eligibility, the pressure to compete and win may lead to more playing time than medically indicated. Furthermore, as many college athletes tend to hide or minimize symptoms in their drive to compete, coaches and training staff can easily become complicit in ignoring injuries. Concussions have received the most attention in recent years, with concussion protocols now more rigidly enforced. This vigilance likely should be applied to other injuries as well.

Medical costs for athletes may be covered for the duration of their enrollment, but lasting injuries that extend beyond graduation often provide a financial hardship for students. This raises the question regarding whether universities should be expected to provide more responsible long-term health care for injured athletes. These are extremely complicated issues that require careful medical, financial, and, of course, ethical consideration throughout college sports.

Athletic competition provides rich opportunities to teach and encourage the attributes of character and ethical conduct reflected in the RRICC model. At a time of life when identity is an imperative, young adults are eager to absorb behaviors and values evidenced and encouraged by adults and peers they highly respect. Universities can positively influence students by defining standards and expectations, teaching strategies for ethical decision making, and encouraging and rewarding sportsmanlike behavior that reflects the attributes of respect, responsibility, integrity, competence, and concern, both on and off the field.

CONCLUSION

College athletics has come to represent both the best and the worst of ethical values. While scandals abound, particularly in big-money athletics, the vast majority of athletes and coaches strive to uphold the values of sportsmanship and integrity. The passionate competition between teams can evoke tremendous loyalty in fans, but often this spills over into overtly rude, bullying, or even violent behavior. Colleges can take the lead in overseeing the ethics of their athletic programs on the player, coach, booster, and fan levels through the thoughtful and deliberate integration of ethical guidelines and leadership.

Chapter 15

Best Practices: Campus Judicial Procedures

Restorative dialogue . . . [is where] the problem rather than the person is put in the center of the circle.
—David Karp, *The Little Book of Restorative Justice for Colleges and Universities*, p. 13

While many thoughtful efforts can be made to maximize good ethical teaching and formation among students during their college years, it is inevitable that problematic and unethical behavior will occur among some students. Probabilities alone would suggest that regardless of the incorporation of best practices in ethical formation on campus, college students will at times, in fact, behave very badly. Some students on virtually every campus will inevitably make terrible decisions regardless of comprehensive on-campus ethics training. And when their egregious behavior violates the rights of others or puts them or members of the campus community in danger or at risk, then immediate and meaningful interventions must occur. One such key intervention involves comprehensive campus judicial procedures utilizing restorative justice approaches.

Certainly, when students commit actual crimes violating the law, local law enforcement and the civil or criminal justice system must intervene and take appropriate action through legal and judicial proceedings. In such cases, the court system's oversight of the student usurps the decision-making control of the college or university community and will move to the local, state, or even federal law enforcement authorities for potential prosecution and rehabilitation.

However, many problematic behaviors on campus such as cheating, underage drinking, racism, vandalism, and general disruptive and disrespectful behavior to others are typically managed internally by the campus judicial system without any engagement of local law enforcement. Many schools include student peers as well as university faculty, staff, and administrators in their campus-based judicial process.

Since institutions of higher learning specialize in education, it makes good sense to take an educational approach to the campus judicial procedures and processes. This can be especially challenging when various campus stakeholders (e.g., administrators, fellow students, parents of victims, alums, trustees, local neighbors in the community) may want to take a punitive approach rather than an educative approach to students engaging in acting-out behavior that harms others, harms property, or results in unflattering press for the college or university. For example, a rowdy, drunken, and violent college student party that disturbs and greatly upsets local neighbors may result in unflattering press attention and a great deal of anger from the community. Or students caught on camera harassing or taunting others, or perhaps engaging in vandalism on campus that goes viral on the Internet, would often be met with calls from various stakeholders for punishment and expulsion. And certainly any kind of sexual misconduct, including date rape or sexual assault of any kind, may result in immediate expulsion and prosecution to the fullest extent of the law.

Yet educational institutions, at their best, must provide an educational approach to problematic student behavior on campus while fully cooperating with law enforcement when crimes have been committed. More often, however, student violations involve noncriminal behavior committed by otherwise well-meaning young adults, and students must be adjudicated and rehabilitated within the college community. Best practices in judicial processes on campus can be used to further ethical training, decision making, and ultimately the positive growth of the offending student. Hopefully the campus judicial process that is attentive to ethical formation can use the student behavior violation as an important teaching moment to assist the offending student or students to better learn from their experience, make appropriate reparations, and change their subsequent thinking and behavior for the better.

At Santa Clara University, for example, the goal of the university judicial system "is to promote the personal growth of those who commit a violation." This growth highlights "accountability, awareness, concern, commitment, and contrition." The student is led through a process of active reflection so that they "consider different viewpoints and examine how one's behavior is not consistent with being a person for and with others" (Santa Clara University, 2015). At Santa Clara the five-step pedagogical process used for adjudication of cases includes examining (1) the *context of learning* (i.e., reviewing the student's life history and their readiness to learn and grow from the problematic behavior), (2) *experience* (i.e., examining activities that make it difficult for the student to consider new ideas), (3) *reflection* (i.e., a thoughtful reconsideration of the student's behavior and its impact on others), (4) *action* (i.e., moving forward with behavior that is more consistent with renewed clarity and conviction for improved behavior), and (5) *evaluation* (i.e., an ongoing review of the personal growth that occurs through the judicial process).

Various questions are asked during the prehearing, hearing, and posthearing judicial process with these five pedagogical goals in mind. In essence, students are asked to actively reflect upon themselves and their behavior, and to evaluate it through the lens of ethical principles using the RRICC model. Thus, examining the important values of respect, responsibility, integrity, competence, and concern for self and others is carefully discussed and evaluated. Restorative justice models are used to consider an action plan for reconciliation with those who have been harmed as well.

Perhaps an example can be helpful. In one situation, students decided to host a "hood" theme party where students came dressed and behaved in offensive, stereotypical African American inner-city manner. A number of African American students on campus felt angry, disrespected, and insulted by the party. The offending students committed no crime and naively didn't think that their party was offensive, proclaiming that they didn't mean to hurt anyone and that they didn't see themselves as racist. The judicial process resulted in a gathering of both the party hosts as well as those who felt victimized by the event. A student peer mentor and a student life staff member facilitated the meeting. Honest and thoughtful conversation ensued over several hours. Ultimately, sincere apologies were offered, some tears were shed, and at the end of the meeting there were even some hugs and handshakes reflecting degrees of reconciliation. The offending students learned something about the unintended consequences of their insensitive and naive behavior while gaining new insight and respect for students of color on campus. RRICC themes of respect, responsibility, integrity, concern, and competence for others were highlighted and filtered through the conversation. Restorative justice was achieved with apologies, donations to the multicultural center on campus by the party hosts, and plans for a collaborative and inclusive party in the future.

This represents a campus adjudication process at its best, and of course not all students or victimized individuals are amenable to such growth and reconciliation. Punitive measures do of course have an important place in college life. Violations may result in suspension or expulsion, loss of on-campus housing privileges or attendance at campus events, derecognition of a fraternity or sorority, or an automatic failing grade in instances of clear cheating. Universities may also require students to obtain counseling, attend diversity seminars or anger management trainings, or undergo drug or alcohol treatment as a requirement for continued studies. Still, punishment is only useful insofar as it forms a part of a larger action plan to educate, repair, and rehabilitate. These more positive goals can be challenging to achieve and require a sophisticated staff and administration geared toward the ultimate character formation of their students.

RESPONDING ETHICALLY WHEN STUDENTS MAKE MISTAKES

Young adults will invariably make mistakes. Some of these errors will be small missteps involving decisions that ultimately have little consequence to oneself or others but that may be regretted nonetheless. At other times, students will make egregious mistakes having huge consequences that place their own or others' health, well-being, and academic standing at grave risk. Colleges vary in their protocols for responding to significant violations of conduct or law, and often students emerge unnecessarily damaged and bitter when punitive measures are carried out in a spirit that is dehumanizing or villainizing and leaves little opportunity for repair. In this chapter, we argue that colleges should behave in these instances by doing what they do best, and that is to *teach*. Responding to the crimes and misdemeanors committed by college students can be viewed as the ultimate "teachable moment," in that how institutions model ethical principles of reconciliation, restorative justice, and compassion will likely make a lasting impression on students' own future responses to injustice and the failures of others.

The Role of Colleges

Many colleges will summarily suspend, expel, and reprimand students who misbehave, with little attention to helping students grow, make amends, and improve their ethical commitments in the future. Several ethical principles that follow from using the RRICC model can be high-lighted as critically important to include in the college adjudication process: reconciliation, restorative justice, and compassion. As has been said, one cannot teach someone to be kind by being mean or vengeful. Providing students an opportunity to make restitution for their misdeeds and grow in their own compassion and integrity should be deemed an imperative educational duty. Rather than simply instituting punishment, humiliation, criticism, and even complete banishment in response to student lapses in ethics and behavior, colleges have an opportunity to teach students the ethical tools of reconciliation, restorative justice, and compassion with which to confront future challenges.

Two Scenarios: Campus A has determined that a student violated the clear rules on possessing and consuming hard liquor on campus. This 19-year-old student was apprehended by campus police and his case turned over to administrators. The university has a strict policy against hard liquor and swiftly acts to suspend the student for the term. The student, chastened and humiliated, is ejected from campus until the fall and sent home to confront his parents and his own disrupted life.

Campus B determines that a 19-year-old student has committed the same hard liquor violation. The protocol for responding to violations is different here than at campus A. First, the student is assigned a faculty mentor to guide and support him through the next steps. This mentor talks with the student and listens patiently to his story. Fully aware of the Four I's and their importance in contextualizing the choices of young adults, the mentor seeks to understand the developmental challenges that might have contributed to this poor choice. Clearly, this is a student with poor impulse control and a high need to fit in and be accepted. Thus, intimacy and impulse control issues are clearly at play. Furthermore, the student asserts that the liquor ban is a "dumb rule," and his defiance of it was partly a misdirected act of independence. Clearly, more productive ways of arguing against this rule were available to the student, but this choice proved highly detrimental to the student and the integrity of campus policies designed to protect the health and safety of all students. Though the student would like to see himself as someone not confined by "dumb rules" and "random authority," his poor choice in exerting his free will must be addressed through education and a program allowing growth.

Understanding the developmental conflicts at play helped the mentor feel compassion for the student, yet still uphold the campus policy. The mentor told the student that the consequence of this alcohol violation necessitated that he demonstrate reconciliation, restorative justice, and compassion as a means of making amends and remaining a student in good standing. The student and his mentor discussed ways to accomplish these goals. First, the student agreed to read a packet of articles explaining the basis for the liquor ban, including reports on the incidence of emergency room visits and sexual assault incidents associated with hard liquor consumption on college campuses. The student was asked to attend a series of 10 Alcoholics Anonymous meetings, if only just to listen and observe, in order to gain some insight into the potential consequences of excessive drinking.

In order to make amends to the college, his parents, and his dorm mates (who were also censured for the hard liquor being on-site), the student wrote letters of apology with a commitment to never repeat this behavior. He also voluntarily surrendered to his parents the credit card he used to purchase the alcohol and reimbursed them from his savings. After completing all of the requirements, he met with his mentor and the dean to discuss what he had learned, how he plans to better express his independence in the future, and his commitment to follow the rules in the future.

The student was humbled by this process and quite grateful that he was not suspended or expelled. He actually felt cared about by the university and could see how immature his behavior had been. The compassion and guidance he received inspired him to be a better citizen of the campus and work to uphold its rules and values in a manner that also reflected his autonomy and integrity.

Restorative Justice and Reconciliation

How colleges respond to rule violators and undesirable behavior shines a bright light on the institution's own ethics and morality. Schools that simply pontificate, judge, and punish unwittingly convey a lack of concern or compassion for the individual under scrutiny. Expelling and even banishing students from ever setting foot on campus can bolster a school's reputation for not tolerating such violations, but at the same time damages its own mission and identity by behaving in a vindictive and uncaring manner. Furthermore, the victims of the violation often receive inadequate attention in the effort to find and punish a perpetrator. As stated by David Karp, a leading expert on college judicial procedures, the restorative justice approach "is different because it is balanced between its attention to offenders and to victims. It is different because it is a harm-centered approach. Instead of 'Who did it, and what should we do to him or her?' restorative justice asks, 'What is the harm and how can it be repaired?'" (Karp, 2015, p. 84).

Restorative justice is a more ambitious, thoughtful, and impactful model which involves a comprehensive resolution process that includes the needs of victims, offenders, and the university. As defined by David Karp in his book *The Little Book of Restorative Justice for Colleges and Universities* (2015):

Restorative justice is a collaborative decision-making process that includes harmed parties, offenders, and others who are seeking to hold offenders accountable by having them: a) accept and acknowledge responsibility for their offenses, b) to the best of their ability, repair the harm they caused to harmed parties and the community, and c) work to rebuild trust by showing understanding of the harm, addressing personal issues, and building positive social connections. (p. 4)

There are three key elements involved in this form of accountability: violators must (1) accept responsibility for their offenses, (2) seek to repair the harm they caused to victims and communities in a meaningful way, and (3) build positive social ties to the offended community in order to build compassion and reduce the likelihood of re-offense. Restorative justice is a means of making reparations directly to the victims of a misdeed and learning in great depth about the consequences such misbehavior can have. For instance, young adults accused and deemed guilty of a sexual assault will obviously have to contend with legal authorities. Yet when met by the university judicial panel, a program of restoration and rehabilitation can be determined. This might include volunteering at a battered women's shelter to gain compassion and achieve a greater sense of solidarity with victims of physical and sexual abuse. It might involve researching and writing an in-depth paper about the effects of sexual assault on victims. It may further involve directly apologizing to the actual victim and seeking to make at least some form of meaningful amends directly to the person who has suffered.

Another example, involving racist or discriminatory behavior, can be adjudicated in a similar fashion. Meaningful apologies and amends to the victims of such damaging behavior, as well as an immersion experience with the offended group, can pave a path toward redemption and reconciliation. If the incident involved, for example, insulting and demeaning a transgender dorm mate, the violator might be required to attend meetings with the campus's sexual and gender diversity group. Similarly, hearing from transgendered individuals about their struggles, as well as their completely healthy and productive qualities, can help humanize and educate ignorant attitudes.

The restoration and reconciliation process might involve meetings with a faculty or student mentor as a means of supporting and helping the student integrate their new knowledge and reexamine past biases. By achieving a more educated view of victims, having an opportunity to know them as human beings, and seeking to make restitution as much as possible, violators may experience the education of their lifetime. The growth and betterment of the violator, as well as the effort to reconcile with the victim, generate far more benefits and long-term outcomes for society than simple judgment and punishment. In addition, the broader ethical influence of such procedures impacts the greater university community: "The beauty of restorative justice is that it adapts to any environment and by its very nature changes a culture over time" (Deborah Eerkes, p. 61, in Karp, 2015).

Accountability must be an active process, as simply being judged and sanctioned does not involve true acknowledgment and insight. Inclusive decision making in making repair should ideally involve both the offenders and the harmed parties in determining necessary reparations. Instead of humiliating and crushing the offender, restorative justice is aimed at making amends and facilitating healing, restoring the dignity of all. By seeking to rebuild damaged relationships, harmed parties can begin to feel safe again, and offenders experience a chance at redemption. Furthermore, by engaging students in an ethical dialogue about the harmfulness of the offense, internalization of new understanding can take place. Where this isn't achieved, a deterrent approach is more necessary, even including extreme measures termed "incapacitation approaches," such as removal from housing or suspension, designed to eliminate the risk of anyone being further harmed.

Restorative justice approaches have been studied and found to be highly effective in campus environments. The results of the STARR Project (Student Accountability and Restorative Research) studied 659 cases of misconduct from 18 colleges around the United States (Karp & Sacks, 2014). The results determined that the restorative justice model produced low numbers of appeals, high rates of compliance, and relatively few repeat offenders. They also achieved significant improvements in learning. Harmed parties consistently expressed strong appreciation and a greater sense of satisfaction and safety from the program and the opportunity to participate directly. David Karp has published an extremely useful handbook for colleges in directing and implementing their efforts to bring restorative justice to their campuses (Karp, 2015).

The University of Colorado at Boulder is possibly the first school in the nation to institute a restorative justice program. The CU-Boulder program brings victims, offenders, and community members together for a group conference in which the incident is discussed. Importantly, offenders in this program must have already admitted wrongdoing and indicated a desire to make amends. Thus, the focus of the group discussion is on the harm done to individuals, groups, and property. Together the group determines how to repair the harm and joins with the offender toward reconciliation. Some of the first cases handled in this manner at CU-Boulder included property damage, objects thrown from balconies at a staff member, and students using a laser pointer directed at the eyes of a police officer. Some of the restorative steps included an offender riding with a police officer to witness the issues he faced, alcohol counseling, and a letter of apology to the campus community. To learn more about the development and implementation of this program at CU-Boulder, see Tom Sebok and Andrea Goldblum's article in *the Journal of the California Caucus of College and University Ombuds* (1999). Additional information on similar types of victim-offender mediations and restorative justice can be found at the following Web sites:

- Center for Restorative Justice and Peacemaking
- Campaign for Equity and Restorative Justice
- Restorative Justice Online
- Victim Offender Mediation Association

Appendix D provides an example of the judicial procedures determined for reviewing student violations in the areas of sexual misconduct and alcohol and drug offenses at Santa Clara University. Many educational sanctions are central to the disciplinary action, providing students an opportunity to learn and gain insight into the negative consequences of their behavior. Making a presentation, writing a thorough paper, attending an alcohol or sexual assault educational program, and engaging in therapy and the like all provide opportunities to demonstrate learning and growth. Furthermore, service and restitution requirements afford the student a chance to gain lived experience and contribute to the impacted community, and also to make tangible amends through reimbursements and other means of making direct reparations. Fines and other punishments can be productively levied, and warnings regarding the future consequences for repeated violations given. These, however, cannot help rehabilitate the student to the same extent without the additional opportunities for education and repair.

THE IMPACT OF TITLE IX: CHALLENGES, BENEFITS, AND OPPORTUNITIES FOR ETHICAL ENHANCEMENT

In 1972, all educational institutions receiving federal funding were required by law to allow no student to "on the basis of sex, be excluded from participation in, be denied the benefits of, or be subjected to discrimination." This ruling targeted sexual discrimination, harassment, and assault, mandating that colleges appoint Title IX coordinators to institute and ensure compliance with programs aimed at preventing such abuses. One immediate impact of Title IX involved huge changes in the athletic status and programming of women's athletics, requiring that equal financial resources be committed to both men's and women's sports on campus.

Title IX required an integrated and ongoing process of implementation and assessment of programs designed to protect women from discrimination and sexual violence. The tasks of identifying problematic situations on campus; revising programming, training, and available resources; and determining sanctions for violations and both adjudication and grievance procedures were more powerfully demanded of colleges. In 2014, a White House Task Force added even more protective requirements to Title IX. Now all colleges must provide information and postings about rules, resources, and support services; develop specialized training sessions for Title IX personnel; provide "bystander training" and ongoing awareness and prevention campaigns; incorporate community feedback; and update evolving legal requirements. Needless to say, these policies have placed enormous demands on colleges and have highlighted the widespread problems and renewed priorities in the battle against sexual assault and discrimination.

In addition, the 2014 addendum now designates all faculty members as mandated reporters of sexual harassment and assault. Comprehensive policies prohibiting sexual assault, domestic violence, dating violence, stalking, and other forms of sexual misconduct that create a hostile environment must be clearly explicated to the entire campus community. Furthermore, detailed grievance procedures ensuring the fair investigation of alleged misconduct have challenged universities to develop protective measures, privacy policies, and an equal opportunity for both parties to present evidence and have an advisor assigned to them.

These pervasive imperatives to protect students from sexual victimization and discrimination have highlighted the enormity of the problems and caused universities to devote significant resources toward their amelioration. Implicit throughout this entire enterprise is the dedication to creating an ethical student body and campus environment. Thus, all of the many Title IX programs provide ready-made opportunities to integrate the teaching and high value placed on ethical decision making. Utilizing the mandated Title IX trainings and enforcement can simultaneously help implement sexual discrimination prevention and teach a broader value on ethical awareness, behavior, and decision making. Thus, Title IX creates a powerful vehicle for campuses to generate a culture of ethics throughout their college communities.

PARENTS AS PARTNERS

Enlisting the engaged support of parents in judicial policies and procedures is critical in many cases to successful outcomes for everyone. Parents are far more likely to join with the university in approving and carrying out a plan of restoration and remediation if their child is being afforded a compassionate opportunity to both make amends and grow as an ethical, safer individual. Parents included in the process play an enormous positive role when they convey similar messages of concern and compassion amid their disappointment and disapproval of their child's misconduct. Partnering with parents to join in a journey toward restoration, education, and reentry into the college's good graces vastly improves the likelihood of successful outcomes.

Since students are legally adults once they've reached the age of 18, colleges are often reluctant to inform or include parents directly. By making explicit the behaviors and circumstances that will trigger parental notification in pre-orientation materials, describing codes of conduct and judicial procedures, this tension can be alleviated. Much like occasions where students become seriously ill or injured, colleges need to set thresholds and guidelines for notifying parents. Neglecting to do so in many circumstances neglects the best interests of the student. Thus, notifying students and parents of university policies in this regard provides families with informed consent.

Parents are apt to respond angrily and sometimes defensively to charges and disciplinary actions taken toward their children. Softening the judgment and penalty of misconduct with clear efforts to emphasize compassion, education, and restorative justice in lieu of simple punishment is likely to enhance parents' willingness to work with the university and student toward reconciliation. When parents can mirror this same compassion, educational emphasis, and road to redemption, students who have committed violations can feel greatly supported, heartened, and inspired to improve themselves and make reparations.

Throughout this process, sensitivity to the Four I's can enhance compassion and understanding for the young adults who make these errors. Often, poor judgment and impulsive actions are the result of normal developmental drives toward intimacy, self-definition, independence, and "blowing off steam" from responsibilities requiring diligence and self-discipline in classes, sports, or other pursuits. Helping parents, faculty, administrators, victims, and the student appreciate these underlying drives can help humanize their mistakes and utilize errors as teachable moments where thoughtful intervention can greatly facilitate better choices in the future.

CONCLUSION

It has often been suggested that the manner in which a society treats its offenders is a measure of its own civility. Colleges are frequently faced with the challenge of responding to violations, large and small, committed by students. It is a difficult yet developmentally significant lesson that must be conveyed through the resolution of misbehavior. In this chapter, we underscore the significant modeling that occurs when students witness how justice is delivered within their colleges. Restorative justice has been increasingly studied and implemented in college settings with excellent results for violators, victims, and communities. In addition, the pervasive policies of Title IX challenge colleges to institute thoughtful, fair, and conscientious procedures for resolving violations. The principles of restorative justice encourage an optimal process of resolving violations with a lens toward ethically informed education and repair.

Chapter 16

Best Practices: Alumni, Donor, and Community Relations

It is not enough to be nice; you have to be good. We are attracted by nice people; but only on the assumption that their niceness is a sign of goodness.

—Roger Scruton

A college's alumni are often thought to reflect the quality and values of their alma mater. The relationship between universities and students does not end at graduation; in fact it can be strengthened and cultivated over time. Each graduating class holds a pool of potentially involved alumni and donors, and it is in both the university's and the graduate's best interests to maximize the relationship and exchange of resources each can provide. In particular, as pertains to our focus on ethical development, select alumni can be identified and engaged to provide living models of the values and ethics the college trumpets.

Universities take great pride in their successful and humanely notable alumni. Conversely, they are often deeply embarrassed or even damaged by those graduates who commit crimes and other unethical actions of infamy. Much like parents who revel in their children's good character and achievements and despair in their failings, colleges are invested in their graduates as reflections and ambassadors of the college's highest goals. Thus, focusing personnel and resources into relationships with alumni who best represent the school's values can pay huge dividends beyond financial donations. Similarly, alumni and donors usually welcome and greatly value opportunities to give back to their college communities through engagement, mentorship, employment opportunities, and the like.

Put simply, prominent alumni are often highlighted as shining examples of what the university seeks to instill and the types of citizens they hope their graduates will become. This natural tendency provides tremendous opportunities to convey to undergraduates the most deeply held ideals of the college, particularly in the domains of ethics, philanthropy, volunteerism, and innovation that positively impact the world. These exemplary alumni can be ethical models and engaged mentors to students.

For example, commencement speakers are often selected for this very purpose. Placing a model of integrity and achievement before a class of new graduates and their families conveys clearly that this is the type of person and societal contribution the university holds in high esteem. Such models can further be selected and honored with honorary degrees, lectures, awards, endowed chairs, scholarships, and public opportunities to speak and tell their stories. Alumni magazines, newsletters, events, Web sites, and featured stories can further convey to the university community at large what the university seeks to stand for on both the local and the global stage.

Students can also benefit tremendously from one-on-one mentoring or small group discussions with alumni who often take great pleasure in advising and guiding young people from their own alma maters. Pairing selected students with well-matched mentors in their fields, avocations, athletics, arts, faith communities, and academic pursuits provides invaluable guidance and inspirational modeling through a mutually rewarding relationship. Importantly, the goal is to select mentors who reflect the realized ethical values universities wish to instill. Too often universities focus solely on recognizing wealthy alums, sometimes overlooking the unsung ethical heroes that students can more readily emulate and benefit from knowing. Certainly, alumni who achieve distinction in their fields through intellectual, artistic, or athletic realms are important for universities to highlight, yet it makes a bold statement to honor ethical leaders with the same regard and attention.

EXPANDING GROUPS OF STAKEHOLDERS

It is often the case that alums choose to settle close to the community where they attended college. Some may have been born and raised near their college community, while others decided to remain near their college after graduation, perhaps finding a satisfying job or relationship where settling close to their alma mater made good sense. In either case, there is often a rich local community of alums and friends of the college nearby. These friends include spouses and other family members of alums and community members who enjoy campus events such as athletic, music, and theater performances, as well as lectures, films, and other activities. Nurturing these relationships is in the best interest of not only the college and their alums but the local community as well. Too often there are "town versus gown" conflicts that might be avoided when careful attention to ethical principles and ethical behavior occurs. Certainly, the local community can expect to be upset and angry when students misbehave or when their activities, including loud parties and alcohol-induced rowdiness, spill into the local neighborhoods. Additionally, colleges likely employ many local businesses for a wide range of services from food supply and distribution to construction and staffing. Colleges trying to be good local citizens involves behaving in ethical and thoughtful ways to everyone in the local community with the goal of developing goodwill between the college and the surrounding environment.

There are a variety of best practices highlighting ethical formation that can be considered when reflecting upon the relationship between colleges and the local community. For example, at Santa Clara University all students, regardless of academic major, participate in at least one community-based learning course where they work in the local community and enroll in an appropriately paired class that highlights the academic portion of their community involvement. A course on abnormal psychology, for example, works with a local homeless shelter for mentally ill clients. A Spanish class uses a local inner-city school location for students to help Spanish-speaking students with their homework. A computer science and engineering course works with local nonprofits to help them with their information technology needs. An ethics in psychology class works with local health- and mental health–care facilities where students interact with patients and clients while learning about ethical approaches to care. In all of these cases and courses, students work closely with local community partners as part of their academic course work, highlighting the relationship between academic material and practical community-based applications. These experiences help students learn about their local neighbors and help neighbors learn about and develop satisfying relationships with students as well. Nurturing these relationships between "town and gown" can provide a rich opportunity for ethical formation and development using real-world and practical applications for students to engage in with close and thoughtful campus faculty and staff supervision.

Additionally, colleges also often invite the local community to campus events such as lectures, athletic events, and musical, dance, film, and drama performances, which all provide opportunities to not only develop and nurture good relationships between the local community members and the college but also highlight strong ethical commitments as well. Being a gracious host, highlighting topics that underscore ethical decision making and principles, and so forth can help enhance the relationships between "town and gown."

Another example of this collaboration includes the Thriving Neighbors Initiative at Santa Clara University. A close university collaboration with one particular low-income neighborhood in San Jose, California, offers a wide variety of collaborative projects between the university and the neighborhood. This includes hands-on data for faculty research, students conducting academic tutoring services for elementary school children, computer and engineering faculty and staff helping with technology needs, and so forth. In addition to providing a practical and local environment for faculty and students to engage in academic work, the community benefits equally from the free services and intellectual contributions of the university community. Additionally, a sense of collaboration and goodwill is enhanced with mutual benefits to all parties.

And finally, another excellent example is annual alumni days of giving, where alums gather for a day of community service and engagement with local nonprofit organizations to provide service to the community. Typically, these events also include socializing with fellow alums and perhaps a festive dinner after a day of volunteer activities assisting others. These initiatives have become popular with both secular and religiously affiliated universities, providing an opportunity for alums to reconnect with their college and one another, as well as providing helpful service to local organizations who need their support. Ethical values, such as those emphasizing the common good and concern for others, are highlighted during these events, thus underscoring the values that the college holds near and dear relating to community and alumni engagement for the benefit of others.

SPECIAL TOPICS IN ETHICS MENTOR GROUPS

Many students find it challenging to find a faculty mentor to help them sort through the many decisions and obstacles on their chosen career paths. Honoring a model alum to host an ongoing mentorship group with students in specific fields offers a forum for career advice and integration of professional ethics into their fields. Alumni-led mentor forums in business, law, health care, psychology, education, journalism, government, and any number of fields can highlight the added benefit of ethical decision making and practices. Emphasizing ethical principles of integrity and responsibility throughout one's professional career brings to life their applied relevance through the considered experience of the mentor. A monthly gathering to discuss such topics on both a professional and personal level can readily integrate the ongoing challenges and benefits of ethical practice in a host of careers.

Students are often drawn to pursue change and involvement in the many pressing social issues of our time. Climate change, human rights, poverty, health care, discrimination, and nuclear disarmament are some examples of ethically charged social causes that alumni mentors are in an excellent position to spearhead with student groups. Notable alumni who work in politics, science, medicine, social services, and the like can lend their experience and knowledge of these current topics from the leading edge and help students pursue their beliefs and interests with the highest ethical standards. Again, having monthly mentor meetings creates personal continuity for students to learn on a more intimate and real-life level.

Another means of integrating alumni as standard-bearers of ethical awareness is through a speakers' series. For example, having alumni speak on campus quarterly regarding their personal experience with ethical dilemmas in their careers can bring to life the complexity and importance of thoughtfully resolving such conflicts. Speakers could share examples of a significant ethical challenge that they faced during their careers, thus modeling for students the normality of such struggles and the decision-making processes that go into ethical choices.

THE POWER OF ATHLETES TO INSPIRE

For better or worse, star college athletes are often revered by their fellow students, as well as by staff, faculty, and alumni. Star athletes carry an aura of heroism and frequently shine as inspirational speakers. A college's alumni athletic standouts can serve a huge role in modeling and inspiring ethical pursuits in undergraduates. Students seek out contact with star athletes and both admire and wonder at what makes them tick. By engaging alumni athletes who have demonstrated laudable ethics and a commitment toward making the world a better place, the often magical gifts of these stars can be enlisted to convey strong models and messages to students regarding the value and strength of being an ethical leader. Through talks to other athletes and the student population at large, the heroics of these athletes *off* the playing field take center stage. The power of athletes to inspire can be well utilized in encouraging non-athletic strivings, including the honorable importance of integrity and ethics. As posted on a plaque in the Dartmouth College gymnasium, "Remember that no person has ever been honored for what he received. Honor is the reward for what he gave" (Charlie Zimmerman).

CONCLUSION

Colleges maintain a relationship with their students long after they graduate. Alumni and many other stakeholders, such as the local community, are important groups to engage for lifelong relationships, learning, and ethical formation. Much can be done to nurture these partnerships and emphasize ethical principles and decision making in the process. Creatively engaging key alumni from a range of fields and life experiences provides students with a forward-looking vision of how ethics may be relevant to their long-term career and life pursuits. Highlighting ethical models among graduates provides students with admirable individuals to emulate and possibly seek out as invaluable mentors. This can be accomplished through speakers, ongoing discussion groups, all forms of campus literature, and key events such as graduation speakers. Furthermore, the richness of surrounding communities can fruitfully be mined to create opportunities for students to engage with, contribute to, learn from, and experience broad segments of society. Immersion and service are often more valuable experiences for the student than for the community members they may be seeking to help. In sum, taking advantage of the extensive network of alumni and community members that model and engage students in ethical thought and pursuit is filled with rich possibilities.

Part IV

Conclusions and Resources

Chapter 17

Putting It All Together: Best Ways to Nurture Ethical Development in Colleges

Until he extends the circle of his compassion to all living things, man will not himself find peace.

—Albert Schweitzer

In our book, we have discussed the imperatives underlying the need for colleges to ascribe significant attention and resources to teaching and advancing ethical formation and character development in their students. The developmental tasks confronted by adolescents and young adults as they grapple with increasing levels of independence and complexity in their lives have been underscored with the use of the Four I's: independence, intimacy, identity, and impulse control. The foundations of moral philosophy and developmental perspectives on the evolution of moral thinking in youth have been presented, along with numerous common college dilemmas that call upon these skills for positive resolutions. The many scandals and high-risk behaviors increasingly described in the media and in government statistics underscore the more destructive consequences of poor decision making in the realms of college alcohol consumption, sexual behavior, and academic integrity. Providing students with the intellectual skills to intentionally develop and live by their own personal codes of ethics is essential to any comprehensive educational endeavor.

We have also sought to delineate the many ways in which colleges can teach, emphasize, and model ethical standards through academics, orientation procedures, student life, judicial practices, residential life, athletics, and other extracurricular programs. Below we highlight the top strategies recommended for colleges to utilize in designing and integrating their own ethical values into a comprehensive college culture and curriculum.

HONOR CODES

Many colleges and universities have developed honor codes that students are required to read, sign, and abide by during their tenure as students within the college. Collegiate honor codes have been evident since the mid-1800s, with the University of Virginia offering the first. Today, most colleges that use honor codes focus specifically on academic integrity, basically stating that students won't cheat or plagiarize their academic course work. Thus, most colleges and universities restrict their honor codes to the classroom experience. Also, many honor codes depend on students not only agreeing to the terms of the college or university honor code document but also agreeing to turn in their peers when they witness honor code violations on campus.

Some colleges and universities, however, expand their honor code system beyond the classroom and academic experience to include non-academic behavior as well. This is especially true at both military and religiously affiliated colleges and universities. These institutions often make explicit their interest in forming people of high moral character in and outside the standard academic activities. They use the honor code system to assist in promoting the virtues and values that they hold near and dear to their particular institution and tradition. Typically, these non-academically based values are consistent with our RRICC model of respect, responsibility, integrity, competence, and concern for others. They also may add additional values and guidelines that are unique to their particular institutions and the mission of the particular military branch or religious denomination associated with the college or university.

Honor codes can be very helpful in providing clear and well-articulated guidance for expected moral and ethical behavior on campus. They make very clear how students should and should not behave, especially as they engage in their academic course work. Yet having and asking students to sign an honor code before enrolling in classes or even before each exam is completed or term paper is turned in is really not sufficient. The routine and all-too-often unthinking signing of the honor code can easily fail to truly register or impact students. It can be done as automatically as signing a check. Few students may take the time and energy to fully understand exactly what they are agreeing to, and even fewer may actually reflect on the meaning of the document they are asked to sign. Making an honor code come alive is challenging but clearly needed to truly integrate the values that are articulated in these codes in the lived experience of students on campus. Moreover, requiring students to determine their own personal ethical beliefs and standards of behavior far exceeds the value of merely prescribing dos and don'ts

Providing a positive frame of reference to honor codes can be an important step to make them come alive and better integrate them into the overall campus experience. Rather than confining them to the classroom environment or interacting with them only before a major exam is completed or term paper turned in, institutions can proudly display their codes as well as the values that are addressed in their honor codes (e.g., integrity, honesty, responsibility) in various places throughout the campus community. In doing so they remind all members of the university community that this is a place where these values and expectations are taken seriously and are integrated into the entire fabric of campus life, both in and out of the classroom setting. These values and virtues ideally should be shared with all members of the campus community, including faculty, staff, and senior administrators. In this way, these values and expectations are proudly proclaimed and a common set of themes expressed, hopefully resulting in more incorporation by all parties associated with the college community.

NEW STUDENT ORIENTATION

From the get-go, incoming students should begin their familiarization with the college's ethical philosophy once admitted. Pre-orientation communications to students and parents should highlight the school's commitment to ethical development and outline the programs and resources in place to support these efforts. Students and parents can review the school's honor code and be asked to complete a brief assignment demonstrating that they have read and discussed these policies and expectations. Pre-orientation materials can also outline the college's approach to teaching ethical decision making (such as the RRICC model or other), emphasizing that the goal is to help students develop and live by their own personal code of ethics, not any particular ideology. Furthermore, every parent and student should be aware of the heightened freshman vulnerability to high-risk behavior, including excessive alcohol abuse, involvement in sexual assault, plagiarism and cheating, and overinvolvement in social activities to the exclusion of maintaining minimal academic standards. Framing this developmental vulnerability in the context of the Four I's can help students and parents grasp the underlying drives and challenges that often lead young adults to make poor decisions. The value of an intentional, practical strategy for making difficult and ethically charged decisions will enable families to understand the benefits of engaging in the college's efforts to help educate and equip them in this manner.

Universities have increasingly invested time and resources into the process of new student orientation. From peer-bonding backpacking trips to a series of organized lectures, social events, meet and greets, and small group activities, colleges have embraced the necessity and benefits of providing a thorough and engaging orientation process for new students. During this often extensive experience, students are introduced to both the spoken and the lived values of the college. They will adeptly glean whether mere lip service is paid to high and mighty ideals or whether the campus demonstrates and models the ethical standards it purports to uphold. Orientation can involve introducing students to campus leaders, professors, and student life advisors devoted to assisting students in carefully making the ethical decisions that best reflect the people they strive to be.

New student orientation is the first and best opportunity for colleges to reach students at their most open and eager point of arrival. All eyes and ears, incoming students are seeking to understand the heart and soul of the college community to which they long to belong. Making character and ethical development an explicit and visible aspect of those first impressions and messages is key to helping students become alert to ethics from the beginning of their college journey.

MAINTAINING AN ORGANIZATIONAL CULTURE OF ETHICS

As we discussed earlier, teenagers arrive on campus with well-developed core personality structures and a fundamental though often unexamined set of core values. Nonetheless, in a broad array of organizations and institutions throughout academia, government, business, and the like, individuals gravitate toward the prevailing cultural values in which they are immersed. Thus, students who perceive their administrators and professors as unengaged and uninspired are likely to behave like unengaged and uninspired students. Where students perceive their leaders as corrupt, they are likely to view integrity as an unhelpful quality for success within the college. But where students believe their professors demonstrate integrity, compassion, and commitment, such qualities are likely to influence them to behave in kind. Much has been studied and written about the power of an organization's culture to influence and motivate its employees. Thus, the culture of any organization—and most certainly that includes the culture at colleges and universities—influences and develops students who strive to emulate and reflect these prevailing values. From the top down, university professionals and student leaders model and convey where ethics do or don't exist within the university's priorities and ethos.

Colleges are currently battling a scourge of sexual assaults, racist incidents, cheating scandals, and binge-drinking problems. University officials are increasingly being educated and enlightened regarding how to make their campuses safer, more inclusive, and more in keeping with academic standards of integrity. Integral to any of these discussions is the ethical thinking and conduct necessary to combat such destructive choices. Critically, the necessary ethics and conduct must begin with those in these very positions of power and leadership. University boards and administrators face an imperative to thoughtfully examine their own ethical thinking and behavior and ensure that these are consistent with their institutional goals and beliefs.

It can be helpful to codify in words and writing clear expectations for staff and students. Some schools may have mottos, such as Santa Clara University's "Three Cs: Conscience, Compassion, and Competence," or Florida State University's "Strength, Skill, Character," or Middlebury College's "Truth and Virtue," or Wake Forest University's "For Humanity," all of which handily and frequently express the core values at the heart of the university. In all aspects of university life—including residence halls, social environments, athletic competitions, and classrooms—faculty, staff, and students should know clearly what is encouraged and what is discouraged in the actions of participants. For example, at Dartmouth College, "The Good Samaritan" policy makes clear that if another student is deemed dangerously intoxicated, bystanders must call for help, and can do so without punitive consequences. Similarly, many schools make explicit that knowledge of another's cheating must be reported. These types of rules regarding the "big ticket items" of sexual assault, cheating, racism, discrimination, and binge drinking in many ways are clear and even obvious.

However, many decisions students make are mired in more ambiguity and require careful and deliberate thought to reach a sound resolution. This is where it is especially important for colleges to provide a framework for ethical decision making. In this book, we discuss many perspectives from moral philosophers and add our own model (i.e., RRICC), which we believe provides a quick, easy, yet powerful reference for evaluating most ethical dilemmas. Colleges can generate a common conversation and shorthand for discussing ethics by highlighting one model that enables individuals to intentionally discern and evaluate their own ethical choices.

Colleges add veracity to their championing of ethical values by rewarding students and faculty who best represent exemplary ethics in thought, scholarship, and behavior. Endowing a faculty chair in the field of ethics, awarding student leaders in ethics public commendation and other rewards, and emphasizing ethical integrity in all aspects of hiring, admissions, and evaluation all powerfully convey the school's value on ethics. These tangible rewards demonstrate more loudly than words the college's commitment to an educational environment steeped in ethical values.

CURRICULAR AND EXTRACURRICULAR INTEGRATION

The inclusion of one mandatory ethics course into college curricula can only pay dividends. Ethics courses can be offered through a variety of academic departments, including philosophy, psychology, business, biology, journalism, etc. The goal of requiring a formal ethics course is not to prescribe any particular beliefs but rather to teach students how to think about ethics from a variety of perspectives. Without elevating ethics to inclusion in the standard curriculum, colleges miss an opportunity to underscore the importance of ethics and impart ethical problem-solving skills to their students. When all students participate in at least one such course, a campus-wide conversation can proceed, with students sharing and discussing their various perspectives. Most important, education in ethics develops alertness to the very presence of ethical considerations, equipping students with a means of understanding and resolving their own ethical dilemmas throughout their professional and personal lives.

Ethical instruction can readily be extended to extracurricular activities, including athletics, fraternities and sororities, clubs, and various causes. Recently, the University of Missouri suffered a spate of racially offensive outbursts against black students, escalating to the point of the president of the university being forced to resign. Further student protests have since ensued—including outrage at Yale University regarding perceived racism on campus—raising a host of ethical issues regarding inclusivity, diversity, journalism, leadership, and communication between student groups and also with school officials. Clearly, providing training in ethical behavior for all organized student groups and activities can only improve the tenor of discourse. Athletic teams routinely discuss sportsmanship and the type of behavior expected of athletes as representatives of the university. Similarly, relevant ethical content should be conveyed within the various extracurricular communities on campus.

Similarly, highlighting student groups and clubs that demonstrate exemplary ethical comportment in the course of their activities can underscore the college's commitment to ethical citizenship throughout the university. Selecting student leaders and representatives to offer information and corrective feedback can also provide some authority to individuals best equipped to engage around difficult issues with other students.

DISCIPLINARY AND JUDICIAL PROCEDURES: RESTORATIVE JUSTICE

The process of restorative justice can serve to exemplify the ethical strivings of a university. How colleges respond to rule violators, and to those harmed by them, vividly illustrates their own educational and moral philosophy. When disciplinary opportunities are confronted from an educational and development perspective, as opposed to violations quickly being addressed through blunt punishments, students and communities benefit richly. Schools that simply judge and punish expediently, overlooking the responsibility to educate violators and help victims recover and repair, unwittingly perpetuate a polarizing culture rather than one of collaboration, healing, and growth.

Restorative justice in college settings has gained important interest and adoption. The three key elements involved in this form of accountability require that violators accept responsibility for their offenses, work toward repairing the harm they have caused, and develop positive engagement with the harmed individual or community in order to build compassion and ensure reformed behavior. Restorative justice involves a comprehensive process of making reparations directly to the victims of a misdeed and learning through personal connection about the harmful consequences of their actions and how to become better citizens.

This approach clearly requires a significant commitment of university resources but can be adapted to meld into existing structures and programs. In a sense, it is part and parcel of an engaged educational program that demands true participation by students and staff alike. Potentially, restorative justice programs can be a model of mediated dialogue, problem solving, and real change within the most edifying environments of academia.

THE BOTTOM LINE

The bottom line is that if we want to graduate college students of honor, who possess a sound intellectual and personal strategy for ethical behavior and ethical decision making, then we must take ethics seriously on college campuses. Most schools already highlight and expect academic integrity and personal responsibility from their students as well as from their faculty and staff. College students, often living away from home for the first time in their lives, are confronted with numerous opportunities to make good and bad choices, often involving sexuality, alcohol consumption, academic cheating, inclusion, and so forth. These students will, regardless of any ethics training, make decisions for themselves that will be either intentional and well informed or not. We strongly believe that students can be given helpful tools based on thousands of years of reflection and writing in moral philosophy and ethics that can make their decisions in life well informed, thoughtful, reasoned, and intentional. We are not advocating exactly what students should or should not do, and it would be counterproductive to seek to take away their freedoms to decide how they alone should live. Rather, we aim for strategies that are reflective, based on good evidence, and communicated and taught with sound understanding of the developmental challenges faced by these emerging adults.

For colleges to help students develop character and good ethical decision-making skills, they need to approach these issues from multiple angles and have everyone associated with the college, from top to bottom of the organizational chart, be attentive, mindful, and engaged with thoughtful, ethical decision making. Certainly not everyone will agree when it comes to what principles or processes are needed to make ethical decisions, but creating an environment where ethical reflection is valued and considered in all campus activities is an important step in the right direction. We believe that ethical principles using our RRICC model of respect, responsibility, integrity, competence, and concern are likely to be appealing to most college campuses. Using the RRICC model or other variations on this theme—such as Santa Clara's Three Cs, competence, conscience, and compassion—to underscore the virtues that colleges hold near and dear acts as a springboard for discussion, reflection, and problem solving of ethical challenges. Having faculty, staff, administrators, and student leaders all model these qualities can help create the kind of college environment where behaviors are consistent with values articulated in promotional brochures and Web pages.

Colleges that remain mindful of the unique developmental tasks that college students face in striving to develop their skills regarding impulse control, intimacy, identity formation, and independence can be far more thoughtful in helping their students move positively through these developmental stages. The good news is that students are often hungry for learning about strategies for healthy development and are often engaged by thoughtful ethical reflection. Also, there is good news in that efforts to create an environment that supports and nurtures ethics don't need to cost a great deal of money or require a great deal of time to accomplish. Rather, having clear, consistent, and well-articulated values, and incorporating these values into all aspects of college life with excellent models for behavior, can go a very long way toward helping students develop good ethical decision-making skills and thus graduate with distinct honor.

FINAL CONCLUSION

Ethics can be nurtured and enhanced when colleges and their stakeholders (e.g., parents, alums, donors, local community members) have a clear vision of the principles that they wish to live by and advocate. These principles can be thoughtfully incorporated into all aspects of campus life, from the classroom and the boardroom to the athletic fields and the dormitories. Making ethics and ethical decision making a top priority need not be a burden or a significant expense. Rather, it requires a commitment from the entire campus community, top to bottom, that thoughtful reflection on ethical principles, behavior, and decision making is important and is taken seriously throughout all aspects of campus life. In doing so, colleges make students more likely to absorb and integrate these tools and values of thoughtful ethical reflection. Championing these truest forms of honor that students discover within themselves gives added meaning to the concept of "graduating with honor." Our future society certainly needs to have many more citizens who take ethics seriously in order for our world to survive and thrive. Our central thesis asks: Why not use these formative college years to teach and mold students toward these inarguably valuable ethical goals? The quality and longevity of our lives on this planet may actually depend on it.

Appendix A

Sample Syllabi for Applied Ethics Classes

ETHICAL ISSUES IN SOCIETY

PHIL 5 – Section 10510

MWF 2:15–3:20 p.m.

SHANNON VALLOR, PH.D.

OFFICE: **Bannan 251**

OFFICE HOURS: **MON/WED 4:00–5:00, THURS 1:30–2:30 or by appointment**

PHONE: **(408) 554-5190**

E-MAIL: **svallor@scu.edu**

COURSE DESCRIPTION

Ethics, interpreted most broadly, is concerned with the good life and how it is achieved in our actions. Interpreted more narrowly, ethics concerns the moral dimension of human existence—that is, how we *ought* to act toward others and ourselves.

Ethics, as far as we know, is a uniquely human endeavor. We alone seem to have the capacities for reflection and self-awareness that allow us to judge our actions in the past and plan for the actions that will make our future. These capacities are liberating—rather than being completely enslaved to heredity and instinct, human beings possess a power of self-determination. We can, to a significant extent, choose the person we want to become. But with this freedom comes responsibility. If we can choose how we act and what we become, then we are also morally accountable for our actions and our lives. The study of ethics is the study of this responsibility and how it can be met.

Philosophers study ethics in two ways—theoretical and applied ethics. *Theoretical* studies of ethics explore the basis of our ethical obligations (metaethics) as well as the specific principles or rules of action we are ethically obligated to follow (normative ethics). *Applied* studies of ethics explore how those normative theories can guide our actual decisions and choices in life.

We will begin the course with a general review of some of the major normative ethical theories. However, this course is primarily devoted to applied ethics. Our goal will be to work out the application of normative ethical theories to some of the most pressing dilemmas in contemporary society. The course is designed to help you become familiar with various types of ethical theory, to become skilled in moral reasoning and decision making, and to learn to apply these skills to concrete, practical issues in society that demand an ethical response.

COURSE REQUIREMENTS

1) **Attendance and participation**—This is an <u>essential</u> requirement for achieving the goals stated in the course description. The classroom is a forum for the open exchange of ideas and insights, and for this reason students are expected to be present and prepared to discuss the readings at each class session. You should be aware that due to the high level of in-class work required, including occasional group activities, your combined attendance and participation level will factor significantly into your course grade (see details on grading).

2) **Paper**—Three short papers (four, five, and six pages) are required. Grades will be based on understanding of the relevant issues and texts; strength of ethical analysis; organization and clarity of expression; and proper grammar. The paper will not involve additional research or sources beyond what is given in the class texts, lectures, and discussions. I will be happy to meet during office hours or schedule another time to discuss the paper before you turn in the final product. However, once the final version is submitted for grading, no rewrites will be allowed. One-half letter grade will be deducted for each day that a paper is late.

3) **Short Writing Assignments**—There will be several in-class short writing assignments based upon the assigned reading for the day, given in the first ten minutes of class and unannounced. Of these, the lowest grade will be dropped and the remainder averaged.

GRADING

Attendance and participation – 15%

Short Writing Assignments – 10%

1st Paper – 15%

2nd Paper – 25%

3rd Paper – 35%

DISABILITY ACCOMMODATION POLICY

To request academic accommodations for a disability, students must contact Disability Resources located in The Drahmann Center in Benson, room 214, (408) 554-4111; TTY (408) 554-5445. Students must provide documentation of a disability to Disability Resources prior to receiving accommodations.

ACADEMIC INTEGRITY

The issue of honesty and integrity is taken seriously in any academic discipline, and certainly no less so in philosophy. In particular, the issue of plagiarism can be problematic in this field, given the delicate balance between the requirement for originality of thought and the necessity of the free exchange of ideas. For written assignments in this class it is essential to cite <u>any</u> outside source used for particular ideas, statements, or facts contained in your paper. This includes information taken from any published source such as books, journals, or newspapers, as well as information obtained from individual persons or the Web—even if you are unable to trace the information back to its original source. The work you submit is graded according to the content and clarity of *your* thought alone, and for this reason, any uncited use of outside sources (whether intentional or not) will be treated as a serious offense according to the guidelines published in the Undergraduate Bulletin and Community Handbook. To give you a sense of how these guidelines will be applied, a paper that contains a plagiarized sentence or paragraph will receive an F with no rewrite allowed, and the incident will be reported to the Assistant Dean for Student Life for a hearing to determine if further action is warranted. Papers containing more than a paragraph of plagiarized material will result in an F for the entire course, in addition to referral to the Assistant Dean for Student Life for further action.

REQUIRED TEXTS

• John Arthur, *Morality and Moral Controversies* (7th Ed.)

CALENDAR

DATE	TOPIC	READING ASSIGNMENT
9/20	Introduction to Ethics	N/A
9/22	Morality and Self-Interest	Hobbes (Arthur, pp. 1–8)
9/24	Morality and Self-Interest (Pt. 2)	Brody (Arthur, pp. 8–15)
9/27	Morality and Religion	Arthur, pp. 15–22
9/29	Morality and Conscience	Bennett (Arthur, pp. 23–30)
10/1	Normative Theories of Ethics (Virtue Ethics)	Aristotle (Arthur, pp. 50–56)
10/4	Normative Theories of Ethics (Kantian Ethics)	Kant (Arthur, pp. 56–65)
10/6	STUDENT PLANNING DAY (No Classes)	N/A
10/8	Normative Theories of Ethics (Utilitarianism)	Mill (Arthur, pp. 65–72)
10/11	Critical Reflections on Ethical Theory	O'Neill, Brandt (Arthur, pp. 78–89)
10/13	Feminist Reflections on Ethical Theory	Held (Arthur, pp. 89–93)
10/15	"Terrorism" "On the Morality of War"	Frey/Morris, Wasserstrom (Arthur, pp. 95–108)
10/18	"The Morality of Pacifism" "Korematsu v. United States"	Ryan, U.S. Supreme Court (Arthur, pp. 109–116)
10/20	"All Animals Are Equal" ***FIRST PAPER DUE ON THIS DATE**	Singer (Arthur, pp. 146–154)
10/22	"Speciesism & the Idea of Equality" "People or Penguins"	Steinbock, Baxter (Arthur, pp. 155–165)
10/25	"The Land Ethic"	Callicott (Arthur, pp. 166–177)

10/27	"JFK Memorial Hospital v. Heston" "Comparing Human Lives" "An Alternative to the Ethic of Euthanasia"	N.J. Supreme Court, Godwin, Dyck (Arthur, pp. 237–244)
10/29	"Active and Passive Euthanasia" "Defective Newborns"	Rachels, Brandt (Arthur, pp. 245–255)
11/1	"Aging and the Ends of Medicine" "The Survival Lottery"	Callahan, Harris (Arthur, pp. 256–267)
11/3	"Texas v. Johnson" "Is Patriotism a Virtue?"	U.S. Supreme Court, MacIntyre (Arthur, pp. 408–418)
11/5	"Crito" "Taking Rights Seriously"	Plato, Dworkin (Arthur, pp. 419–429)
11/8	"Civil Disobedience" "On Not Prosecuting Civil Dis." **FILM DAY (PART ONE):** *The Weather Underground*	Rawls, Dworkin (Arthur, pp. 429–443)
11/10	**FILM DAY (PART TWO):** *The Weather Underground*	No Assigned Reading
11/12	Film Discussion	No Assigned Reading
11/15	"On the Liberty of Thought" "Village of Skokie v. National Socialist Party" ***SECOND PAPER DUE ON THIS DATE**	Mill, Illinois Supreme Court (Arthur, pp. 521–527)
11/17	"Prohibiting Racist Speech" "Political Correctness"	Lawrence & Gunther, Dershowitz (Arthur, pp. 527–534)
11/19	"On Racism and Sexism" "Social Movements & the Politics of Difference"	Wasserstrom, Young (Arthur, pp. 559–574)
11/22– 11/26	THANKSGIVING BREAK	N/A
11/29	"Morality and the Liberal Ideal" "Multiculturalism"	Sandel, Raz (Arthur, pp. 586–602)
12/1	"Reason Before Identity" "The Question of Inherited Guilt"	Sen, Pettigrove (Arthur, pp. 602–610 + handout)
12/3	"Reparations and 'The Debt'" **LAST DAY OF CLASS**	McWhorter (Arthur, pp. 615–625)
12/8	***THIRD PAPERS DUE BY THIS DATE (PAPER COUNTS AS THE FINAL)**	

SANTA CLARA UNIVERSITY

Psychology Department

ETHICS IN PSYCHOLOGY (PSYC 114)

Instructor:	Thomas G. Plante, Ph.D., ABPP
Office:	Psychology Department (Alumni Science 203)
Telephone, Fax:	408-554-4471 (Office), 408-554-5241 (Fax)
E-Mail & Web:	tplante@scu.edu, www.scu.edu/tplante
Office Hours:	generally before and after class or by appointment
Course Meeting Room:	Kenna 216
Course Meeting Times:	Tuesdays and Thursdays, 2:00 p.m.–3:40 p.m.

REQUIRED READING:

Texts:

Rachels, J. & Rachels, S. (2012). *The Elements of Moral Philosophy* (7th Edition). NY: McGraw-Hill. ISBN: 9780078038242

Koocher, G.P., & Keith-Spiegel, P. (2008). *Ethics in Psychology and the Mental Health Professions: Standards and Cases* (3rd Edition). NY: Oxford. ISBN: 9780195149111

Plante, T.G. (2004). *Do the Right Thing: Living Ethically in an Unethical World.* Oakland, CA: New Harbinger. ISBN: 1572243643

APA Ethics Code also located at http://www.apa.org/ethics/code/index.aspx#.

Additional readings may be provided during the class.

COURSE EVALUATION:

Class Quizzes		100 points
Class Behavior		+/-
Midterm Learning Adventure 1:	Feb 4	100 points
Midterm Learning Adventure 2:	Mar 4	100 points
Final Learning Adventure:	Mar 18	200 points
Term Paper	Mar 13	100 points
Class Participation and Scholarly Enthusiasm:		+
+/- can improve or decrease course grade		

COURSE DESCRIPTION

Ethics in psychology involves the role of ethical behavior and decision making in the field of psychology and related behavioral, medical, and social sciences (e.g., medicine, public policy, nursing, occupational therapy, physical therapy). In accordance with the university's statement of purpose, the course seeks to "prepare students to assume leadership roles in society through an education that stresses moral . . . values . . ., seeks to answer . . . 'what should be' . . . and [promotes] justice . . . and the common good." Class topics include issues related to competence; integrity; professional, scientific, and social responsibility; respect for others' rights and dignity; concern for others' welfare; and other topics. Suggested prerequisites include PSYC 1 or 2 as well as PSYC 40, 43.

LEARNING OBJECTIVES:

(from University Core Curriculum Requirements)

1.1 Be able to reason ethically by drawing on major ethical theories and traditions (e.g. virtue ethics, feminist ethics, deontological or consequentialist theories); by normatively assessing individual, professional, and institutional decisions; and by articulating their personal engagement with the meaning of the right and the good. (Arts & Humanities, Ethical Reasoning, Critical Thinking)

1.2 Be able to analyze, critically evaluate, and apply major ethical theories and traditions to significant personal, professional, and institutional decisions. As part of such efforts, students will be able to articulate how they understand some central ethical concepts such as justice, happiness, the good, virtue, dignity, rights, and equality. (Arts & Humanities, Critical Thinking, Ethical Reasoning)

1.3 Be able to demonstrate appreciation of nuance and ambiguity, as well as clarity and precision, in their thinking and writing about moral problems, concepts, and ideals. (Critical Thinking, Complexity)

1.4 Reflect on their own ethical decisions and actions, on their roles as morally responsible members of the human community, and on what it means to be a good person. (Critical Thinking, Complexity)

COURSE GOALS:

(1) To understand ethical issues and ethical decision making in the field of psychology and related fields.

(2) To provide a framework for understanding and thinking about ethical issues in psychology and other behavioral, social, and medical sciences.

(3) To provide the foundation for students taking additional courses and advanced training in psychology and other behavioral and social science fields.

SEQUENCE OF TOPICS AND READINGS:

Week 1 (Jan 7 & 9):	Introduction to Course & Introduction to Ethics	R# 1–6*, P 1
Week 2 (Jan 14 & 16):	Methods and Perspectives in Ethical Decision Making	R 7–13, P 2
Week 3 (Jan 21 & 23):	Application of Ethical Decision Making to Psychology and Related Fields	K 1–3 & Appendix A
Week 4 (Jan 28 & 30):	Competence & Integrity	K 4, 5, 6; P 3–4
Week 5 (Feb 4 & 6):	Professional & Scientific Responsibility *Midterm Learning Adventure 1: Tues, Feb 4* (Assessing Learning Objectives 1.1–1.4)	K 16, 19; P 5

Week 6 (Feb 11 & 13):	Respect for People's Rights and Dignity	K 8, 9, 13; P 6
Week 7 (Feb 18 & 20):	Concern for Others' Welfare	K 10, 11, 12; P 7
Week 8 (Feb 25 & 27):	Social Responsibility	K 7, 14, 15
Week 9 (Mar 4 & 6):	Special Issues: e.g., Legal & Work Issues *Midterm Learning Adventure 2: Tues, Mar 4* (Assessing Learning Objectives 1.1–1.4)	K 17, 18
Week 10 (Mar 11 & 13):	Future Trends, Hot Topics, & Conclusions *Term Paper Due: Thurs, Mar 13, at 2:00 p.m.* (Assessing Learning Objectives 1.1–1.4)	P 8–9

* Please have readings completed during the first class session of each week.
\# R = Rachels book, K = Koocher book, P = Plante book
NOTE: *Final Learning Adventure: Tues, Mar 18, at 1:30 p.m.*

ADDITIONAL ITEMS:

1. *Laptops and cell phones.* Laptops and cell phones are not allowed to be used in class (unless you have a documented learning disability that requires the use of these technologies). Students typically use them more to check their e-mail, Facebook and other social networking sites, and surf the Web more than they tend to use them for taking notes. They try to multitask (which doesn't work according to the cognitive science research) and then wonder why they didn't do well on class learning adventures or don't recall what was said or not said in class. Research demonstrates that the grade performance for those using laptops tends to approximate the performance of those who don't attend class. I think that says it all. Violations of this policy will result in being failed for the week (10 points, first offense), failed for the month (second offense, 50 points), failed for the course (third offense, all points).

2. *Class Quizzes* will occur weekly on the reading material. They will generally include three questions asked in class. You are expected to answer two of the three correctly to pass the quiz. Less than two correct answers will result in a fail for the week (10 points loss). Responses should be made on *index cards* and handed in to the professor. You should have 10 index cards available for the class. You cannot pass the quiz unless an appropriate index card is used.

3. *Attendance.* You'll be asked to sign in for each class period and attendance will be recorded. You are expected to be in class for at least 80 percent of

the class sessions. Less than 80 percent (without doctor's or coach's written statement) results in failing the class attendance and behavior portion of the grade.

4. *Expected classroom behavior.* Please note the following expectations regarding classroom behavior:

   a. *Arrive on time.*

   b. *Don't pack up books and such before class is completed.*

   c. *Turn off cell phones.*

   d. *Use restrooms before and after class and during the midclass break.*

   e. *Don't leave class once started (if you do, please don't return that day).*

   f. *If you miss class, get notes from other students.*

   g. *Read the textbook as required.*

   h. *Participate in class discussions.*

   i. *Cheating in any form won't be tolerated and will result in being failed from the class.*

5. Please note that makeup learning adventures are not possible. If you miss one of the midterm learning adventures with an *excused* absence, the final learning adventure will count for 300 rather than 200 points (400 points if both midterms are missed). Missing the final or failing to submit the term paper will result in being dropped or failed from the course. Learning adventures will primarily be short essay and/or multiple guess and will be graded using a curve (only if needed).

6. Term papers should also be handed in via Canvas in the Turn.it.in.com drop box. Choose an ethics issue that you are interested in, but be sure to choose something that isn't straight out of the texts. Papers won't be accepted after the final and will be reduced by 10 points per day after the due date.

7. Please be prompt to class. We will make every effort to begin and end each class on time.

8. If you would like to speak with me individually, please feel free to do so. Please try to schedule your visit during scheduled office hours. If it is impossible for you to attend office hours due to a class conflict, then please make an appointment rather than an unscheduled visit. Additionally, feel free to e-mail me 24/7.

9. In keeping with the mission of the university, relating the course material to the "greater glory of God and to the common good" as well as helping to educate leaders with *competence, compassion, and conscience* will be integrated into class material where appropriate.

10. In order to make the most of this course (and your tuition dollars), please attend each class session, keep up with the assigned reading, and participate in class activities and discussions with scholarly vigor. *Ad Majorem Dei Gloriam*

To request academic accommodations for a disability, students must be registered with Disabilities Resources, located in Benson, room 216. In order to register, please go online to www.scu.edu/disabilities. You will need to register and provide professional documentation of a disability prior to receiving academic accommodations. It is best to read "Required Documentation" on the Web site before starting the registration process in order to determine what is needed. You may contact Disabilities Resources at 408-554-4109 if you have questions.

This course is associated with the Applied Ethics Pathway. If you choose to declare this Pathway, you may use a representative work from this course in the Pathway Portfolio you will complete during your senoir year. Therefore, keep electronic copies of your work. Students who began studies at Santa Clara in 2009 or 2010 will post their work for the Pathway on Camino; students who began studies at Santa Clara in 2011 or later will post their work on their TaskStream e-Portfolio.

Appendix B

Sample Syllabi for Freshman 100/101 Classes

University 101-034

Fall 2012

MW- 2:30-3:45; Capstone Hall

CONTACT INFORMATION

Instructors:	Dr. Dan Friedman	Katie Kortier
E-mail:	friedman@sc.edu	kortierk@yahoo.com
Phones:	C: 422-7526; Office: 777-9506	C: 678-234-5248
Office:	1728 College St	NA

Office Hours: By appointment. I am generally available from 8:00–4:00 each day, M–F.

PURPOSE

The purpose of University 101 is to help new students make a successful transition to the University of South Carolina, both academically and personally. This course aims to foster a sense of belonging, promote engagement in the curricular and cocurricular life of the university, articulate to students the expectations of the university and its faculty, help students develop and apply critical thinking skills, and help students continue to clarify their purpose, meaning, and direction.

GOALS & OBJECTIVES

I. Foster Academic Success

As a result of this course, students will:

a) Adapt and apply appropriate academic strategies to their courses and learning experiences.

b) Demonstrate how to effectively evaluate information sources and utilize university libraries and information systems for academic inquiry.

c) Recognize the purpose and value of academic integrity and describe the key themes related to the Honor Code at the University of South Carolina.

d) Use written and oral communication to discover, develop, and articulate ideas and viewpoints.

e) Identify and apply strategies to effectively manage time and priorities.

f) Identify relevant academic policies, processes, and procedures related to advising, course planning, and major exploration.

II. Help Students Discover and Connect with the University of South Carolina

As a result of this course, students will:

a) Identify appropriate campus resources and opportunities that contribute to their educational experience, goals, and campus engagement.

b) Develop and apply skills that contribute to building positive relationships with peers, staff, and faculty.

c) Describe what it means to be a Carolinian in context of the history, traditions, and culture of the university.

III. Prepare Students for Responsible Lives in a Diverse, Interconnected, and Changing World

As a result of this course, students will:

a) Examine how their background and experiences impact their values and assumptions and explain the influence these have on their relationships with others.

b) Describe concepts of diversity and recognize diverse perspectives.

c) Describe and demonstrate principles of responsible citizenship within and beyond the campus community.

d) Describe processes, strategies, and resources, and explain the implications of their decisions, related to their overall wellness.

COURSE READINGS & MATERIALS

1. Sewell, M. E., & Friedman, D. (Eds.). (2012). *Transitions: Building a new community*. Columbia, SC: University of South Carolina.

2. Myers-Briggs Type Indicator. $15. Please visit the Career Center on the sixth floor of the Business Administration building to purchase your access to this instrument. Must be completed by August 29.

3. Digital subscription to *New York Times*. Visit www.nytimes.com/collegeds for ordering information. Subscriptions will need to begin on September 10 and run through November 21.

4. Other readings available on Blackboard (chapters or articles).

COURSE REQUIREMENTS & GRADING

Attendance & Participation	15%
E-mail Journal (5 entries)	10%
Assignments & Quizzes	10%
Academic Success Activity	10%
Beyond the Classroom Learning	5%
Resident Expert Presentation	20%
MBTI Analysis Paper (midterm)	15%
Final Exam	15%

GRADING SCALE

90–100 = A	87–89 = B+
80–86 = B	77–79 = C+
70–76 = C	67–69 = D+
60–66 = D	Below 60 = F

ATTENDANCE POLICY & CLASS PARTICIPATION

You are expected to attend all class meetings and outside events. This is a seminar course in which attendance and participation are vital. Full credit will be given for perfect attendance. Ten points will be deducted from your attendance grade for each unexcused absence. Five or more absences may result in a failing grade for the course. Participation will be evaluated based on your engagement in the class, substantial contributions to class discussions, evidence of having completed the readings, and positive attitude. You will also be required to schedule a one-on-one meeting with your instructors as a way to check in about your progress this semester. More information will be provided about this later.

CLASSROOM BEHAVIORS

You are encouraged to openly engage in class discussions, ask questions, share ideas, and express your thoughts. Please be respectful of others by avoiding disruptive behaviors such as side conversations, cell phone use, arriving late, leaving early, etc.

E-MAIL JOURNAL

You will be required to submit regular journal entries via e-mail as a means of reflective writing. **You are required to submit five entries over the course of the semester.** Topics and deadlines will be posted to Blackboard. Your journal entries should demonstrate considerable reflection and thought and should be at least two paragraphs long.

ACADEMIC SUCCESS STRATEGIES ASSIGNMENT

One goal of this class is to help you be successful in your other academic courses. In order to help foster habits and behaviors that lead to academic success, you will be required to earn 50 points by choosing activities from the list below. You do not need to do all the activities on the list, but you do need to accumulate 50 points over the course of the semester (in any combination you choose). Evidence (paper, confirmation slip, etc.) is due one week from when you attend an event or complete a task.

Required

_____ Complete the Semester at a Glance activity on page 76 of *Transitions* (10 points) **Due August 29.**

Earn 40 more points from the list below.

_____ Attend an SI session (10 points each)—bring signature from SI leader

_____ Type your notes for one of your classes (10 points per week)

_____ Make study guide for one of your exams (10 points)

_____ Make an outline for a chapter in one of your textbooks (10 points)

_____ Take a paper for another class to the Writing Center for review (10 points)

_____ Take professor out to lunch—write one-page reaction paper (20 points)

> *For more information about how to get a free lunch ticket for your professor, as well as potential discussion questions to ask over lunch, please visit the ACE Web site at: http://www.housing.sc.edu/ace/otl.html.*

_____ Attend ACE coaching session—bring signature from ACE Coach (10 points)

MBTI PAPER

Please explain what each letter in your Myers-Briggs type means about you. Do not just give a summary or (even worse) directly quote the paraphrased responses about your type. You need to **synthesize** and **analyze** your Myers-Briggs type. How can understanding your MBTI type help you succeed in college? You should give examples for **each** scale about how it can help **and** hinder your college success. Please be as detailed and specific as possible while providing a thoughtful analysis.

This answer must be typed, double spaced, and should be around three to four pages. This should be in essay form, with an introduction, conclusion, and transition between ideas. You will be evaluated based on:

- Grammar & spelling (25 points)
- Organization, structure, introduction/conclusion, & transitions (15 points)
- Explanation of MBTI Type (20 points)
- Analysis of type and connection to college success (40 points)

RESIDENT EXPERT RESEARCH PRESENTATION

To further explore the course learning outcomes, particularly information literacy, you will develop a research presentation that contributes to our learning in this course. This project will be your opportunity to enhance and practice your research, writing, group work, and presentation skills.

In small groups, you will develop a research question, collect information, and create an informative and engaging presentation for your classmates. Each member of the group will also be responsible for submitting two summaries and evaluations (annotated bibliographies) of articles being considered for the project.

Possible topics might include (but certainly are not limited to):

- Can college students (or people in general) effectively multitask?
- How much sleep do we really need?
- Is the freshman 15 a real thing?
- What do we know about the effects (physical, ethical) of ADHD medication for those without ADHD?

BEYOND THE CLASSROOM LEARNING (USC CONNECT)

In order to foster your ability to integrate your learning (make connections between your coursework and what you are learning beyond the classroom), you will be asked to attend at least one beyond-the-classroom learning opportunity (cultural event such as a play, recital, or dance; campus lecture; etc.) and write a one- to two-page reflection that addresses the following components:

1) Describe something you learned from this experience (150-200 words).
2) Describe how the beyond-the-classroom experience connects to a larger concept, topic, issue, or UNIV 101 learning outcome (such as diversity, wellness, academic success, etc.) and/or to specific aspects of an area of study (history, math, science, etc.). Be specific as to how your experience reinforced, contradicted, or provided a concrete example related to the larger concept you identified (200 words or more).

We may choose to attend an event as a class or you may choose an opportunity on your own. The reflection paper must be submitted to Blackboard by 5:00 p.m. on November 19.

OTHER ASSIGNMENTS

There will be several in-class and short out-of-class assignments. These will include: a quiz on the syllabus, a time management project, a meeting with the instructor(s), and other similar activities. In addition, each student will be asked to provide one "Do You Know" to start the class. For this activity, you will research a university resource, agency, policy, or opportunity and educate your classmates on this topic or area (two minutes). This will be a way we can learn about all the university has to offer students. You should utilize your *Transitions* text and USC Web pages to find the appropriate information.

FINAL EXAM

You will be asked to create a three-minute media presentation (movie, slide presentation, art collage, etc.) and write a letter to yourself that synthesizes your first semester of college. More information will be provided later in the semester. We will hold a "film festival" at our final exam period (Wednesday, December 10, at 12:30 p.m.).

University 101

Fall 2012; MW 2:30–3:45

Date	Class Topic	Assignment for Today	Notes
8/27	Introductions & Overview of Syllabus		Take syllabus quiz on Blackboard; chapter 1 in *Transitions*
8/29	Build Community; How We Learn	Have completed syllabus quiz by 2:00 p.m. today; Deadline to complete MBTI	Sign up for "Did You Know"; take ENGAGE Inventory
9/3	No Class—Labor Day		
9/5	Campus Safety	Meet in Russell House room 305; have read *Transitions* pages 195–199	Journal 1 due Friday
9/10	High School v. College: Understanding College Professors		Semester at a glance activity due
9/12	Campus Involvement & USC Connect	Have read chapter 3 in *Transitions*	Introduce USC Bucket List (competition)

9/17	Alcohol Use in College	Have read pages 181–185 in *Transitions*	
9/19	Understanding Your Personality Preferences: The Myers-Briggs Type Indicator (MBTI)		Journal 2 due Friday
9/24	MBTI; Time Management		
9/26	Advising Issues	Four-year plan & career aspirations; have read pages 122–131 in *Transitions*.	Undergraduate Bulletin scavenger hunt due (p. 132 *Transitions*); get in groups for Resident Expert Project
10/1	My 30 Values Activity		Time Management Project due
10/3	Writing Workshop & Academic Integrity	MBTI paper due; have read pages 155–164 in *Transitions*	
10/8	Library & Information Literacy		Journal 3 due Friday
10/10	Digital Identities	Have read pages 141–154 in *Transitions*	
10/15	Photo Contest		
10/17	Fall Break—No Class		
10/22	Carolina History & Traditions		
10/24	Discuss/analyze sources for presentation		
10/29	Effective Presentations		Journal 4 due Friday
10/31	Responsible Citizenship & Election Issues		Calculate GPA; presentation outlines due; take inventory on isidewith.com
11/5	Responsible Citizenship & Election Issues		
11/7	Career Center	Have read pages 110–121 in *Transitions*	
11/12	Resident Expert Presentation		
11/14	Resident Expert Presentation		Journal 5 due Friday

(Continued)

(*Continued*)

Date	Class Topic	Assignment for Today	Notes
11/19	Resident Expert Presentation		
11/21	Thanksgiving Break		Beyond the classroom reflection paper due
11/26	International Conversations— Thinking Globally		
11/28			
12/3			
12/5	Last Day of Class	Final exam due	

Appendix C

Sample Honor Codes

Dartmouth College Honor Code

ACADEMIC HONOR PRINCIPLE

On February 13, 1962, the Dartmouth College Faculty passed unanimously the following resolution; the text was updated by Faculty vote on May 17, 1999: Whereas, on February 1, 1962, a majority vote of the student body adopted the principle that "all academic activities will be based on student honor" and thereby accepted the responsibility, individually and collectively, to maintain and perpetuate the principle of academic honor. Therefore be it resolved that,

1. The Faculty of Dartmouth College, in recognizing the responsibility of students for their own education, assumes intellectual honesty and integrity in the performance of academic assignments, both in the classroom and outside. Each student upon enrollment at Dartmouth College accepts this responsibility with the understanding that any student who submits work which is not his or her own violates the purpose of the College and is subject to disciplinary actions, up to and including suspension and separation.

2. The Faculty recognizes its obligation: (a) to provide continuing guidance as to what constitutes academic honesty; (b) to promote procedures and circumstances which will reinforce the principle of academic honor; (c) to review constantly the effective operation of this principle.

3. The practice of proctoring examinations is hereby discontinued, though a teacher may be present at appropriate times for the purpose of administration or to answer questions.

4. The Committee on Standards shall undertake: (a) to publish and interpret the Resolution on Academic Honor to the student body each year; (b) to adjudicate reported violations according to established procedures; (c) to review constantly the effective operation of this principle and, if necessary, make recommendations to the Faculty for maintaining the spirit of this Resolution. The Faculty, administration, and students of Dartmouth College recognize the Academic Honor Principle as fundamental to the education process. Any instance of academic dishonesty is considered a violation of the Academic Honor Principle.

Fundamental to the principle of independent learning are the requirements of honesty and integrity in the performance of academic assignments, both in and out of the classroom. Dartmouth operates on the principle of academic honor, without proctoring of examinations. Any student who submits work which is not his or her own, or commits other acts of academic dishonesty, violates the purposes of the college and is subject to disciplinary actions, up to and including suspension or separation.

The Academic Honor Principle depends on the willingness of students, individually and collectively, to maintain and perpetuate standards of academic honesty. Each Dartmouth student accepts the responsibility to be honorable in the student's own academic affairs, as well as to support the Principle as it applies to others.

A number of actions are specifically prohibited by the Academic Honor Principle. These focus on plagiarism and on academic dishonesty in the taking of examinations, the writing of papers, the use of the same work in more than one course, and unauthorized collaboration. This list of examples covers the more common violations but is not intended to be exhaustive.

1. Examinations. Any student giving or receiving assistance during an examination or quiz violates the Academic Honor Principle.

2. Plagiarism. Any form of plagiarism violates the Academic Honor Principle. Plagiarism is defined as the submission or presentation of work, in any form, that is not a student's own, without acknowledgment of the source. With specific regard to papers, a simple rule dictates when it is necessary to acknowledge sources. If a student obtains information or ideas from an outside source, that source must be acknowledged. Another rule to follow is that any direct quotation must be placed in quotation marks, and the

source immediately cited. Students are responsible for the information concerning plagiarism found in Sources and Citation at Dartmouth College, available in the Deans' Offices or at <u>Sources and Citations</u>.

3. Use of the Same Work in More Than One Course. Submission of the same work in more than one course without the prior approval of all professors responsible for the courses violates the Academic Honor Principle. The intent of this rule is that a student should not receive academic credit more than once for the same work product without permission. The rule is not intended to regulate repeated use of an idea or a body of learning developed by the student, but rather the identical formulation and presentation of that idea. Thus the same paper, computer program, research project or results, or other academic work product should not be submitted in more than one course (whether in identical or rewritten form) without first obtaining the permission of all professors responsible for the courses involved. Students with questions about the application of this rule in a specific case should seek Faculty advice.

4. Unauthorized Collaboration. Whether or not collaboration in course work (labs, reports, papers, homework assignments, take-home tests, or other academic work for credit) is permitted depends on expectations established in individual courses. Students are sometimes encouraged to collaborate on laboratory work, for example, but told to write their laboratory reports independently. Students should presume that collaboration on academic work is not permitted, and that submission of collaborative work would constitute a violation of the academic honor principle, unless an instructor specifically authorizes collaboration. Students should not presume that authorization in one class applies to any other class, even classes in the same subject area. Students should discuss with instructors in advance any questions or uncertainty regarding permitted collaboration.

Faculty Guidelines for Responding to Violations of the Academic Honor Principle (Voted by the Faculty of Arts and Sciences, May 23, 1983)

An instructor who suspects that a student may have violated the Academic Honor Principle of the College should observe the following guidelines:

1. The instructor may want to discuss the suspected violation with the student(s) in order to determine that there has been no misunderstanding between the instructor and the student(s).

2. The instructor is strongly encouraged to test the validity of his or her suspicion by consulting a colleague or the department/program chair.

3. If, after consultation, the instructor believes that the suspicion is valid, the instructor should immediately bring the matter to the attention of the COS

and should inform the department/program chair. Under no circumstances should the instructor who suspects a violation of the Academic Honor Principle attempt to resolve the matter independently or in camera with the student in question.

Academic Honor Principle Sanctions

Given the fundamental nature of the Academic Honor Principle in an academic community, students should expect to be suspended if they engage in acts of academic dishonesty. Any student who submits work which is not his or her own, or commits other acts of academic dishonesty, violates the purposes of the College and is subject to disciplinary action, up to and including suspension or separation.

The COS will consider aggravating and mitigating factors, sanctions imposed in other Academic Honor Principle cases, and the student's prior disciplinary history in determining appropriate sanctions in individual cases. If a student is found responsible for violating the Academic Honor Principle, the COS acknowledges that the Faculty may reserve the right to fail the student for the exercise, the course, or both.

Santa Clara University: Honor Code

THE HONOR CODE PLEDGE

All students who apply to Santa Clara University must agree to sign the Honor Pledge. At an Honor Code induction ceremony at the start of a student's first year at Santa Clara, the student will write and sign the pledge as follows:

I am a person of integrity. I pledge, as a member of the Santa Clara University community, to abide by and uphold the honor code.

The Honor Pledge will be included in the Undergraduate Bulletin and on all faculty syllabi. On the first day of class, students should write and sign the Honor Pledge as it is written above.

Students should also write and sign the pledge before taking any tests or completing any papers and assignments worth 20 percent or more of the course grade. Faculty are encouraged to ask students to write the pledge by hand before signing it, as this method is most successful for discouraging dishonest academic behavior in class.

FACULTY RESPONSIBILITIES

All members of the University faculty will be required to become aware of the policies and procedures as outlined in the Honor Code and to uphold these within their classes.

A. *Education of the faculty*

The Honor Code Council will be responsible for orienting all new full-time and part-time faculty to the Honor Code and training them in its procedures. The Council will also be responsible for reinforcing the Honor Code as a priority among returning faculty members at the beginning of each academic year. This "orientation" at the beginning of each year should, when possible, be done prior to faculty activities in the classroom.

B. *Communicating standards of conduct to students*
1. Faculty members will assist in the education of students regarding appropriate academic behavior by referencing the Honor Code on their syllabi.
2. Faculty members should dedicate time at the beginning of and several times throughout the quarter to explain to their students the importance of the Honor Code. This discussion will include a conversation about why academic integrity is of such importance and why making an ethical commitment to honesty in one's academic work is a core characteristic of a student's academic life at Santa Clara.
3. Faculty are expected to clearly explain to students how the Honor Code applies in the context of their course. The following list is meant to be suggestive but not exhaustive of the kinds of issues that faculty could address: plagiarism and the documentation of sources (especially with regard to online research); permissible and impermissible group work and collaboration; standards for laboratory work; use of solution manuals; dual submissions (e.g., one paper submitted by a student for credit in two classes).

C. *Honor Code Pledge*

At the beginning of the academic quarter, after discussing the Honor Code and its provisions with students, faculty should require students to write out and sign the Honor Code Pledge.

Faculty members should also require students to write out and sign the Honor Code Pledge on all exams, papers, and assignments worth more than 20 percent of the final grade. If students do not turn in the

Pledge, the faculty member should approach the student about why he or she failed to do so.

D. *Responsible actions*

All faculty members or individuals with the responsibility of teaching or assisting in a course will not tolerate academic dishonesty. *Under the Honor Code, all faculty members will have the authority to determine an appropriate academic sanction for any violation of the Honor Code.*

If a faculty member becomes aware of a situation in which dishonest behavior may have occurred, he or she should take the following course of action:

1. Discuss the situation with the student(s) suspected of violating the Honor Code. If the discussion results in the decision that the original suspicion was unjustified, no additional actions need be taken. If, however, there is still a reason to suspect dishonesty, regardless of the intent or severity of the suspected violation, the faculty member should do the following:

   a. Determine an appropriate academic sanction for the violation. Faculty members may use their discretion in determining an academic sanction; however, they should first consult the sanctioning guidelines that the Honor Code Council has created before making their decision. These recommended sanctioning guidelines can be found in section E under Faculty Responsibilities.

   b. After determining the appropriate academic sanction, the faculty member should fill out an Honor Code Violation Report, which will contain a description of the alleged violation and the academic sanction decided upon. Once completed, the faculty member will send the Report to the Honor Code Council, and it will then be added to the student's Honor Code file.

While a faculty member may use his or her discretion in determining an appropriate academic penalty, faculty members are still *required* to report any violation to the Honor Code Council.

In cases where a faculty member delegates responsibility to another person for supervising academic work (e.g., supervising laboratory work, proctoring examinations), the faculty member must explain to that person the implications of the Honor Code in the context of the course and appropriate methods for reporting suspected violations to the faculty member. The faculty member teaching the course is ultimately responsible for following the procedures listed above.

E. Sanctioning guidelines

Faculty are expected, in making their determination of an academic sanction, to consult sanctioning guidelines created and promulgated by the Honor Code Council. These guidelines have been created to help achieve greater consistency of sanctions for similar violations across different departments and schools at Santa Clara University. In making their decision, faculty should be guided by the following broad distinction between different kinds of academic integrity offenses and the potentially corresponding academic sanctions.

1. A minor offense is a less serious violation, which normally carries the sanction of zero credit for the work with respect to which the violation occurred. Such an offense has some of the following characteristics: the dishonesty involved a more limited portion of the work submitted; it would not have considerably increased the student's grade in the course; and the student did not engage in extensive premeditation and planning prior to the act.

2. A major offense is a more serious violation which normally carries the penalty of an F in the course. Such an offense is one which has some of the following characteristics: the dishonesty involved a substantial portion of the work submitted; it would have considerably increased the student's grade in the course; and there is evidence of fairly extensive premeditation and planning prior to the act.

3. A flagrant offense is a violation of an unusually grave nature, which normally carries the penalty of F in the course and may warrant suspension or permanent dismissal of the student from the University. A flagrant offense would be one that has all the characteristics of a major violation listed above plus further features which make the offense more grave. For example, the student may have convinced a substantial number of classmates to participate in serious acts of dishonesty and led them in this endeavor, or the student may have engaged in several serious acts of dishonesty in the course in question, or serious acts of dishonesty in a number of courses.

Sample Paradigm for University Judicial Procedures

Santa Clara University

Ignatian Pedagogical Paradigm and the University Judicial Process

A goal of the University Judicial System is to promote the personal growth of those who commit a violation. This growth is characterized by accountability, awareness, concern, commitment, and contrition. For a student to experience this type of growth, one must engage in active reflection in a safe learning environment that challenges the student to consider different viewpoints and examine how one's behavior is not consistent with being *a person for and with others*.

THE FIVE PEDAGOGICAL STEPS:

- Context of Learning: the student's life experience and readiness to learn
- Experience: any activity that challenges the student with new ideas
- Reflection: a thoughtful reconsideration
- Action: to do something consistent with a new conviction
- Evaluation: a thoughtful review of the personal growth through this experience

REFLECTION QUESTIONS FOR SCU HEARING OFFICERS IN PREPARATION FOR MEETING WITH STUDENTS

Pre-Hearing Questions (Context of Learning)

- Do you think you behaved in a way that is contrary to how you want to act? Why or why not?
- Do you think you violated the Student Conduct Code? Why/not?
- Was your behavior consistent with what you want to achieve at SCU? What are you trying to achieve? Who do you want to be? How do you want to live your life (now and in the future)?
- What does it mean to be respectful to our community members?
- What role does being honest, just, and fair play in maintaining your personal integrity?
- Do you have all the resources you need to maintain your integrity?
- What can you do to repair the harm to yourself, others, the community that you may have caused?

Hearing Questions (Experience-Reflection)

- How could you have been more respectful to those involved and/or to yourself in this incident?
- At the point when you could have chosen to do the right thing, why didn't you choose to make a responsible decision? Can you accept that responsibility now?
- If you had acted with integrity, what would that have looked like?
- Did you have the competency to do the right thing? If not, why not?
- What was it that you were concerned about at that moment (self-interest, others, the community)? What concerns do you have now with regards to yourself, those involved, and the greater community?
- Did you treat people with dignity and respect during and after the incident?

Post-Hearing Question (Reflection-Action-Evaluation)

- How could you have been more respectful to those involved and/or to yourself?

Pre-Hearing Questions (Context of Learning)

- How has this incident impacted the community?
- Was the reported behavior consistent with what we expect from SCU students?

- Do you have all the resources you need in preparation for this upcoming hearing?
- As a hearing officer, what approach would be most effective in resolving the reported incident?

Hearing Questions (Experience-Reflection)

- How could the student have been more respectful to those involved and/or to oneself?
- At the point when the student could have chosen to do the right thing, why didn't the student choose to make a responsible decision? How can I help him/her accept that responsibility now?
- Did the student have the competency to do the right thing? If not, why not?
- Was the behavior inconsistent with his/her values?
- Did the student treat people with dignity and respect during and after the incident?
- What was the student most concerned about at that moment (self-interest, others, the community)?
- Is the student conscious of the connection between his/her behavior and current and future goals?

Post-Hearing Questions (Experience-Action-Evaluation)

- Did the student understand how she/he could have been more respectful to those involved and/or to her/himself?
- Does the student know how to repair the harm to oneself, others, or the community?
- Did the student have the competency to do the right thing? If not, why not?
- What concerns do I have now regarding those involved and the greater community?

"Ignatian Pedagogy: A Practical Approach," International Commission of the Apostolate for Jesuit Education (1993).

"Ignite the Leader in You," Fordham University, Principals of Good Practice for Student Affairs at Catholic Colleges and Universities, and Introduction to Ex Corde Ecclesiae. NJSLC (2010).

Appendix E

A Framework for Ethical Decision Making

Markkula Center for Applied Ethics

Santa Clara University

This document is designed as an introduction to thinking ethically. We all have an image of our better selves—of how we are when we act ethically or are "at our best." We probably also have an image of what an ethical community, an ethical business, an ethical government, or an ethical society should be. Ethics really has to do with all these levels—acting ethically as individuals, creating ethical organizations and governments, and making our society as a whole ethical in the way it treats everyone.

WHAT IS ETHICS?

Simply stated, ethics refers to standards of behavior that tell us how human beings ought to act in the many situations in which they find themselves—as friends, parents, children, citizens, businesspeople, teachers, professionals, and so on.

It is helpful to identify what ethics is NOT:

- Ethics is not the same as feelings. Feelings provide important information for our ethical choices. Some people have highly developed habits that make them feel bad when they do something wrong, but many people feel good even though they are doing something wrong. And often our feelings will tell us it is uncomfortable to do the right thing if it is hard.

- Ethics is not religion. Many people are not religious, but ethics applies to everyone. Most religions do advocate high ethical standards but sometimes do not address all the types of problems we face.

- Ethics is not following the law. A good system of law does incorporate many ethical standards, but law can deviate from what is ethical. Law can become ethically corrupt, as some totalitarian regimes have made it. Law can be a function of power alone and designed to serve the interests of narrow groups. Law may have a difficult time designing or enforcing standards in some important areas and may be slow to address new problems.

- Ethics is not following culturally accepted norms. Some cultures are quite ethical, but others become corrupt—or blind to certain ethical concerns (as the United States was to slavery before the Civil War). "When in Rome, do as the Romans do" is not a satisfactory ethical standard.

- Ethics is not science. Social and natural science can provide important data to help us make better ethical choices. But science alone does not tell us what we ought to do. Science may provide an explanation for what humans are like. But ethics provides reasons for how humans ought to act. And just because something is scientifically or technologically possible, it may not be ethical to do it.

WHY IDENTIFYING ETHICAL STANDARDS IS HARD

There are two fundamental problems in identifying the ethical standards we are to follow:

1. On what do we base our ethical standards?
2. How do those standards get applied to specific situations we face?

If our ethics are not based on feelings, religion, law, accepted social practice, or science, what are they based on? Many philosophers and ethicists have helped us answer this critical question. They have suggested at least five different sources of ethical standards we should use.

FIVE SOURCES OF ETHICAL STANDARDS

The Utilitarian Approach

Some ethicists emphasize that the ethical action is the one that provides the most good or does the least harm, or, to put it another way, produces the greatest balance of good over harm. The ethical corporate action, then, is the one that produces the greatest good and does the least harm for all who are affected—customers, employees, shareholders, the community, and the environment. Ethical warfare balances the good achieved in ending terrorism with the harm done to all parties through death, injuries, and destruction. The utilitarian approach deals with consequences; it tries both to increase the good done and to reduce the harm done.

The Rights Approach

Other philosophers and ethicists suggest that the ethical action is the one that best protects and respects the moral rights of those affected. This approach starts from the belief that humans have a dignity based on their human nature per se or on their ability to choose freely what they do with their lives. On the basis of such dignity, they have a right to be treated as ends and not merely as means to other ends. The list of moral rights—including the rights to make one's own choices about what kind of life to lead, to be told the truth, not to be injured, to a degree of privacy, and so on—is widely debated; some now argue that nonhumans have rights, too. Also, it is often said that rights imply duties—in particular, the duty to respect others' rights.

The Fairness or Justice Approach

Aristotle and other Greek philosophers have contributed the idea that all equals should be treated equally. Today we use this idea to say that ethical actions treat all human beings equally—or if unequally, then fairly based on some standard that is defensible. We pay people more based on their harder work or the greater amount that they contribute to an organization, and say that is fair. But there is a debate over CEO salaries that are hundreds of times larger than the pay of others; many ask whether the huge disparity is based on a defensible standard or whether it is the result of an imbalance of power and hence is unfair.

The Common Good Approach

The Greek philosophers have also contributed the notion that life in community is a good in itself and our actions should contribute to that life. This approach suggests that the interlocking relationships of society are the basis of ethical reasoning and that respect and compassion for all others—especially the vulnerable—are requirements of such reasoning. This approach also calls attention to the common conditions that are important to the welfare of everyone. This may be a system of laws, effective police and fire departments, health care, a public educational system, or even public recreational areas.

The Virtue Approach

A very ancient approach to ethics is that ethical actions ought to be consistent with certain ideal virtues that provide for the full development of our humanity. These virtues are dispositions and habits that enable us to act according to the highest potential of our character and on behalf of values like truth and beauty. Honesty, courage, compassion, generosity, tolerance, love, fidelity, integrity, fairness, self-control, and prudence are all examples of virtues. Virtue ethics asks of any action, "What kind of person will I become if I do this?" or "Is this action consistent with my acting at my best?"

PUTTING THE APPROACHES TOGETHER

Each of the approaches helps us determine what standards of behavior can be considered ethical. There are still problems to be solved, however.

The first problem is that we may not agree on the content of some of these specific approaches. We may not all agree to the same set of human and civil rights.

We may not agree on what constitutes the common good. We may not even agree on what is a good and what is a harm.

The second problem is that the different approaches may not all answer the question "What is ethical?" in the same way. Nonetheless, each approach gives us important information with which to determine what is ethical in a particular circumstance. And much more often than not, the different approaches do lead to similar answers.

MAKING DECISIONS

Making good ethical decisions requires a trained sensitivity to ethical issues and a practiced method for exploring the ethical aspects of a decision and weighing the considerations that should impact our choice of a course of action. Having a method for ethical decision making is absolutely essential. When practiced regularly, the method becomes so familiar that we work through it automatically without consulting the specific steps.

The more novel and difficult the ethical choice we face, the more we need to rely on discussion and dialogue with others about the dilemma. Only by careful exploration of the problem, aided by the insights and different perspectives of others, can we make good ethical choices in such situations.

We have found the following framework for ethical decision making a useful method for exploring ethical dilemmas and identifying ethical courses of action.

A FRAMEWORK FOR ETHICAL DECISION MAKING

Recognize an Ethical Issue

1. Could this decision or situation be damaging to someone or to some group? Does this decision involve a choice between a good and bad alternative, or perhaps between two "goods" or between two "bads"?

2. Is this issue about more than what is legal or what is most efficient? If so, how?

Get the Facts

1. What are the relevant facts of the case? What facts are not known? Can I learn more about the situation? Do I know enough to make a decision?

2. What individuals and groups have an important stake in the outcome? Are some concerns more important? Why?

3. What are the options for acting? Have all the relevant persons and groups been consulted? Have I identified creative options?

Evaluate Alternative Actions

1. Evaluate the options by asking the following questions:
   - Which option will produce the most good and do the least harm? (The Utilitarian Approach)
   - Which option best respects the rights of all who have a stake? (The Rights Approach)
   - Which option treats people equally or proportionately? (The Justice Approach)

- Which option best serves the community as a whole, not just some members? (The Common Good Approach)
- Which option leads me to act as the sort of person I want to be? (The Virtue Approach)

Make a Decision and Test It

1. Considering all these approaches, which option best addresses the situation?
2. If I told someone I respect—or told a television audience—which option I have chosen, what would they say?

Act and Reflect on the Outcome

1. How can my decision be implemented with the greatest care and attention to the concerns of all stakeholders?
2. How did my decision turn out and what have I learned from this specific situation?

This framework for thinking ethically is the product of dialogue and debate at the Markkula Center for Applied Ethics at Santa Clara University. Primary contributors include Manuel Velasquez, Dennis Moberg, Michael J. Meyer, Thomas Shanks, Margaret R. McLean, David DeCosse, Claire André, and Kirk O. Hanson. It was last revised in May 2009.

Appendix used with permission from the Markkula Center for Applied Ethics, Santa Clara University.

Appendix F

Fifteen Principles for the Design of College Ethical Development Programs

by Gary Pavela

The subject of applied ethics is returning to American colleges and universities. In the late 1980s, Derek Bok (then president at Harvard University) began to stress the importance of student "character development" (see Bok, "Ethics, the University and Society," *Harvard Magazine*, May-June, 1988, p. 39). Bok observed that "[m]oral development was a central responsibility of the American college in the last century," and argued that schools and colleges have an ongoing responsibility to affirm basic ethical principles "that have been held to be important by almost every human society of which we have any knowledge" ("Developing 'character' again at American universities," *Christian Science Monitor*, July 27, 1987, p. 21).

Bok was joined by President James O. Freedman at Dartmouth, who wrote in a 1989 *Washington Post Education Review* article that "moral development will once again become an explicit part of liberal education" ("Five Areas of Concern," August, 6, 1989, p. 18).

The views expressed by Bok and Freedman—also seen in the work of Ernest Boyer, among others—are now reflected in an array of tangible developments, like the establishment of the National Center for Academic Integrity, the creation of the Kenan Ethics Program at Duke University, and the blossoming of "ethics and the professions" and "civic responsibility" education programs at schools as diverse as Washington and Lee University and Arizona State University.

APPLIED ETHICS AND THE SCIENCES

A renewed focus on student ethical development does not require revival of traditional religious perspectives. It is in the sciences where discussion of applied ethics seems most pronounced, harkening back to Darwin's original observation in *The Descent of Man* (Norton Critical Edition, 1979, pp. 200–201) that "the development of moral qualities" in human beings "lies in . . . social instincts" that can be "strengthened by exercise or habit." Edward O. Wilson (University Research Professor and Honorary Curator in Entomology at the Museum of Comparative Zoology at Harvard University) recently wrote in this regard that:

We are learning the fundamental principle that ethics is everything. Human social existence . . . is based on the genetic propensity to form long-term contracts that evolve by culture and moral precepts and law. The rules of contract formation were not given to humanity from above, nor did they emerge randomly from the mechanics of the brain. They evolved over tens or hundreds of millennia because they conferred upon the genes prescribing them survival. . . . We are not errant children who occasionally sin by disobeying instructions from outside our species. We are adults who have discovered which covenants are necessary for survival, and we have accepted the necessity of securing them by sacred oath. (*Consilience*, Knopf, 1998, pp. 297–298)

Current interest in college ethical development programming remains comparatively unfocused. Careful thought and planning are required if continued progress is to be made. The following "fifteen principles for the design of college ethical development programs" are written to encourage continued reflection, discussion, and revision.

FIFTEEN PRINCIPLES FOR THE DESIGN OF COLLEGE ETHICAL DEVELOPMENT PROGRAMS

1. Identify and affirm the basic values and virtues necessary for community life.

Commentary
Ethical development programming will fail if it is not grounded in a broad community consensus. At secular institutions, that consensus is most likely to be based on what Sissela Bok (*Basic Values*, University of Missouri Press, 1995) calls "minimalist" ethical standards—perhaps the kind summarized by Ernest L. Boyer in *The Basic School: A Community for Learning* (Carnegie Foundation for the Advancement of Teaching, 1995):

Honesty

"Each person carries out his or her responsibilities carefully and with integrity, never claiming credit for someone else's work and being willing to acknowledge wrongdoing . . .

Respect

Each person responds sensitively to the ideas and needs of others without dismissing or degrading them . . .

Responsibility

Each person has a sense of duty to fulfill willingly the tasks he or she has accepted or been assigned . . .

Compassion

Each person is considerate and caring. There is a recognition that everyone, from time to time, feels hurt, confused, angry, or sad. Instead of ignoring such conditions, people reach out to one another . . .

Self-discipline

Each person agrees to live within limits . . . At the simplest level, self-control reflects habits of good living . . .

Perseverance

Each person is diligent, with the inner strength and determination to pursue well-defined goals . . .

Giving

Each person discovers that one of life's greatest satisfactions comes from giving to others, and recognizes that talents should be shared, through service.

2. **Recognize the fallibility and complexity of human nature.**

Commentary

Young people are skilled at detecting hypocrisy. They know human beings aren't capable of moral perfection. Affirming and teaching ethical values requires awareness of the reality of human fallibility, and the importance of viewing ethical development as a committed, life-long striving to define and lead a better life. The complexity of human nature also suggests that good and evil are somehow bound together in the human personality, and that it is the experience—and overcoming—of evil (or unrestrained self-regard) that can create great personalities, like a St. Augustine, or a Malcolm X. Microbiologist Rene Dubos wrote in this regard that:

Every perceptive adult knows he is part beast and part saint, a mixture of folly and reason, love and hate, courage and cowardice. He can be at the same time believer and doubter, idealist and skeptic, altruistic citizen and selfish hedonist. The coexistence of these conflicting traits naturally causes tension but it is nonetheless compatible with sanity. In a mysterious way, the search for identity and the pursuit of self-selected goals harmonize opposites and facilitate the integration of discordant human traits into some kind of working accord. (*The God Within*, Scribners, 1972, p. 84)

3. Address the life of the spirit, and the lifelong task of forming a self.

Commentary
Colleges aren't the only places where applied ethics may be taught. Business is paying at least as much attention to issues of personal character, usually in terms of the "emotional intelligence" needed to work productively with colleagues. The danger in the "business" approach, however, is that ethical development may be constricted, and defined to serving corporate ends.

Educational institutions have a broader mission, reflected in Alfred North Whitehead's observation that "education is the guidance of the individual towards a comprehension of the art of life" (*The Aims of Education*, Free Press, 1929, p. 39). In the broadest sense, the "art" of life encompasses learning how to understand the self, mold the self, and share the self—perhaps to the point of grasping the illusion of the self, at least as something disconnected from the world and other living beings.

There is no simple formulation to guide educators in addressing matters that touch on ultimate or "spiritual" concerns. The first step is to recognize the artificial limits that have been imposed on exploring such matters (which are not limited to the realm of religion). Those limits may reflect the fact that colleges are teaching the equivalent of "business ethics" because colleges are becoming more and more like businesses.

4. Help students consider questions and goals of pressing interest to them, including the pursuit of happiness in relationship with others.

Commentary
Students are likely to pay attention to topics that interest them. What interests students? It doesn't take extensive survey techniques to know that students (like everyone else) are interested in discovering how happiness can be found; exploring the nature of love and friendship; and wondering what to do with their lives. These are topics philosophers have pondered from the beginning of time. Students will appreciate the opportunity to reflect upon them too. What educators have to do is ask the right questions at the right time, in a climate of mutual respect and freedom.

5. Promote ethical development through experience, collaboration, conflict, and guided reflection, rather than formal "instruction" alone.

Commentary
It's a common (and astute) observation that students don't learn ethics by lectures, or out of books—any more than people learn how to ride bicycles by reading instruction manuals. Ethical development is more likely to occur in a climate of action and experience (including the experience of failure), followed by opportunities to think and reflect. What educators have to do is stimulate experience (occasionally setting limits, for safety); suggest ways to think about what has been learned; and encourage students to explore anew.

Student accomplishment in service learning or other experiential programs should be recognized in campus awards ceremonies and on transcripts. Colleges that give appropriate awards for ethical action are also likely to promote ethical thinking and a sense of concern for others.

6. Create and maintain attractive physical environments designed to promote a sense of community.

Commentary
People are attracted to beauty, and fellowship in partaking of beauty. Nurturing and commemorating beautiful places (often by rituals and ceremonies) also helps build a sense of community. With the sense of community comes the heightened possibility of moral discourse, grounded in mutual responsibility. Particularly in academic settings, discussions about obligations to a particular community can be expanded to include

consideration of broader obligations to build and maintain a better world for everyone—including the generations to come.

7. Foster periods of silence, peace, and reflection.

Commentary
"Speed," time, and noise all have important impacts on human behavior. One does not have to observe metropolitan traffic patterns long to understand that the accelerating pace of life contributes to aggression and incivility. Wilhelm von Humboldt's famous "five conditions of a true university" included solitude—and for good reason. It is in moments of peace and solitude that the incessant clamoring of the self fade away, and a sense of eternity (whatever is outside of time) appears. For many, a sense of timelessness is associated with feelings of harmony, trust, love, and empathy—perhaps the highest attributes of ethical development.

8. Recruit students, administrators, and faculty members who are truth-seeking and intellectually and ethically alive.

Commentary
Being intellectually and ethically alive means being attentive to interpreting experiences with empathy and reason in an effort to define and live by values that help oneself and others lead a life of love and fulfillment, including the fulfillment of productive work. These are capabilities students can demonstrate in high school, as organizers of community service programs, leaders of honor societies or religious groups, or social or political activists. Targeted recruitment efforts should be made to find such students—by regular contact with teachers and guidance counselors and careful attention to press reports (including school newspaper stories) about the activities of outstanding candidates. Once students are recruited, an emphasis on ethical development can be reflected in application questions or essays that raise ethical questions (e.g., "How do you plan to add to the building of the world?").

For teachers and administrators, being intellectually and ethically alive also suggests the kind of spiritual vitality and commitment described by Page Smith in *Killing the Spirit: Higher Education in America* (Viking, 1990, p. 203):

[T]he true person has some vision of higher things . . . [that] touch the deepest levels of our consciousness and solace us, inspire us, reconcile us to our humanity. They are the wellsprings of life. The most familiar and most mysterious is love. . . . Love is the mortar of our perilously fragile lives . . . it is indistinguishable from grace. None of us [is] worthy of it, and yet all of us must have it to live. It can't be taught. We can have any number of courses on sex education (sex has little to do with love, although love of course may include sex, rather as an afterthought), but who can imagine a university course on love? . . . Teachers who love their students are of course by that very fact teaching their students the nature of love, although the course may in fact be chemistry or computer science. . . . And, in a curious way, the professor, although he seldom realizes it, needs them as much as they need him. So long as he refuses to take them to heart, they are simply an inconvenience, a burden, a part of his "teaching load."

9.   Design a curriculum that poses challenging ethical questions and helps students acquire the knowledge and experience to address them.

Commentary
History, literature, art, and all the humanities can promote student ethical development by telling stories rich with human drama. Good teaching can bring the drama alive and use it to raise timeless moral questions. The sciences have the capacity to make an equally powerful contribution. Scientific inquiry is grounded in identifiable virtues like honesty, courage, dedication, and the willingness to accept criticism and learn from failure. Students will learn to appreciate those virtues by seeing living examples of how scientists practice them on a daily basis.

The evolution of college curricula is also shifting toward experiential learning and internships. That's a desirable outcome for student ethical development, since experiential learning (particularly in circumstances where clients or customers require care or assistance) can be designed to foster a sense of empathy. Regardless of the setting, experiential learning also provides immediate, personal experience with inevitable human conflicts and issues of professional ethics. Teachers managing internship experiences have an obligation to ask questions that can bring ethical issues into focus and help students formulate principled responses.

Many campuses are also weaving leadership training programs into the curriculum. Those programs should emphasize what experience (and research) has demonstrated: the foundation of good leadership is integrity, especially the ability to inspire and maintain trust.

10. Affirm and teach academic integrity as a core institutional value.

Commentary
Just as monasteries preserved ancient learning during the dark ages, college and university academic integrity policies helped maintain a foundation

for moral discourse on college campuses during the last three decades of the twentieth century. It's virtually impossible to find any other component of academic life that permitted reference to concepts like "honor," "trust," or "integrity." Student leaders, faculty members, and administrators need to strengthen the institutional commitment to academic integrity—perhaps by developing new forms of student-managed honor codes—and use expanded and creative forms of academic integrity programming to reach a broader segment of the campus community.

11. **Give students structured opportunities to discuss, formulate, and administer student conduct policies and related ethical development programming.**

Commentary
Giving students significant responsibility to formulate and administer student conduct policies helps them acquire immediate insights into the challenges and complexities of any legal system—especially the careful balance that has to be drawn between procedural rights and community interests. The experience students gain in helping to resolve contested cases has the potential to enhance their own ethical development (particularly if issues and conflicts are discussed in the context of broader principles) and the programming they might develop for fellow students. Above all, as Derek Bok has suggested, disciplinary systems should be designed to encourage thoughtful conversation about why particular rules are necessary, and the ethical principles those rules may be based upon.

12. **Distinguish legal requirements from ethical obligations.**

Commentary
Colleges are awash in programs designed to alert students to their legal responsibilities, usually involving substance abuse, sexual harassment, sexual assault, and misuse of computer facilities. There's a growing danger that legal analysis will be substituted for ethical judgment. Generally, the law should be regarded as a floor, not a ceiling. Whenever legal requirements are identified, ethical issues should also be raised, preferably by role playing or other devices designed to elicit sympathy and understanding.

13. **Use the popularity and prominence of athletic programs to affirm institutional values and foster character.**

Commentary
Whether academics like it or not, intercollegiate athletics has assumed a powerful "teaching" role in the lives of many students. It can affirm virtues

like courage, tenacity, commitment, self-sacrifice, and teamwork—or qualities like greed, cynicism, hypocrisy, and rudeness. Whether intercollegiate athletics helps or hinders student ethical development depends on forceful leadership by college presidents and athletic directors, including a willingness to hold even the most prominent coaches and players to basic standards of civility and honesty.

14. **Implement "wellness" and substance abuse programs that include an awareness of responsibilities to self and others.**

Commentary
"Wellness" programming, just like programming on legal requirements, can disguise ethical issues and inhibit ethical development. It is not "blaming the victim" to suggest that each person has at least some ultimate responsibility for his or her own conduct, including the decision to use alcohol and other drugs. Eric Fromm had an important insight in this regard in his book *The Heart of Man* (Harper and Row, 1964, p. 133):

The argument for the view that man has no freedom to choose the better against the worse is to some considerable extent based on the fact that one looks usually at the last decision in a chain of events, and not at the first or second ones. Indeed, at the point of final decision the freedom to choose has usually vanished. But it may still have been there at an earlier point when the person was not yet so deeply caught in his own passions. One might generalize by saying that one of the reasons why most people fail in their lives is precisely because they are not aware of the point when they were still free to act according to reason, and because they are aware of the choice only at the point when it is too late for them to make a decision." Educators could also benefit from studying a broad range of ways to limit substance abuse and other forms of self-destructive behavior. Research has shown, for example, that Alcoholics Anonymous (AA) can be an effective program for motivated participants (see Morganstern, J., Department of Psychiatry, Mount Sinai School of Medicine, "Affiliation with Alcoholics Anonymous after Treatment," *Journal of Clinical and Consulting Psychology*, 65: 768–777, 1997). Essential components of the AA program (e.g. making "a searching and fearless moral inventory" and making "direct amends" to people harmed by participants' abusive drinking) highlight the sense of hope that comes with ethical insight and personal accountability.

15. **Encourage staff members to develop and use the skills of ethical dialogue.**

Commentary
Many college and university staff members have opportunities to discuss serious, sometimes intensely personal matters with students. Those

conversations may be remembered for years, especially by students who hunger for mature wisdom and guidance. Staff members don't need formal training in philosophy to ask thoughtful questions designed to promote ethical thinking (Socrates also lacked a doctorate). It's probably sufficient to know that the best questions—and subsequent discussions—will usually encompass variations of two classic formulations: *How is a good life defined?* and *How will the values and habits you are acquiring now help you lead a good life?*

Appendix G

Additional Resources

The following is a list of resources that can be helpful in ethics formation among college students. This is not meant to be an exhaustive list by any means. Those interested in general and specific categories of ethics may find the following information and Web sites of value.

NOTABLE ETHICS CENTERS FOCUSED ON IN THIS VOLUME

Markkula Center for Applied Ethics, Santa Clara University

The Markkula Center for Applied Ethics at Santa Clara University is one of the preeminent centers for research and dialogue on ethical issues in critical areas of American life. The center promotes the role of ethics in everyday life, providing practical tools for ethical living and action. The center attempts to create a meaningful, positive impact on the ethical behavior of institutional leaders and of individuals in their institutional, professional, and personal lives by helping them make more informed ethical choices. http://www.scu.edu/ethics/

Ethics Institute, Dartmouth College

The Ethics Institute at Dartmouth has interests in applied and professional ethics ranging from medical, business, legal, and engineering ethics to the ethics of teaching and research. Dartmouth faculty who teach ethics have acquired a national reputation for their commitment to the objectivity and rationality of moral values. This perspective adds a distinctive dimension to their teaching and research in areas such as medical and business ethics. http://www.dartmouth.edu/~ethics/

COLLEGE STUDENT ETHICS TRAINING AND FORMATION RESOURCES

Campus Clarity

Campus Clarity offers online training for students, faculty, and staff on a variety of campus related issues inspired by Title IX and the SaVE Act. It is a subdivision of LawRoom, which has been offering online training for organizations since 1994. Student-centered training offers modules on dating, sexual assault, alcohol use and abuse, and other topics. https://home.campusclarity.com/

National Resource Center — First Year Experience and Students in Transition

The National Resource Center - First Year Experience and Students in Transition offers a wide variety of resources, including over 20 sample syllabi from across the country on Freshmen 101–style classes. The center offers policies, scholarship, and best practice associated with students transitioning from high school to college environments. The University of South Carolina hosts the center and maintains their Web site. http://sc.edu/fye/

The International Center for Academic Integrity (ICAI)

The International Center for Academic Integrity (ICAI) focuses on student cheating, plagiarism, and academic dishonesty in higher education institutions. It also seeks to advance a culture of integrity within academic communities across the globe. ICAI offers assessment services, resources, and consultations to member institutions, and hosts an annual conference. http://www.academicintegrity.org/icai/about-1.php

ALCOHOL & OTHER DRUGS

Monitoring the Future: National Survey Results on Drug Use, 1975–2013, Volume 2, College Students and Adults Ages 19–55. This research from a team at the University of Michigan offers insightful information about alcohol consumption by college-age students. http://www.moni toringthefuture.org//pubs/monographs/mtf-vol2_2013.pdf

A Call to Action: Changing the Culture of Drinking at U.S. Colleges, April 2002. This National Institute of Alcohol Abuse and Alcoholism (NIAAA) document thoughtfully discusses the need to change the culture of college-student drinking on campus. http://www.collegedrinking prevention.gov/media/taskforcereport.pdf   http://www.collegedrinking prevention.gov/niaaacollegematerials/taskforce/taskforce_toc.aspx

SEXUAL VIOLENCE

Rape and Sexual Assault Victimization among College-Age Females, 1995–2013. This report from the U.S. Department of Justice outlines the best available data on sexual assaults on campus. http://www.bjs.gov /content/pub/pdf/rsavcaf9513.pdf

One in Four, Inc.

One in Four, Inc., is a nonprofit organization focused on the prevention of sexual assault by the application of theory and research to sexual assault prevention programming. One in Four provides presentations, trainings, and technical assistance with a focus on single-sex programming targeted toward colleges, high schools, the military, and local community organizations. http://www.oneinfourusa.org/statistics.php

Not Alone: The First Report of the White House Task Force to Protect Students from Sexual Assault, April 2014. http://www.whitehouse.gov /sites/default/files/docs/report_0.pdf

NOTABLE BOOKS

Brooks, D. (2015). *The road to character.* New York: Random House.

Damon, W. (2008). *Moral child: Nurturing children's natural moral growth.* New York: Simon and Schuster.

Firestone, R., & Catlett, J. (2009). *The ethics of interpersonal relationships.* London: Karnac Books.

Karp, D. R. (2015). *The little book of restorative justice for colleges and universities: Repairing harm and rebuilding trust in response to student misconduct.* New York: Skyhorse Publishing.

Plante, T. G. (2004). *Do the right thing: Living ethically in an unethical world.* Oakland, CA: New Harbinger Publications.

Smith, C., Christoffersen, K., Davidson, H., & Herzog, P. S. (2011). *Lost in transition: The dark side of emerging adulthood.* New York: Oxford University Press.

References

Bandura, A. (1986). *Social foundations of thought and action: A social cognitive theory.* New York: Prentice-Hall, Inc.

Bowman, N. A. (2013). How much diversity is enough? The curvilinear relationship between college diversity interactions and first-year student outcomes. *Research in Higher Education, 54*(8), 874–894.

Brooks, D. (2015). *The road to character.* New York: Random House.

Carpendale, J. I. (2000). Kohlberg and Piaget on stages and moral reasoning. *Developmental Review, 20*(2), 181–205.

Damon, W. (1988). *The moral child. Nurturing children's natural moral growth.* New York: Free Press.

Damon, W. (2008). *Moral child: Nurturing children's natural moral growth.* New York: Simon and Schuster.

Damon, W., & Colby, A. (1987). Social influence and moral change. In W. M. Kurtines & J. L. Gewirtz (Eds.), *Moral development through social interaction* (pp. 3–19). New York: Wiley.

Fabes, R. A., Carlo, G., Kupanoff, K., & Laible, D. (1999). Early adolescence and prosocial/moral behavior I: The role of individual processes. *The Journal of Early Adolescence, 19*(1), 5–16.

Facts & stats. (2015, February). Retrieved from http://www.plagiarism.org /resources/facts-and-stats/

Feldman, R. S. (2007). *Adolescence.* Upper Saddle River, NJ: Pearson/Prentice Hall.

Firestone, R., & Catlett, J. (2009). *The ethics of interpersonal relationships.* London: Karnac Books.

Florida State University. (n.d.). *Florida State University 2016–2017 general bulletin —undergraduate edition: Academic integrity and grievances: A summons to responsible freedom, values and moral standards at Florida State University.* Retrieved from http://registrar.fsu.edu/bulletin/undergrad/info/integrity.htm

Gill, J. (2008, April 24). Cultural insight can help tackle plagiarism. *Times Higher Education*. Retrieved from https://www.timeshighereducation.com/news/cultural-insight-can-help-tackle-plagiarism/401564.article

Gilligan, C. (1982). *In a different voice*. Boston, MA: Harvard University Press.

Goleman, D. (1997). Foreword: Emotional intelligence in context. In P. Salovey & D. J. Sluyter, *Emotional development and emotional intelligence* (p. 8). New York: Basic Books.

Hart, D., Burock, D., London, B., & Atkins, R. (2003). Prosocial tendencies, antisocial behavior, and moral development. In A. Slater & G. Bremner (Eds.), *An introduction to developmental psychology* (pp. 334–356). Malden, MA: Blackwell.

Karp, D. R. (2015). *The little book of restorative justice for colleges and universities: Repairing harm and rebuilding trust in response to student misconduct*. New York: Skyhorse Publishing.

Karp, D. R., & Sacks, C. (2014). Student conduct, restorative justice, and student development: findings from the STARR project: A student accountability and restorative research project. *Contemporary Justice Review*, *17*(2), 154–172.

Kingree, J. B., & Thompson, M. P. (2013). Fraternity membership and sexual aggression: An examination of mediators of the association. *Journal of American College Health, 61*(4), 213–221. doi:10.1080/07448481.2013.781026

Kohlberg, L. (1984). *The psychology of moral development: The nature and validity of moral stages* (Vol. 2). New York: HarperCollins College Division.

Korn, M. (2015, March 26). Stanford University latest top school to face cheating claims: The school is probing "an unusually high number" of claims of academic dishonesty among students. *Wall Street Journal*. Retrieved from http://www.wsj.com/articles/stanford-university-latest-top-school-to-face-cheating-claims-1427387107

Lih-Juan ChanLin (2015). Tablet reading service for college students. *Procedia - Social and Behavioral Sciences, 197*, 231–235.

Lythcott-Haims, J. (2015). *How to raise an adult*. New York: Macmillan.

Mayhew, M. J., Seifert, T. A., & Pascarella, E. T. (2010). A multi-institutional assessment of moral reasoning development among first-year students. *The Review of Higher Education, 33*(3), 357–390.

Mills, B. A., Bersamina, R. B., & Plante, T. G. (2007). The impact of college student immersion service learning trips on coping with stress and vocational identity. *The Journal for Civic Commitment, 9*, 1–8.

Mottola, A. (Trans.). (1964). *The spiritual exercises of St. Ignatius: St. Ignatius' profound precepts of mystical theology*. New York: Doubleday.

National Collegiate Athletic Association. (2005). *NCAA division one manual*. NCAA.

National Collegiate Athletic Association. (n.d. a). *Fairness and integrity*. Retrieved from http://textlab.io/doc/9202268/ncaa-game-day-environment-and-fan-code-of-conduct-ncaa

National Collegiate Athletic Association. (n.d. b). *NCAA game day environment and fan code of conduct.* Retrieved from https://www.ncaa.org/sites /default/files/Fan%2BCode%2Bof%2BConduct.pdf

National Football League. (2014). NFL introduces award to recognize outstanding sportmanship. Retrieved from http://www.nfl.com/news/ story/0ap3000000414839/printable/nfl-introduces-award-to-recognize-outstanding-sportsmanship

National Institutes of Health Task Force of the National Advisory Council on Alcohol Abuse and Alcoholism. (2002, April). *High-risk drinking in college: What we know and what we need to learn.* Retrieved from http:// www.collegedrinkingprevention.gov/media/FINALPanel1.pdf

Park, A., Sher, K. J., & Krull, J. L. (2008). Risky drinking in college changes as fraternity/sorority affiliation changes: A person-environment perspective. *Psychology of Addictive Behaviors, 22*(2), 219–229. doi:10.1037/0893 -164X.22.2.219

Park, J. J., & Kim, Y. K. (2013). Interracial friendship and structural diversity: Trends for Greek, religious, and ethnic student organizations. *Review of Higher Education, 37*(1), 1–24. Retrieved from http://search.proquest .com.libproxy.scu.edu/docview/1465331477?accountid=13679

Piaget, J. (1932). *The moral development of the child.* London: Kegan Paul.

Pino, N. W., & Smith, W. L. (2003). College students and academic dishonesty. *College Student Journal, 37*(4), 490.

Plante, L. G. (2007). *Bleeding to ease the pain: Cutting, self-injury, and the adolescent search for self.* Westport, CT: Greenwood Publishing Group.

Plante, T. G. (2004). *Do the right thing: Living ethically in an unethical world.* Oakland, CA: New Harbinger Publications.

Plante, T. G., Lackey, K., & Hwang, J. (2009). The impact of immersion trips on development of compassion among college students. *Journal of Experiential Education, 32,* 28–43.

Powell, M. (2016, March 4). The tragedy of hall of fame coach and his star recruit. *New York Times.* Retrieved from http://www.nytimes.com/2016/03/06 /sports/ncaabasketball/smu-keith-frazier-larry-brown-corruption.html

Santa Clara University. (2015). *Santa Clara University student handbook 2015– 16.* Retrieved from https://www.scu.edu/media/offices/student-life /purge/SCU_Student_Handbook_2015-16_FINAL.pdf

Sauter, M. B., Stebbins, S., Frohlich, T. C., & Comen, E. (2015, September 11). Highest paid public employee in every state. *Wall Street Journal.* Retrieved from http://247wallst.com/special-report/2015/09/11/highest-paid-emplo yee-in-each-state/

Sebok, T., & Goldblum, A. (1999). Establishing a campus restorative justice program. *Journal of the California Caucus of College and University Ombuds, 2*(1) 13–22.

Seider, S., Huguley, J., & Novick, S. (2013). College students, diversity, and community service learning. Retrieved December 1, 2015, from http:// www.tcrecord.org.libproxy.scu.edu/library/content.asp?contentid= 16880

Skidmore College. (n.d.). Project on restorative justice at colleges and universities. Retrieved on January 10, 2016, from http://www.skidmore.edu/campusrj/

Smith, C., Christoffersen, K., Davidson, H., & Herzog, P. S. (2011). *Lost in transition: The dark side of emerging adulthood.* New York: Oxford University Press.

U.S. Department of Justice. (2014). *Rape and sexual assault victimization among college-age females, 1995–2013.* Washington, DC: Author.

U.S. Department of Health and Human Services. (2002). *A call to action: Changing the culture of drinking at U.S. colleges.* Washington, DC: Author.

Wechsler, H., Davenport, A., Dowdall, G., Moeykens, B., & Castillo, S. (1994). Health and behavioral consequences of binge drinking in college: A national survey of students at 140 campuses. *Journal of the American Medical Association, 272*(21), 1672–1677.

White House Task Force to Protect Students from Sexual Assault. (2014, April). *Not alone: The first report of the White House task force to protect students from sexual assault.* Washington, DC: Author.

Williams, A. E., & Janosik, S. M. (2007). An examination of academic dishonesty among sorority and non-sorority women. *Journal of College Student Development, 48*(6), 706.

Index

Absolute moral rules, 30–31
Academic demands: ethical challenges with, 83; student perspective on, 92–95
Accountability as active process, 148
Activism, best practices, 117–120
Adolescence: stages of, 9
Alcohol use: additional resources, 219–220; data on, xi–xii; Greek life, best practices, 128–132; identity formation and, 15; RRICC decision making example, 46–47; student perspectives, 95–96. *See also* Campus judicial procedures, best practices
Alternative spring break, 70–71
Alumni boosters: athletes, as inspirational speakers, 157–158; athletics, 136; best practices, overview, 153–154; expanding stakeholder groups, 154–156; mentoring groups, 156–157
Applied ethics: program design principles, 208–217; sample class syllabi, 171–181
Aristotle, 123
Athletics, best practices: alumni boosters, 136; athletes as inspirational speakers, 157–158; community service, 135–136; current ethical issues, 138–139; health concerns, 138–139; modeling by coaches and leaders, 135; nurturing ethical behavior, 137–138; overview of, 133–135, 166–167; students as avid fans, 136–137
Autonomous cooperation stage, 9
Autonomy: ethical challenges with, 82

Bandura, Al, 53
Behavior reinforcement, 54–55
Best practices: organizational culture and, 56–57. *See also* Athletics, best practices; Campus judicial procedures, best practices; Community relations, best practices; Curriculum, best practices; Extracurricular activities, best practices
Black Lives Matter Protest, Dartmouth, 119–120
Brooks, David, 51, 75
Byrne, Allison, 97

Campus Clarity, 219
Campus Crusade for Christ, 71–72

Campus judicial procedures, best
practices: overview, 141–142, 167–
168; parents as partners, 151–152;
restorative justice and reconciliation,
146–149; role of colleges, 144–146;
Santa Clara University sample
paradigm, 199–201; Title IX, impact
of, 150–151
Camus, Albert, 27
Chalaka, Sonya, 98–99
Chalkboards, public, 116–117
Character, student decisions about,
86–88
Cheating: data on, xii–xiii; NCAA
rules, 134–135; student
perspectives on, 98–101. *See also*
Campus judicial procedures, best
practices
Chief ethics officer, 55
Code of conduct. *See* Campus judicial
procedures, best practices
Cognitive development, 9
College: examples of ethical
situations, 5–8; as unique
experience, 3–4. *See also*
Universities and ethical thought
Commencement speakers, 154
Common good, 33, 204–205
Community relations, best practices:
expanding stakeholder groups,
154–156; mentoring groups,
156–157; overview, 153–154
Community service: alternative spring
and semester breaks, 70–71; by
athletes, 135–136; best practices,
113–114; Greek life, best practices,
129–130
Compassion, RRICC model and,
42–43
Competence, RRICC model and,
41–42
Concern, RRICC model and, 42–43
Corrective feedback, 57
Counseling services, 72
Crime. *See* Campus judicial
procedures, best practices

Cultural relativism, 28–29
Culture: academic pressure, student
perspectives, 92–95; plagiarism
in China, 94–95. *See also*
Organizational culture of
ethics; Universities and ethical
thought
Curriculum, best practices: applied
ethics class, sample syllabi, 171–
181; daily life applications, 108–
109; ethical development program
design, 208–217; foundations in
moral philosophy, 107; Freshman
101 course, 109–110; Freshman
101 course, sample syllabi, 182–
190; overview, 105–107, 166–167;
specific discipline applications,
107–108

Daily life, ethical application in,
108–109
Damon, William, 11
Dartmouth Black Lives Matter Protest,
119–120
Dartmouth College Ethics Institute,
218–219
Dartmouth College Honor Code,
191–194
Deamer, Christian, 97–98
Decision making. *See* Ethical decision
making
Detachment, Four Ds, 56
Development, moral: Gilligan on,
10–11; high-risk students, 22–25;
Kohlberg on, 9–10; Piaget on, 9;
through adolescence, 8–11. *See also*
Four I's
Developmental status, ethics
education and, 65–66
Direction, Four Ds, 57
Discernment, Four Ds, 56–57
Discipline. *See* Campus judicial
procedures, best practices
Discovery, Four Ds, 56
Discussion groups, ethics topics,
72–74

Donors: best practices, overview, 153–154; expanding stakeholder groups, 154–156; mentoring groups, 156–157

Dorms. *See* Residential life, best practices

Economic forces, delayed independence and, 14

Edison, Thomas, 67

Education, ethical thought and: applied ethics class, sample syllabi, 171–181; college promotional materials, 78–79; culture of ethics, maintaining, 164–166; developmental considerations, 65–66; ethical development program design, 208–217; ethics curriculum, 62; ethics events, status of, 64; faculty and staff models, 63–64; Honor Code, Dartmouth College, 191–194; Honor Code, Santa Clara University, 196–198; honor codes, 162–163; overview of, 59; pre-orientation and orientation, 61–62, 163–164; student governance and adjudication, 64–65; student leaders and models, 63; value of ethics skill building, 168–169. *See also* Curriculum, best practices

Egoism, 29–30

Environment, moral development and, 11

Ethical decision making: ethical development program design, 208–217; five-step approach for, 34–36; Four Ds, 56–57; framework for, 202–207; in practice, 43–47. *See also* RRICC model

Ethical development program design, 208–217

Ethics Bowls, 116

Ethics curriculum. *See* Curriculum, best practices

Ethics Institute, Dartmouth College, 218–219

Ethics ombudsman, 56

Expectations, setting of, 52–53

Extracurricular activities, best practices: community services activities, 113–114; Ethics Bowls, 116; Greek life, 115–116; overview, 113, 166–167; public chalkboards, 116–117; student activism and protest, 117–120; student clubs and organizations, 114–115

Extracurricular activities, ethics in, 62

Faculty: as ethical leaders, 63–64

Fair, James, 100

Faith communities: alternative spring and semester breaks, 70–71; counseling services, 72; overview of role, 67–69; Shabbat dinners, 71–72; speakers and discussion groups, 72–74

Feedback, corrective, 57

Females: moral development of, 10–11

Florida State University (FSU), Spiritual Life Project, 69

Four Ds, 56–57

Four I's: high-risk students, 22–25; identity, 14–15; impulse control, 20–22; independence, 16–17; intimacy, 17–20; overview of, 13–14; parent use of, 77–78

Framework for ethical decision making, 202–207

Fraternities, 97–98, 115–116, 128–132

Freshman 101 ethics course, 109–110; sample syllabi, 182–190. *See also* Curriculum, best practices

Friendships, intimacy and, 17–20

Gender, moral development and, 10–11

Gilligan, Carol, 10–11

Golden Rule, 38–39

Goldstein, Noah, 100

Goleman, Daniel, 20

Gomez, Phil, 100
Greek life: best practices, 115–116; residential life, 128–132; student perspectives on, 97–98

Hillel Centers, 71–72
Hines, Zach, 92
Honorary degrees, 154
Honor codes, 162–163; Dartmouth College, 191–194; Santa Clara University, 196–198
Hookups, 18

Identity, sense of, 14–15; high-risk students, 22–25
Impulse control, 20–22; high-risk students, 22–25
Incipient cooperation stage, 9
Independence, 16–17; ethical challenges with, 82; high-risk students, 22–25
Integrity, RRICC model and, 40–41
International Center for Academic Integrity (ICAI), 219
International student perspectives, 93–95
Internships, RRICC decision making example, 44–45
Intimacy, 17–20; high-risk students, 22–25

Judicial procedures. See Campus judicial procedures, best practices
Justice: as moral philosophy, 32, 204; restorative justice, 146–149, 167–168

Kant, Emmanuel, 30–31
Karp, David, 141, 146–147
Kohlberg, Lawrence, 9–10

Leadership: as behavior model, 53–54; behavior reinforcement, 54–55; coaches and team leaders, 135; commencement speakers, 154; faculty and staff, 63–64; honorary

degrees, 154; student character choices and, 88; student leaders and models, 63
Living arrangements. See Residential life, best practices

Males, moral development of, 10–11
Maltzer, Ian, 96
Markkula Center for Applied Ethics, 202–207, 218
Marriage, median age of, 14
Mentors, 154, 156–157
Mischel, Walter, 20
Mission statements, 59, 129
Modeling behavior: coaches and team leaders, 135; commencement speakers, 154; honorary degrees, 154; organizational culture, 53–54
Moral absolutism, 30–31
The Moral Child: Nurturing Children's Moral Growth (1988), 11
Moral development: Gilligan on, 10–11; high-risk students, 22–25; Kohlberg on, 9–10; Piaget on, 9; through adolescence, 8–11
Moral philosophy: absolute moral rules, 30–31; common good, 33, 204–205; cultural relativism, 28–29; curriculum best practices, 107; decision making, five-step approach, 34–36; egoism, 29–30; justice approach, 32, 204; overview of, 27–28; rights approach, 31–32, 204; social contract, 31; sources of ethical standards, 203–204; utilitarianism, 30, 203–204; virtue, 33–34, 205. See also RRICC model

National Resource Center-First Year Experience and Students in Transition, 219
NCAA rules, 134–135, 137. See also Athletics, best practices
New student orientation, 61–62, 163–164. See also Universities and ethical thought

Olhausen, Jessica, 98
One in Four, Inc., 220
Organizational culture of ethics: behavior reinforcement, 54–55; corrective feedback, 57; expectations, setting of, 52–53; modeling behavior, 53–54; overview, 51, 164–166; skill building and problem solving, 55; tools for acting ethically, 56–57

Parents, role of: campus judicial policies and, 151–152; discussing ethical situations, 81–83; Four I's, use of, 77–78; opening a dialogue, 77; overview, 75–76; review college materials for ethics content, 78–79; RRICC model, use of, 79–81; trust, building of, 76
Paulson, Henry, 113
Pavela, Gary, 208–217
Philosophy, moral: absolute moral rules, 30–31; common good, 33, 204–205; cultural relativism, 28–29; decision making, five-step approach, 34–36; egoism, 29–30; justice approach, 32, 204; overview of, 27–28; rights approach, 31–32, 204; social contract, 31; sources of ethical standards, 202–203; utilitarianism, 30, 203–204; virtue, 33–34, 205. See also RRICC model
Piaget, Jean, 9
Plagiarism, Chinese culture and, 94–95. See also Campus judicial procedures, best practices
Plante, Lori, 13–14
Plante, Tom, 37
Problem solving, 55
Protests, best practices, 117–120
Public chalkboards, 116–117

Reconciliation, 146–149
Relationships: ethical challenges in, 81–82; high-risk students, 22–25; intimacy and, 17–20

Religion, ethical principles of, 37–38. See also Faith communities
Residential life, best practices: bulletin board use, 127–128; Greek life and, 128–132; initial dorm meetings, 127; monthly ethics conversations, 127; overview, 123–126; written statement of ethical goals, 126
Respect, RRICC model and, 38–39
Responsibility, RRICC model and, 39–40
Restorative justice, 146–149, 167–168; Santa Clara University judicial procedures, 199–201
Rights approach, moral philosophy, 31–32, 204
Romantic relationships, intimacy and, 17–20
Roosevelt, Teddy, 37
RRICC model: competence, 41–42; concern, 42–43; decision making in practice, 43–47; integrity, 40–41; overview of, 37–38; parent use of, 79–81; respect, 38–39; responsibility, 39–40

Santa Clara University: alternative spring break, 70; community outreach programs, 155–156; Ethics Board, 116–117; ethics course requirement, 106; framework for ethical decision making, 202–207; honor code, 196–198; Markkula Center for Applied Ethics, 218–219; mission statement, 59; paradigm for judicial procedures, 199–201. See also Student perspectives
Schiel, Megan, 92–93
Schweitzer, Albert, 59, 161
Scrunton, Roger, 153
Self, sense of, 14–15
Self-regulation: ethical challenges with, 82; impulse control, 20–22
Semester breaks, 70–71

Sexual activity: additional resources, 220; ethical challenges with, 82–83; high-risk students, 22–25; intimacy and, 17–20. *See also* Campus judicial procedures, best practices

Sexual assault, data on, xi–xii

Shabbat dinners, 71–72

Singer, Peter, 85

Skill building, 55

Smith, Christian, 3, 13, 105

Social contract, 31

Social learning: moral development and, 11

Sororities, 97–98, 115–116, 128–132

Speakers on campus, 72–74, 157–158

Spiritual Exercises, 56

Spiritual traditions. *See* Faith communities

Sports. *See* Athletics, best practices

Spring breaks, 70–71

Staff, as ethical leaders, 63–64

STARR Project, 148

St. Ignatius of Loyola, 56

Student activism and protest, 117–120

Student clubs and organizations, best practices, 114–115

Student perspectives: on academic pressure, 92–95; on alcohol, 95–96; on building ethical muscles, 91–92; on cheating, 98–101; Greek life, 97–98

Student roles: applied ethics class, sample syllabi, 182–190; as avid sports fans, 136–137; character decisions, 86–88; developmental considerations, 65–66; ethics governance and adjudication, 64–65; Freshman 101 ethics course, sample syllabi, 182–190; Honor Code, Dartmouth College, 191–194; Honor Code, Santa Clara University, 196–198; overview,

85–86; student leaders, 63; understanding the benefits of ethics, 88–90. *See also* Universities and ethical thought

Title IX, impact of, 150–151

Tools for acting ethically, 56–57

Trust, between parent and child, 76

Turgeon, Michael, 99–100

Twain, Mark, 133

Universities and ethical thought: applied ethics class, sample syllabi, 171–181; culture of ethics, maintaining, 164–166; developmental considerations, 65–66; ethical development program design, 208–217; ethics curriculum, 62; ethics events, status of, 64; faculty and staff models, 63–64; Honor Code, Dartmouth College, 191–194; Honor Code, Santa Clara University, 196–198; honor codes, 162–163; overview of, 3–8, 59; pre-orientation and orientation, 61–62, 163–164; promotional materials, 78–79; student governance and adjudication, 64–65; student leaders and models, 63; value of ethics skill building, 168–169. *See also* Curriculum, best practices

University of Colorado Boulder, restorative justice program, 149

Utilitarianism, 30, 203–204

Virtue, 33–34, 205

Volunteer services: by athletes, 135–136; best practices, 113–114; Greek life, best practices, 129–130

Wickstron, Teresa, 96

Yang, Evangeline, 95

About the Authors

THOMAS G. PLANTE, PhD, ABPP, is the Augustin Cardinal Bea, S. J. University Professor and directs the Spirituality and Health Institute at Santa Clara University. He is also an adjunct clinical professor of psychiatry and behavioral sciences at Stanford University School of Medicine. He recently served as vice chair of the National Review Board for the Protection of Children and Youth for the U.S. Conference of Catholic Bishops and is past president of the Society for the Psychology of Religion and Spirituality (Division 36) of the American Psychological Association. He has authored or edited 20 books, including *Religion, Spirituality, and Positive Psychology: Understanding the Psychological Fruits of Faith* (2012, Praeger), *Sexual Abuse in the Catholic Church: A Decade of Crisis, 2002–2012* (2011, Praeger), *Spiritual Practices in Psychotherapy: Thirteen Tools for Enhancing Psychological Health* (2009), and *Do the Right Thing: Living Ethically in an Unethical World* (2004). He has published over 200 scholarly professional journal articles and book chapters as well. He teaches courses in abnormal, clinical, health, and general psychology as well as ethics and maintains a private clinical practice as a licensed psychologist in Menlo Park, California.

LORI G. PLANTE, PhD, is a licensed psychologist maintaining a clinical psychology practice in Menlo Park, California, for over 25 years. She is a retired clinical faculty member in psychiatry and behavioral sciences at

Stanford University School of Medicine. She has specialized advanced training in the treatment of adolescents and young adults, as well as psychotherapy and assessment of adults with a wide variety of difficulties. Her practice spans the range of relational problems (with children, partners, colleagues), developmental transitions, affective disorders (e.g., depression, anxiety, bipolar illness), loss and grief, trauma, eating disorders, behavioral problems, self-injury, and a host of issues impacting academic achievement, career challenges, and social functioning. She has also published several books and professional articles, including *Bleeding to Ease the Pain: Self-Injury, Cutting, and the Adolescent Search for Self* (2010, Praeger).